THE
ENGLISHMAN AND HIS BOOKS
IN THE EARLY NINETEENTH CENTURY

The attempt to describe the effects of the Sublime & Wonderful is dedicated to M.G. Lewis Esqr M.P.

TALES of WONDER!

A Satirical Print by James Gillray, to illustrate the Effects
of reading Tales of Mystery and Horror

Fr.

AMY CRUSE

THE ENGLISHMAN
AND
HIS BOOKS

in the early
nineteenth
century

BENJAMIN BLOM   New York/London   1968

London 1930
Reissued 1968
by Benjamin Blom, Inc. Bronx, New York 10452
and 56 Doughty Street London, W.C. 1

Library of Congress Catalog Card Number 68-20218

Printed in United States of America

PREFACE

IN a former book, *The Shaping of English Literature*, the author attempted to tell the story of the readers of books in England from the earliest times to the closing years of the eighteenth century. This book takes up the story and carries it on to the accession of Victoria. The period dealt with, therefore, is—even allowing for some inevitable overlapping—less than fifty years, as compared with the thirteen hundred years covered by *The Shaping of English Literature*. There were in those later days so many more Englishmen who read books and so many more books for them to read that the story is a much fuller one, and has to be told in a different fashion. All this is discussed in the introductory chapter, in which the author has tried to tell what were her aims and ideals in writing this book.

A. C.

CONTENTS

ILLUSTRATIONS

THE ENGLISHMAN AND HIS BOOKS

CHAPTER I

INTRODUCTORY

NO history of literature can be complete unless it takes account of the readers as well as of the writers. To claim that if there were no readers there would be no writers would be going beyond the warrant of proven facts ; it is difficult to imagine that under any conditions the greatest among the creators of our literature could have failed to give expression to the spirit that was in them. But it is certain that there are a great many books which would never have come into existence had it not been that a company of readers was waiting to receive them, and the work even of the greatest writers has been influenced, and its form sometimes determined, by the thought of those into whose hands it would pass. Dr Johnson said that no man but a blockhead ever wrote except for money ; and without readers there can be no money. The plain-spoken Doctor, when he made this statement, was reacting rather violently against the cant that he hated, which professed to regard authorship as an almost sacred calling. John Heminge and Henrie Condell, Shakespeare's first editors, put the case less crudely in a preface which they addressed "To the great Variety of Readers." "The fate of all books," they declared, "depends upon your capacities, and not of your heads alone but of your purses. Well. It is now publique and you will stand for your privileges, we know : to read and censure. Do so, but buy it first." Shakespeare, had he lived to see this first collected edition of his works, would probably have agreed entirely with his editors, for there are many signs in his plays that he had the readers of

his day—or the playgoers, which for our present purpose
is the same thing—in his mind as he wrote. It remained
for John Milton to raise the relation between the author
and his readers to its highest plane in his great aspiration
that he "might perhaps leave something so written to after-
times as they should not willingly let it die."

In the earlier ages, when readers (or hearers) were comparatively few and the supply of literature small and showing little variety, the relations between the author and his
public were evident and simple. As time went on and
readers and books multiplied, these relations became more
and more complex ; and by the beginning of the nineteenth
century they had become highly involved and difficult to
distinguish. There was an enormous body of readers,
drawn from every class in the country, and books of many
types and on all sorts of subjects were coming into existence
almost faster than they could be reviewed or chronicled.
To watch these books pass into the hands of the reader,
to note his reaction to them, and the reaction, in turn, of
his liking or disliking, his enthusiasm or his indifference,
his opposition or his agreement, on the output of new
literature, is a task far too large for complete accomplishment, but it is what this book, in a partial and limited
fashion, attempts to do.

It might seem at first sight that the main difficulty in
writing the story of early nineteenth-century readers would
lie in making a wise selection from an over-abundance of
material; but this is not so. The records, compared with the
greatness of the subject, are scanty. There are biographies,
autobiographies, diaries, letters, publishers' statistics,
reviews, and newspaper paragraphs in plenty, but from
most of these very little useful information can be gathered.
We are told how many copies of a certain book were sold,
and this gives us some notion of its general popularity, but
it does not tell us anything about the people who read the
book, what they thought of it, and how, if at all, it affected
their actions. We can read the critical journals and find
out what the directors of public taste had to say about a
new work, but we are not sure how far the general body of

readers followed them. As for autobiographies, letters, and diaries, the majority of them contain very little about books or reading. People do not, as a rule, write down in any detail their thoughts concerning a book that they have read. They talk about it, and often enter into lively discussions on its merits, but nobody cares to record these conversations, and they are, for the most part, lost; only occasionally, as in the case of Charles Lamb's famous 'Wednesday evenings,' does some small fraction of the talk come down to succeeding generations. We are grateful to Macaulay and Mary Russell Mitford, to Jane Austen, and Clarissa Trant, and Francis Place, and Henry Crabb Robinson, and a few others, who have left us really full and interesting accounts of the books they read and what they thought of them. For the rest we must depend upon scattered references, some detailed, some scanty; a quotation here, an allusion there, a chance remark, or a passing comment.

It is a fascinating business, this following up of first one and then another among the English men and women who have left us any record of their lives, in the hope of picking up some hints about their reading and their opinions concerning it. Every piece of information that falls to us has its significance, though there is a large variation in the interest and the value of the different items. When Southey tells us that if he were confined to twelve English books his choice would be Shakespeare, Chaucer, Spenser, Milton, Jackson, Jeremy Taylor, South, Isaak Walton, Sidney's *Arcadia*, Fuller's *Church History*, and Sir Thomas Browne, we are not greatly thrilled, but we feel that we know something of the tastes of a man of letters who is at the same time a practical man of affairs. Sara Coleridge's dictum that "to be always reading Shelley would be like living on quince marmalade; Milton and Wordsworth are substantial diet for all times and seasons," is more interesting, as reflecting the view likely to be taken by a cultured woman on the poetry of the day. Hazlitt's story of how he and Coleridge once found in the old-fashioned parlour of an inn at Lynton a little worn-out copy of Thomson's *Seasons*, and how

Coleridge exclaimed " *That* is true fame ! " gives an added interest to the other records of books found in inns, and we think respectfully of the copy of *Paul and Virginia* over which Hazlitt spent half a night when he stayed at Tewkesbury, and of the " library piled up in the corner of the window " at " Dobson's " to which, Dorothy Wordsworth tells us, " William soon made his way, and brought out a volume of Enfield's *Speaker*, another miscellany, and an odd volume of Congreve's plays." When Edward Bulwer-Lytton tells us that his grandmother

> never opened a book except (in later life at least) the Bible. She held book learning in utter contempt. She was extremely lively and fond of fashionable amusements. Once, indeed, when I was a very little boy, I lent her the *History of Jane Shore*, a pamphlet popular with housemaids and for which I paid sixpence. It made a great impression on her mind . . .

we feel that we have learned a little about the reading habits of great ladies, housemaids, and small boys. Even such chance allusions as that of Lady Wharncliffe, " I am sorry for Lord Castlereagh, for I believe he is miserable out of office, and become a perfect Lord Glenthorne " (a character in Miss Edgeworth's *Ennui*), and Miss Eden's " A day of misfortunes, like Rosamund's day in Miss Edgeworth's book " must be carefully noted. They prove that the works of this writer were so familiar to the readers of the time that characters from them could be mentioned in ordinary letters in the full assurance that the person addressed would understand and appreciate the allusion.

It is disappointing to find that many readers who describe their serious studies in some detail make only a slight, and often a slighting, reference to the books which they read for recreation. Sydney Smith gives his week's scheme of reading, and adds : " Then I always have a standing book of poetry and a novel to read when I am in the humour to read nothing else." Margaret Gray, the seventeen-year-old daughter of devout evangelical parents, follows the same plan. " For ornamental reading," she says, " one has always both time and inclination." We would give a good deal to hear a discussion between Lamb and his sister on one of those modern tales " whereof," says Charles, " our common reading table is daily fed with assiduously fresh supplies "; and it would be interesting as well as enlightening to know the names of the novels which young Thomas Warren, son of a Norfolk barrister, read while he was at Kingswood School, thereby throwing his mother into a state of almost frantic grief.

When fact fails us we can turn to fiction ; and here we find a mass of evidence which is no less valuable than that of the authentic records. Here are preserved some of those conversations which history and biography have lost ; the novelist has, we may believe, made his characters voice the opinions and the preferences held by the people of his day. To listen to Lady Harriet Duncan in Thomas Lister's *Granby*, or to the company assembled in the drawing-room of Lady Lilfield in Mrs Gore's *Manners of the Day*, is to learn a great deal about the reading of fashionable ladies and gentlemen in the early nineteenth century, before Victoria came to the throne. To hear, in the works of Jane Austen, Catherine Morland talk to Isabella Thorpe, and Marianne Dashwood hold forth to her family on the merits of her favourite poets, is to know what books were read in those days by young ladies just out of the schoolroom. If we visit, with George Eliot, the pleasant parlour of Dorlcote Mill, where Mr Riley is taking his brandy and water with Mr Tulliver, and Maggie is sitting on a low stool by the fire, we shall hear a conversation that will throw some light on the reading of uneducated people in out-of-the-way country places. Even to go with Winthrop Mackworth Praed to the county ball, and listen to the *belle* of the ball as

> She talked,—of politics or prayers,—
> Of Southey's prose or Wordsworth's sonnets,—
> Of danglers—or of dancing bears,
> Of battles—or the last new bonnets,

brings some enlightenment.

Fiction can most usefully be drawn upon to supplement facts when we are trying to find out something about the tastes of the ordinary person. Biographies and autobiographies are for the most part concerned with extraordinary persons. Only occasionally does a quite undistinguished man —or woman—leave us the details of his—or her—reading. We have the book lists of Clarissa Trant, and these are very valuable, because they tell us something about the reading of a well-educated girl of the higher class. We have the records of Thomas Poole, of Nether Stowey, and from these we can learn to what books a thoughtful youth, who loved learning but had few advantages of education, would be likely to turn for help and instruction. Even these readers, though they are not famous, are probably exceptional in the fineness of their literary tastes, and we have not yet reached the ordinary person. But we find him, or something very like him, in the pages of the novelist. When Bulwer-Lytton says of Lord Erpingham, in *Godolphin*, " He was generally considered a sensible man. He had read Blackstone, Montesquieu, Cowper's Poems, and *The Rambler*, and was always heard with great attention in the House of Lords," it is reasonable to suppose that such a course of reading was in those days considered a normal and adequate literary equipment for a second-rate politician. When John Lockhart, in *Reginald Dalton*, describes Mrs Macdonald as travelling with " Dugald Stewart in the chaise pocket and Wordsworth and the Lakers in her reticule " we feel that such were the highbrow ladies of the period who aspired to be abreast of all the latest literary movements. If we want to know the books read by an old-fashioned gentlewoman we can enter the Hertfordshire cottage where Charles Lamb's blind Margaret sits spinning at the door, with her granddaughter Rosamund, who is reading *Julia de Roubigné* by her side : on the shelves behind them are " the Bible, Wither's *Emblems*, Walton's *Compleat Angler*, *The Pilgrim's Progress* and a Cookery Book with a few sprigs of lavender and rosemary stuck here and there between its leaves "—the old lady's favourites in the days when she could see to read them. For the reading of an old-fashioned gentleman we go to Thackeray, who shows us Colonel Newcome travelling across Europe and India with Boswell's *Life of Johnson, Don Quixote, Sir Charles Grandison,* and

14

INTRODUCTORY

The Spectator always among his baggage, because he liked
" to be in the company of gentlemen." The Colonel
denounced *Tom Jones* as " a book that tells the story of a
parcel of servants, of a pack of footmen and lady's maids
fuddling in ale-houses " ; he denounced Gibbon as an infidel
for whose opinion he would not give the end of a cigar. His
friend and housemate, James Binnie, " a jolly young
bachelor, of two or three and forty, lately returned from the
Indian Civil Service," was a devout admirer of the *Decline
and Fall* and of the works of David Hume ; yet he and the
Colonel lived together in perfect peace and amity.

It must be remembered that, in this early nineteenth
century, reading aloud was far more common than it is now.
As we search the records of the time, the picture that meets
us almost more often than any other is that of a family
group gathered in a stiff, comfortable parlour ; the mother
and the daughters are stitching industriously at the shirts
whose making, in those pre-sewing-machine days, embittered
the lives of so many restless or aspiring girls ; the father or
brother is reading aloud from a book certified to be unimpeachable in its moral tone. Harriet Martineau laments
that when she was young it was not thought proper for a
young lady to study very conspicuously ; she was expected
to sit down in the parlour with her sewing, listen to a book
read aloud, and hold herself ready for callers. When the
callers came, conversation often turned naturally on the
book just laid down, which must therefore be very carefully
chosen lest the shocked visitor should carry to the house
where she paid her next call an account of the deplorable
laxity shown by the family she had left. At Steventon,
where the Austens lived, there was reading aloud at all
times of the day. " My father reads Cowper to us in the
mornings, to which I listen when I can," wrote Jane to her
sister Cassandra. In June 1808 they were reading Sir
Walter Scott's new poem. " Ought I to be very pleased with
Marmion ? " asked Jane. " As yet I am not. James reads
it aloud every evening—the short evening, beginning about
ten, and broken by supper." Sometimes Jane herself was
the reader. " We have got the second volume of *Esprella's*

15

Letters" (by Southey), " and I read it aloud by candlelight."
Sometimes they made an unfortunate choice. *Alphonsine*
(by Madame de Genlis) did not do.

> We were disgusted in twenty pages, as, independent of a bad
> translation, it has indelicacies which disgrace a pen hitherto so
> pure ; and we changed it for the *Female Quixote*, which now
> makes our evening amusement, to me a very high one, as I find
> the work quite equal to what I remember it.

The taste for reading aloud seems to have been hereditary
in the Austen family, for more than twenty-five years later,
in 1835, Jane's great-niece wrote from Eastbourne, where
she was spending her honeymoon :

> We have long snug evenings, the Major reading aloud to me
> whilst I work or draw, and we find the hours pass very rapidly.
> We have just finished *The Gypsy*, by G. P. R. James, with which
> we were much pleased. The interest of the tale is well sustained,
> and there are many passages of beautiful sentiment scattered
> through the work. Our little drawing-room looks very cozie
> and snug, with a bright fire, the curtains drawn, and the well-
> polished tea-kettle singing on the hearth.

Leigh Hunt tells of evenings in his childhood when his
father—selfish, learned, and a spendthrift—settled himself
in the most comfortable chair in the room, and his mother,
after brightening the fire and bringing out the coffee, knew
that her husband " was going to read Saurin or Barrow to
her with his fine voice and unequivocal enjoyment. We
struggled on between quiet and disturbance, between placid
reading and frightful knocks at the door "—which knocks
announced the calls of infuriated tradesmen demanding the
money due to them. No such unpleasant interruptions
disturbed the peaceful evenings which Thomas Moore spent
with his pretty actress wife in their country home at May-
field. " I pass my day in my study or in the fields," he
wrote, " after dinner I read to Bessy for a couple of hours,
and we are in this way at present going through Miss
Edgeworth's works." Walter Scott, as all who heard
him testified, was one of the most delightful and inspiring
of readers. During the winter seasons that he spent
in Edinburgh it was his custom to gather a company of

intimate friends to dinner on Sundays at his house in Castle Street. The sound of music in a street of Edinburgh on a Sunday evening would have been considered highly indecorous, so after dinner Scott would entertain his guests in the drawing-room by reading to them. He read scenes from Shakespeare and from Joanna Baillie's *Plays on the Passions*, and poems by Wordsworth and by Crabbe. " In those days," says John Lockhart, " Byron was pouring out his spirit fresh and full ; and if a new piece from his hand had appeared, it was sure to be read by Scott the Sunday evening afterwards." A few years later, in parlours and drawing-rooms all over the land, Scott's own Waverley Novels were being read aloud to the delight of young and old. In the quiet drawing-room of his dignified house on Denmark Hill Mr Ruskin read to his wife and to his small son, who sat still as a mouse in his own particular chair in his own particular corner of the room, until seven o'clock came and he was sent off to bed without regard to the plight in which he left the hero and heroine of the story. Mr Ruskin read also Shakespeare and Crabbe and Byron, and to all of these the fair-haired, blue-eyed little boy listened with grave attention, laying the foundation of a fine literary taste.

This almost universal habit of reading aloud had its effect upon the books that were being produced. The test of a really good book became, for a number of people, its fitness for being read aloud in the family circle, and this caused a certain class of writers to show an excessive carefulness in avoiding the mention of anything that could be called indelicate or improper. Exactly how far this influence went, and whether on the whole it acted for good or for evil, there is not sufficient evidence to determine ; but we can see it at work during the whole of the pre-Victorian period, and on throughout the nineteenth century.

When we turn from books to plays and begin an inquiry into the tastes and opinions of the crowds that filled the theatres during this period, we find the playgoers even more reticent than the readers of books. Actors and actresses will tell us a good deal about their stage experiences and about what happened behind the scenes. Dramatic critics like Hazlitt and Leigh Hunt will give judgment on the play and allot praise or blame to the performers. But very few of the ordinary people who sat in the gallery or the pit, or even in one of the boxes, will tell us how they enjoyed the evening, and what approved and what condemned. Charles Lamb gossips delightfully about his visits to the theatre, but he can certainly not be called an ordinary playgoer. Charles Greville's references to the plays he saw are few and usually not very interesting. Sir Walter Scott and Miss Mitford add something, but not much, to our store of information. We are grateful to Crabb Robinson for many full and interesting references to various plays, and to Lady Wharncliffe for her eloquent descriptions of the performances of the marvellous boy tragedian, William Betty. To Lady Wharncliffe's son, James Stuart Wortley, we give delighted thanks for a spirited and vivid account of the early appearances of Miss Fanny Kemble.

The novels of the day contain disappointingly few references to the theatre; and it becomes a matter of putting together a number of very slight hints and passing comments. These do not take us very far. They do little toward answering any of the theatrical questions of the period: why, for example, so few plays of any merit were written, and why the audiences deteriorated so greatly in character. Answers to these questions have been given by historians of the drama, but it would be interesting to see what light the people themselves could throw upon them.

When we assemble the scraps of evidence we have collected concerning the readers of books and the spectators of the drama, and attempt from them to draw conclusions or to make generalizations, we find the task extremely difficult and full of dangers. We want much fuller knowledge before we can proceed with any confidence. Take, for example, the case of *Robinson Crusoe* and *The Pilgrim's Progress*. The evidence that these two books were among the most widely read—were probably the most widely read —of any books of the time is overwhelming. No matter what biographical account is taken up, there is almost certain to be a mention that *The Pilgrim's Progress* and *Robinson Crusoe* were read by its subject. We might therefore think ourselves justified in concluding that a large number of the most popular books of the day will follow these two types ; but we find this is not so, and we are at a loss to account for their popularity. Charles Dickens does not help us much when he says :

> I have just been propounding to Forster if it is not a wonderful testimony to the homely force of truth, that one of the most popular books on earth has nothing in it to make anyone laugh or cry. Yet I think with some confidence that you never did either over any passage in *Robinson Crusoe*.

" Homely truth " would scarcely seem to be the quality likely to attract the generation that bought in such enormous numbers the extravagant " Tales of Terror " of Mrs Radcliffe and her school, and of which Mrs Piozzi wrote to Madame D'Arblay in 1820 :

> How changed is the taste of verse, prose, and painting since *le bon vieux temps*, dear Madam ! Nothing attracts us but what terrifies and is within—if within—a hair's-breadth of positive disgust. The picture of Death on his Pale Horse [by Benjamin West, exhibited in 1817], however, is very grand certainly—and some of the strange *things* they *write* remind me of Squire Richard's visit to the Tower Menagerie when he says, " They are *pure* grim devils "—particularly a wild and hideous tale called *Frankenstein*.

That it was a generation which desired to be made, if not to laugh, certainly to cry, seems to be proved by the high value which it set on ' sensibility ' as an attractive and almost an indispensable quality of all well-bred young ladies, and by the fact that all the heroines—and a good many of the heroes—of all the fashionable novels had the habit of shedding floods of tears on almost every page.

It is not claimed that the present book gives an account that is near to being exhaustive of the English reader of the time, but an attempt has been made to show him in some of his more important aspects. The period dealt with is that from 1790 to 1837, with some extension at each end ; 1790 rather than 1800 was chosen as the starting-point because so many important movements that came to their fulfilment in the nineteenth century had their beginnings in the years round about the outbreak of the French Revolution. It has been thought better to deal with each division of the subject as a whole instead of attempting a strictly chronological account. Each chapter therefore extends through the whole, or a large portion of the period, and this leads to some slight breaches of the exact order of time ; for example, we meet Master Thomas Babington Macaulay as a young gentleman of fourteen in Chapter II and as a small boy of four in Chapter III.

The great body of the readers here dealt with are those who, like Hazlitt, " set out in life with the French Revolution." But there is also the older generation—the last survivors of the eighteenth century—and there are the later-born who never knew what it was to live under the shadow of Napoleon. To some extent our own age is like theirs. With us too are the elder folks of the last century, the generation that grew up with the Great War, and the children of the New Age. To compare the literary tastes of these three classes to those of their prototypes a hundred years ago should be both interesting and instructive.

CHAPTER II

THE SUBSCRIBERS TO "CAMILLA"

IT has been the fate of many who in their youth were
looked upon as daring innovators, startling and perhaps shocking their own generation, to live to hear
themselves called old-fashioned, and to see themselves
regarded with kindly indulgence by the generations of their
children and their grandchildren. Such was the fate of
Fanny Burney, and such, in a less degree, was the fate of
her readers. When, in 1778, Miss Burney published *Evelina*
she was considered by the reading public as a young lady
of amazing temerity, who had defied the customs of her class
and had, moreover, set a new fashion in literature. Other
young ladies who read the book did so with a pleasing sense
of keeping up with the latest advance both in literature and
in the emancipation of women as preached by the Blue-
stockings. But when, thirty-six years later, Madame
D'Arblay (who was Fanny Burney married) sent out *The
Wanderer* the case was changed. A new generation of
readers, which included the Wordsworthians, the Byron
worshippers, the Minerva Press young ladies, and the
enraptured company fresh from *Waverley*, looked upon the
book as a curious and rather ridiculous survival from an
earlier age, and upon those who upheld its claim to consideration as hopelessly old-fashioned. It is true that there
were still living a sufficient number of people who remembered and respected Madame D'Arblay to ensure for her
book a good sale; but few people read it except those of
her own generation.

Half-way between *Evelina* and *The Wanderer* came
Camilla, in 1796, and at that time Madame D'Arblay had
only become just sufficiently old-fashioned to endear herself to a large and very important section of the English-
reading public. There were still many people, most of them

intelligent, well-bred, and prosperous, who regarded Dr Johnson as the great authority in literature and held in horror the new ideas that had come in with the French Revolution. Madame D'Arblay, this dignified company felt sure, might be trusted to give them a book in the sound tradition of the seventies and eighties, without any of the disturbing notions with which the younger generation was trying to upset the comfort of its elders.

It was on this public that Madame D'Arblay relied when she decided to publish *Camilla* by subscription. It was not an unusual method in those days, and it had been suggested to her when she published her second novel, *Cecilia*, but it was one, we are told, from which " her natively retired temperament had made her recoil." She was older now, and her need of money was more pressing, so the plan was reconsidered and finally accepted. Her influential friends were eager to help her. Great ladies—the Dowager Duchess of Leinster, Mrs Boscawen, widow of Admiral Boscawen, the beautiful Mrs Crewe, daughter of the Duchess of Portland, and the fashionable Mrs Locke, of Norbury Park, Surrey—kept the list and received subscriptions. The work was to be published in five volumes, and the price of each set was to be a guinea ; admirers might subscribe for as many sets as they pleased. Everything was quickly put in train, and in the highest circles of society the publication of Madame D'Arblay's book was eagerly discussed as one of the most important social, as well as literary, events of the season.

The list of subscribers, printed in the first edition of *Camilla* and containing over eleven hundred names, is an interesting and valuable record. By studying it carefully much may be learnt concerning a very important class of readers—the class that was to be the dominant one for at least the next ten years, and was then very slowly to disappear and make way for the great new class that the new movements were bringing into being. All these readers knew exactly the kind of book they wanted. When they put down their guinea for the five volumes of *Camilla* they did so with the definite expectation of receiving another

22

Evelina or *Cecilia*. They wanted a vivid, convincing picture of the life of their day and class—conventional elegance and morality set forward with humour and pathos. They wanted something over which they could laugh and cry and moralize without any real emotional or intellectual disturbance. It is true that some of them were not quite pleased with *Camilla* when they got it, but that was because it did not reach the standard that had been set up. *Camilla* fell far below Madame D'Arblay's earlier works, though it was of the same genus. But the disapproving voices were few, and the chorus of praise was loud enough, almost, to prevent their being heard.

The list of subscribers is headed by two royal dukes, and there are so many people of title included in it that it looks as if no member of the English nobility could have failed to enrol among Madame D'Arblay's supporters. The names of the King and Queen are absent ; they were not ordinary subscribers, but the book is dedicated to her Majesty from her " most obedient, most obliged, and most dutiful servant," and it was in fact written throughout with an eye to the " sweet Queen's " approval. Her gracious acceptance of a copy was humbly entreated by the author, who travelled down to Windsor and was granted an audience. " The Queen was in her dressing-room, with only the Princess Elizabeth," said Madame D'Arblay. " I presented my little, though not small, offering on one knee, placing the volumes as she desired on a table by her side and expressing as well as I could my devoted gratitude for her invariable goodness to me." Before the interview ended the King was summoned, and a second set of volumes presented to him. Both their Majesties acknowledged the presentation by a ' compliment ' of fifty guineas. An even greater compliment, and one which made Madame D'Arblay a proud woman, was the permission given for copies to be presented to the Princesses Elizabeth, Augusta, and Sophia, aged respectively thirty, twenty-eight, and twenty-six. They were allowed to read *Camilla* without the Queen or some other discreet person first looking it through to see that it contained nothing unfit for the eyes of irreproachably

23

brought-up young ladies. *Cecilia* had only been passed for their reading, some years after its publication, by the express sanction of the learned Dr Ross, Bishop of Exeter. But they had been younger then, and, moreover, *Cecilia* had been openly called a novel, a name that had an unladylike and immodest sound in the ears of the stricter section of the reading public. Madame D'Arblay carefully avoided the use of this suspect word in connexion with *Camilla*. " I own I do not like calling it a novel," she had written to her father in June 1795. " It gives so simply the notion of a mere love story that I recoil a little from it. I mean this work to be sketches of character and morals put in action— not a romance."

It was as " sketches of character and morals " that the book was accepted in the royal household. The royal taste in literature was decorous and unimaginative. We know George III's opinion of Shakespeare. " Was there ever such stuff as a great part of Shakespeare ? Only one must not say so. But what think you ? What ? Is there not sad stuff ? What ? What ? " The Queen—according to Fanny Burney—liked serious books on religion and morality, essays of the *Spectator* and *Tatler* type, a little of the poetry of Milton and Cowper, and a few books of travel. These Fanny, while Lady of the Wardrobe, had been in the habit of reading aloud, and her Majesty regretted that *Camilla* could not be read in the same way. " How shall I read it ? " she asked the princesses. " Quick, at once, or comfortably at Weymouth ? " " Why, Mamma," replied the Princess Elizabeth, " I think as you will be so much interested in the book Madame D'Arblay would be most pleased you should read it at once, now, quickly, that nobody may be mentioning the events before you come to them, and then again at Weymouth, slow and comfortably." And so it was done.

The members of the royal household who had been Miss Burney's colleagues followed their Majesties' example and subscribed for *Camilla*. Even Mrs Schwellenberg, the Keeper of the Robes, bought a copy, though she almost certainly did not read it. She was ignorant and illiterate, and she knew little English. She did not like novels—" I won't have nothing what you call novels—what you call romances—what you call histories—I might not read such what you call stuff—not I "—she had rudely declared. She did not like Miss Burney—" I shall do everything I can to assist you to appear for nobody," she had said when she and Fanny had been in attendance on the Queen during a visit to Oxford, and she had acted consistently in the spirit of this pronouncement. But their Majesties set the fashion at Court, and every one, including Mrs Schwellenberg, followed. No one with any pretension to rank or position could venture to neglect *Camilla*.

Statesmen and eminent public men made up another circle of admirers. Canning, then Under-Secretary for Foreign Affairs, subscribed for a set, and so did William Wyndham, the Secretary at War. Edmund Burke, who had always been an admirer of Miss Burney's, took ten sets in his own name and ten in the name of the son he had recently lost. He had sat up all night reading *Evelina* when it came out in 1778. But he was a sick man now, and broken down by the death of his son, and he had no strength or heart for novel-reading. " How ill I am you can easily believe," he said to one lady who came to call upon him, " when a new novel of Madame D'Arblay lies on my table unread." Warren Hastings took three sets, and canvassed his friends enthusiastically to obtain other subscribers. Lord Macartney, who was going out as Governor to the Cape of Good Hope, took a set with him. " This I have not opened," he said,

> nor will I suffer anyone to anticipate a word of it to me, and still less suffer myself to take a glimpse of even a single sentence till I am many leagues out at sea : that then, without hindrance of business or any impediment whatever, I may read the work throughout with uninterrupted enjoyment.

The Blue-stockings stood staunchly by their old associate, and the names of all their surviving members are to be found on the list of subscribers. They were now an aged and a dwindled company. Mrs Vesey and Mrs Delany were dead. Mrs Ord, Mrs Thrale, and Mrs Garrick were over sixty,

Mrs Carter, Mrs Boscawen, Mrs Montagu, and Mrs Chapone over seventy. Hannah More, the youngest of the company, was fifty-one. Of the male Blue-stockings admitted to the *coterie* Horace Walpole was seventy-nine, Bennet Langton, the friend of Dr Johnson, fifty-nine, Sir Lucas Pepys, the physician, fifty-four, Sir William Pepys, Master in Chancery, fifty-six, and Owen Cambridge seventy-nine. By all of these *Camilla* would be judged on its real literary merit, not on its conventional morality. The Blue-stockings, in spite of peculiarities at which their own and succeeding generations have laughed, were women of strong intellect and personality who outraged the opinion of their contemporaries by insisting that women were capable of the same intellectual pursuits and interests as men ; and the male members were broad-minded enough to admit this also. They all read *Camilla*, but not all of them admired it. " Mrs Chapone," Madame D'Arblay wrote to her father, " spoke warmly of *Camilla*, especially of Sir Hugh." Mrs Montagu had been a little scornful of *Cecilia*, and although she took ten sets of the new work, she liked it even less. Hannah More, having now given up the seasons of decorous gaiety in town in which she had been used to indulge, was living at Cowslip Green, near Bristol, with her four sisters, busy with her schools, her tracts, and her parish visiting. She found time to read *Camilla*, and wrote to Horace Walpole concerning it. " I will only reply by a word or two to a question you seem to ask," he wrote, " how I like *Camilla*. I do not care to say how little." Writing to his old friend, the beautiful Miss Mary Berry (whose name, with her sister's, is on the list of subscribers), he was more outspoken. " Next arrived Dr Burney on his way to Mrs Boscawen. He asked me about the deplorable *Camilla*. Alas ! I had not recovered of it enough to be loud in its praise."

Literary-minded people living in provincial towns had in quite a number of cases been inspired by the example of the Blue-stockings to set up small societies of their own. Of these Lichfield shone with a splendour given to it by Anna Seward, the beautiful and talented " Swan of Lichfield " ; her father, the learned Canon ; Dr Erasmus Darwin, the burly, rough-spoken, famous physician, author of *The Loves of the Plants*; the eccentric, unkempt Thomas Day, who wrote that immortal children's classic *Sandford and Merton*; the lovely Honora Sneyd, later to become the second wife of the much-married Mr Lovell Edgeworth; with various others—dignitaries of the cathedral and local men of learning. The fame of the meetings which these book-loving people held monthly at each other's houses brought to the town many notable visitors. Dr Johnson came sometimes; he was Lichfield-born, and though he had early deserted his native town for London, some of his glory was reflected upon it. Thomas Hayley, the friend of Cowper, and William Seward, a minor poet (who was no relation of the great Anna, and annoyed her by insisting on pronouncing his name Su-ward instead of Se-ward, which she considered the more elegant way), both came for long visits in the seventies, when Lichfield reached its highest point of brilliance. By the time *Camilla* was published its lights were burning low, though they were still visible. Dr Darwin had left the town in 1781; in 1784 came the death of Dr Johnson; the Swan was middle-aged, though still elegant and eloquent. Strangely enough, her name is not on the list of subscribers, though those of William Seward, Thomas Hayley, and several Lichfield inhabitants are. But she read *Camilla*, or at least intended to read it, for she wrote in 1797 to a friend, Mrs Gell of Derbyshire (who was herself a subscriber and had probably lent her copy to Miss Seward):

> You will pity me when I tell you that my promised enjoyment of the new effusion of Mrs D'Arblay's fancy is not yet realized. A combination of circumstances have produced this delay. It seems the fashion to decry it, as immeasurably inferior to the elder sisters of her charming pen. But your very different opinion is a host in its favour, while the palm of preference Dr Burney extends to *Camilla* excites expectations which look down upon the verdict of the multitude.

While the Lichfield lights were waning a great illumination was springing up at Norwich. The years immediately before and after the publication of *Camilla* saw it in its highest brilliance. The Norwich society was made up for the most part of cultured Dissenters who aspired to prove themselves as intellectual, as broad-minded, as skilled in the graces and amenities of social life as their contemporaries of the Church of England, who were a little apt to look down on those outside their communion. Several of the group had been connected with the Warrington Academy, which had been established to give Dissenters, who were shut out from Oxford and Cambridge, the benefits of a university education. Most of them attended the then famous Octagon Chapel, where English Presbyterianism was preached, and they were active in all good works in the town. The central light of this society was Mr William Taylor, the noted German scholar of his day, whose translation of Bürger's *Lenore* so strongly impressed young Walter Scott that, as he said, it made him a poet. There was another family of Taylors, Mr and Mrs John Taylor, with their clever sons and daughters, and it was in Mrs John Taylor's *salon* that the gatherings of the Norwich literary *coterie* were held. She was a witty and lively lady, and she led the conversation at these meetings in so spirited a fashion that her admirers called her " the Madame Roland of Norwich." Her guests were most of them as clever, if not as brilliant, as she was herself. There was Dr Enfield, who compiled the famous *Speaker*, a book of extracts read by everybody and used in almost all schools of the day ; Dr Alderson, the physician, with his beautiful daughter Amelia, who afterward married Opie, the painter ; Sir James Mackintosh, philosopher and politician ; Dr Frank Sayers, author of *Dramatic Sketches* ; Basil Montagu, the barrister ; Mrs Martineau, whose son and daughter, James and Harriet, were both afterward to become famous. All those names (except that of Mrs Martineau), with those of several other Norwich residents, are on Madame D'Arblay's list of subscribers. Doubtless the book was discussed when the guests assembled in Mrs John Taylor's pleasant drawing-room on the summer evenings of 1796. The hostess would have many witty things to say about it, and sharp-tongued Mrs Martineau—who was a little looked down upon by the others because her father had been a wholesale grocer and because she could not speak French—would not allow the trifling drawback of not having read the book to prevent her from offering her criticisms. The older members would recall memories of *Evelina* and *Cecilia* and the stir that Miss Burney had made in the literary world when Dr Johnson was its ruler; and visitors like young Henry Crabb Robinson, a lawyer then in attendance on the Norfolk circuit, would be greatly impressed by the wit and culture and literary insight possessed by this renowned circle.

Mrs Anna Letitia Barbauld, though she did not live at Norwich, may be regarded as a member of the group; her father had been a tutor and her husband a student at Warrington Academy; and William Taylor had been a pupil at her husband's school at Palgrave. She often visited at Norwich, and added a new grace to Mrs John Taylor's *salon* by the charming simplicity of her manners and by her learning—she knew Latin as well as French. At the time when *Camilla* was published she and her husband were living in a pleasant house at Stoke Newington, which was then a pretty country district. Her father, Dr Aikin, and various other relatives were also living at Stoke Newington, and the Barbaulds' house in Church Street was the centre of a Nonconformist society, intellectual and in many respects liberal-minded, but entirely opposed to the new, restless spirit which was trying to change the established order and send the world forward to the cry of "Progress!" Some years earlier Mrs Montagu, the Queen of the Blue-stockings, had asked Mrs Barbauld to become the Principal of a Ladies' College she was trying to establish; and Mrs Barbauld had declined the offer, giving her reasons at length.

> A kind of academy for ladies where they are to be taught in a regular manner the various branches of science appears to me better calculated to form such characters as the *Précieuses* or *Femmes Savantes* than good wives or agreeable companions. . . . The best way for a woman to acquire knowledge is by conversation with a father or brother and by such a course of reading as they may recommend.

In 1796 Mrs Barbauld was fifty-three years old; in

intellectual gifts she was equal to any of her male relatives, yet she was still guided by their advice. She read *Camilla*, but as it was subscribed for in Mr Barbauld's name we may conclude that she did so with his permission and good-will. She did not think very highly of the book. " How do you like *Camilla* ? " she wrote to a friend, Miss Dixon. " Not so well, I am afraid, as the former publication by the same hand. I like, however, the story of Eugénie." Eugénie is a sort of secondary heroine of *Camilla*, plain, sickly, and retiring, neglected by many people, but finally appreciated by the youth she loves, and happily married.

Bath was another, though a less important, " little academe," and at Bath *Camilla* had many admiring readers. The names of Mr Thomas Bowdler, his wife, his son, and his two daughters are all on the list of subscribers to Madame D'Arblay's novel. The Bowdlers were well-known and highly respected members of Bath society. In their household, as in Queen Charlotte's, *Camilla* was approved because it was "sketches of character and morals put in action— not a romance." They belonged to a large and increasing body of readers who had been gradually discovering that the outspokenness of the earlier writers, including Shakespeare, and even the author of *Pamela*, was coarse, and quite unfitted for polite ears. These people professed and cultivated an extreme delicacy of taste, which, superadded to the morality of the eighteenth century, led on to the much-ridiculed prudery of the nineteenth. The Bowdlers had a sincere appreciation of good literature, and it pained them deeply to reflect that the great works of Mr Shakespeare must, or at least ought to, remain unread by modest young ladies because of certain regrettable blemishes. So Thomas Bowdler the younger set to work on the plays in the same spirit which he had brought to his other works of social reform. With much toil he produced a purified version of Shakespeare, which he called *The Family Shakespeare*, because it could safely be read aloud in the family circle. It was published in 1818, and Dr Bowdler afterward proceeded to treat Gibbon's *Decline and Fall of the Roman Empire* in the same way. He thus placed the works of both Shakespeare and Gibbon in the class of books that could not " raise a blush on the cheek of modest innocence, nor plant a pang in the heart of the devout Christian." By this test he, and the large class of readers who thought as he did, judged each new book as it appeared, and *Camilla* was one of those which was not found wanting.

There was another household—very different in many ways from these quiet homes, governed by religion and convention—where *Camilla* was admitted only on the strict understanding that it was not a novel or a romance. This was the Irish household, or " settlement," as it might almost be called, of Edgeworthstown, in County Longford. Here lived Mr Lovell Edgeworth—handsome, clever, restlessly energetic—with his third wife (there was to be a fourth later), his fourteen or fifteen children, and a large body of servants and dependants. The household was entirely patriarchal in its method of government, Mr Edgeworth being the ' benevolent despot ' who was admired, adored, and obeyed by all. " I do not think," he boasted, " that one tear per month is shed in this house, nor the voice of reproof heard, nor the hand of restraint felt." Therefore, when we see the name of his eldest daughter, Maria, aged twenty-nine, on the list of subscribers to *Camilla*, we know that it was placed there by his consent and advice, and that the copy which duly arrived at Edgeworthstown was taken into his charge forthwith. Mr Edgeworth held strong and decided views on the subject of literature—as, indeed, he held strong and decided views on most subjects. Poetry and romance he considered not only useless, but harmful. Fairy-tales he held in entire reprobation ; not one of the little Edgeworths had made the acquaintance of Cinderella, or Beauty and the Beast, or Titania, or Puck—at least, not officially. There were no books in Mr Edgeworth's large and solid collection dealing with such unreal and therefore pernicious personages. The gods of his worship were Utility and Morality ; his enemies roundly asserted that he believed in no other. When the family gathered according to custom at the great oblong table in the library—for it was, we are told, Mr Edgeworth's principle to " allow his children to

31

participate in his own occupations and thereby to profit by his example "—such books as the dictator approved were read and discussed. For the children there was *Sandford and Merton*, that embodiment of Mr Edgeworth's creed, written by Thomas Day, who had been the friend of his youth, the sharer of all his ideas, theories, and cranks ; or there were the delightful stories written for them by their elder sister, Maria, or there was Dr Aikin and Mrs Barbauld's *Evenings at Home*, which was read aloud and which they " all admired extremely." For Mr Edgeworth there were the heavy tomes bearing on the particular pursuit that occupied him at the moment ; when he was trying to construct a tower, or invent a telegraph, he read the six volumes of *Machine Approuvis* ; when his head was filled with the idea of a universal language, he delighted in a rare copy which he possessed of *Real Character, or An Essay towards a Universal Philosophical Language.* There was Adam Smith's *Wealth of Nations*, Bentham's *Introduction to the Principles of Morals and Legislation*, Hume's *Treatise on Human Nature*, and other works of the Utilitarian writers, which he read, or allowed his daughter to read to him. For light reading for Mrs Edgeworth and the elder children there was Dr Aikin's letters, Godwin's essays, and *Camilla*, which must have appeared almost frivolous in such company.

The list of subscribers contains the names of many clergymen, and copies of *Camilla* travelled to country parsonages all over England. One set of volumes went to a Miss Jane Austen, Steventon Rectory, Hampshire, and was delivered into the hands of a young lady aged twenty-one. She was a pretty and lively young lady who went to as many balls and assemblies and dinners as t¹ ⌐ select society of the neighbourhood offered, and she enjoyed these festivities all the more if they brought with them the opportunity for a little mild and entirely decorous flirtation. She spent a good deal of time and thought, and as much money as she could afford, on her dress. " I have spent all my money on pink persian," she wrote to her beloved sister Cassandra, who was two years older than herself. " So I hope Edward [her brother] has not bought the furs he thought of for me

The History
OF
SANDFORD AND MERTON,
BY
Mr. Thomas Day.

Tommy's first lesson in humility.
Page 45

LONDON
Published by J. Walker, Paternoster Row, and J. Harris
St. Paul's Church Yard.

TITLE-PAGE TO AN EARLY EDITION (1808) OF
"SANDFORD AND MERTON"

32

as I shall not be able to pay him." She must have been obliged to practise some self-denial to save the guinea that she paid for *Camilla*, but she loved reading, and had so delighted in *Evelina* and *Cecilia* that she felt she must have this new book. She and Cassandra seized eagerly upon it and read it without loss of time. It probably arrived toward the end of July, and in August Jane went to stay with some friends at Rowling. Her brother escorted her there, and was to return later and take her home. On September 1 she wrote to Cassandra, referring to an incident in *Camilla* in a way which shows that the book was already a subject of familiar conversation between the sisters.

> To-morrow I shall be just like Camilla in Mr Dubster's summer-house, for my Lionel will have taken away the ladder by which I came here, or at least by which I intended to get away, and here I must stay till his return. My situation, however, is somewhat preferable to hers, for I am very happy here, though I should be glad to get home by the end of the month.

On September 16 she described a dinner-party :

> Miss Fletcher was one of the guests. She wore her purple muslin, which is pretty, but does not suit her complexion. There are two traits in her character which are pleasing—namely, she admires *Camilla* and drinks no cream in her tea.

Miss Austen is inclined to make the appreciation of *Camilla* a touchstone of character. Stupid or unpleasant people, she seems to maintain, do not like it. Tom Thorpe, the vulgar, boasting undergraduate of *Northanger Abbey*, described it to Catherine Morland as

> " that stupid book, written by that woman they made such a fuss about—she who married the French emigrant."
> " I suppose you mean *Camilla* ? " said Catherine.
> " Yes, that's the book. Such unnatural stuff ! An old man playing at see-saw ! I took up the first volume once and looked it over but I soon found it would not do ; indeed, I guessed what sort of stuff it must be before I saw it. As soon as I heard she had married an emigrant I was sure I should never be able to get through it."
> " I have never read it."
> " You have no loss, I assure you. It is the horridest nonsense you can imagine. There is nothing in it but an old man's

c

playing at see-saw and learning Latin. Upon my soul there is not."

The justice of this criticism was, we are told, unfortunately lost on poor Catherine, but we seem to hear in it an echo of words spoken by some acquaintance of Miss Austen, and by her fully appreciated.

The inhabitants of Steventon Rectory were probably considered by their neighbours as being less particular with regard to the books they read than one would have expected in a clergyman's family. On December 18, 1798, Jane wrote to Cassandra, who was away on a visit :

> I have received a very civil note from Mrs Martin requesting my name as subscriber to her library, which opens January 14, and my name, or rather yours, is accordingly given. My mother finds the money . . . As an inducement to subscribe, Mrs Martin tells me that her collection is not to consist only of novels, but of every kind of literature, etc. She might have spared this pretension to our family, who are great novel-readers, and not ashamed of being so ; but it was necessary, I suppose, to the self-confidence of half her subscribers.

The Austens read and enjoyed the ' horrid ' novels of Mrs Radcliffe and her followers ; they cried over *Evelina* and *Cecilia* ; they spent delightful evenings reading aloud the mawkish love-stories of the Minerva Press, and criticized them devastatingly afterward. They read poetry also. Shakespeare, Southey, Scott, Cowper, and Crabbe provided matter for the reading-circle. Cowper and Crabbe were Jane's favourite poets, and it was a family joke that she intended to become Crabbe's second wife. " Poor woman ! " she wrote to Cassandra, referring to the first Mrs Crabbe, and to what might be expected to happen in the event of that lady's death, " I will comfort *him* as well as I can, but I don't undertake to be kind to her children. She had better not leave any."

More than a dozen provincial book-clubs and reading societies took copies of *Camilla*, and these probably mark the position of small literary *coteries* on the model of Lichfield and Norwich. The book found its way also to the circulating libraries of London. Miss Julia Dawkins, who lived with her mother above a hosier's shop in Holborn, and to whom we are introduced in Mrs Brunton's novel *Self-control*, obtained *Camilla* from one of these. " Having no character of her own, this young lady," we are told, " was always as nearly as she was able, the heroine whom the last read novel inclined her to personate. When *Camilla* was the model for the day she became insufferably rattling, infantile, and thoughtless "—in attempted imitation of what the author intended to be an artless and charming playfulness.

There are many other well-known and interesting names on Madame D'Arblay's list of subscribers, each of which might, if we could continue investigations indefinitely, lead us to a new circle of readers. There is Mrs Siddons, the great tragic actress, the centre and head of theatrical society. There is Thomas Wedgwood, the famous pottery-maker, with his large family and his many friends. There is Richard Heber, Member of Parliament for Oxford, half-brother of the well-known bishop and friend of Walter Scott. There are the Misses Harriet and Sophia Lee, who wrote bad novels after the style of Mrs Radcliffe. There is James Beattie the poet, David Hume, nephew of the historian, Thomas Holcroft the dramatist, and many others.

Even if we could follow all the eleven hundred subscribers to their homes we should still see only a few of those who were eager to read *Camilla*. Within three months only five hundred copies were left out of an edition of five thousand, and the book continued to be read well into the nineteenth century. Charles Lamb read it—probably in a copy borrowed by his sister Mary from the circulating library—for in a sonnet addressed to Sarah Burney he wrote of

that good
Old man, who as Camilla's guardian stood
In obstinate virtue clad like coat of mail.

Hazlitt found a copy at an inn at Bridgewater, where he stayed for a night during a walking-tour, and says, unenthusiastically, that he " got through two volumes." Macaulay read it, of course, and compared its style unfavourably with that of *Evelina* ; every passage that the authoress meant to be fine was, he declared, detestable, and the book was saved from condemnation only by the admirable spirit and force of those scenes in which she was content to be familiar. Byron and Lord Holland had both certainly read it before 1813, when Madame D'Arblay's last novel, *The Wanderer*, was in the press, for at that time Byron wrote to Mr Murray, the publisher :

> Lord Holland is laid up with the gout, and would feel obliged if you could obtain and send as soon as possible Madame D'Arblay's (or even Miss Edgeworth's) new work. I know they are not out ; but it is perhaps possible for your *Majesty* to command what we cannot with much money purchase as yet. . . . I would almost fall sick myself to get at Madame D'Arblay's writing.

If we wished to give in one sentence a general idea of the class of readers who subscribed to Madame D'Arblay's book we could scarcely do better than take the sentence with which she begins her heroine's story. " In the bosom of her respectable family resided Camilla." Nearly all the readers of *Camilla* were respectable, and nearly all resided in the bosoms of their families. It is gratifying to one's sense of poetical justice to reflect that with the proceeds of the sale of the book Madame D'Arblay built Camilla Cottage, where she herself resided " in the bosom of her respectable family " for nearly seven years.

CHAPTER III

WORDSWORTHIANS AND ANTI-WORDSWORTHIANS

IN 1798, just two years after the appearance of *Camilla*, there came another book, which, both in itself and in the circumstances of its publication, was very unlike that fortunate and exemplary work. It was a small book of two hundred and ten pages, bound in paper boards, and its price was one shilling and sixpence. Its title was *Lyrical Ballads*, its contents twenty-three poems, some of them very short, consisting of only a few stanzas. It was published anonymously by an obscure Bristol bookseller, Joseph Cottle, and came into the world quietly, without any heralding by advertisement or by the praises of influential friends. No one except a small group of intimates knew that the authors were two young men who had not so very many years before left Cambridge—William Wordsworth, aged twenty-eight, son of a Yorkshire attorney, and Samuel Taylor Coleridge, aged twenty-six, whose father had been vicar of Ottery St Mary, Devonshire. Coleridge had written four of the poems, including *The Ancient Mariner*, which was by far the longest in the book ; the other nineteen, all dealing with simple, everyday events in humble life, were the work of Wordsworth.

The publisher, Joseph Cottle, was himself a young man of twenty-eight. He was eager and enthusiastic, a poet himself in a humble way, and very ready to admire the books which the new generation of poets was producing. There was at this time assembled in Bristol a group of brilliant young men who were working hard to bring into being the new heaven and the new earth which the French Revolution had seemed to promise. Of these Cottle was the friend and in some sort the patron. He was a fervent admirer of Coleridge, and when the young man read to him some of the poems which were to form part of the book that he and his friend had planned Cottle " perceived in them a peculiar but decided merit," and agreed to publish them, and to pay the authors, who were both nearly penniless, thirty guineas.

Five hundred copies of the book were printed, but very few were sold. Such critical journals as noticed it made it the subject of careless ridicule. *We are Seven* was airily described as " innocent and pretty infantile prattle." Only here and there came a word of commendation. *The Monthly Review* picked out a passage from *Tintern Abbey* for high praise. *The Critical Review* found in the poems " so much genius and originality that we wish to see another publication from the same hand written on more elevated subjects and in a more cheerful disposition." A few seafaring men, taking the title of the first poem, *The Ancient Mariner*, to indicate that it was a book of sea-songs, bought copies and complained roundly when they discovered their mistake. A few copies were sent to friends, a few were sold in Bristol, but most readers followed the example of the reviews and made fun of the poems. " The *Lyrical Ballads*," wrote Sara Coleridge sadly to her husband, " are laughed at and disliked, with few exceptions."

" The sale was so slow, and the severity of most of the reviews so great," wrote Joseph Cottle in his *Early Recollections*,

> that its progress to oblivion seemed ordained to be as rapid as it was certain. I had given thirty guineas for the copyright . . . but the heavy sale induced me to part with the largest proportion of the impression of five hundred at a loss to Mr Arch, a London bookseller.

Soon after this Cottle gave up business and sold his copyrights to the firm of Longmans. The copyright of the *Lyrical Ballads* was valued as *nil* ; Cottle suggested that it should be returned to Wordsworth, and Mr Longman agreed. It seemed as if nobody wanted to read what the two young poets had taken such high and serious delight in writing.

Yet there was a public for the *Lyrical Ballads*, though perhaps not a very large one. It was not a public collected and united into a compact body. It was made up of obscure individuals scattered in ones and twos all over the country. Most of them were young, some very young ; most of them were vaguely discontented, many were not very happy. All of them were looking, consciously or unconsciously, for something that would bring a change into their lives—that would create for them a world of beauty and simplicity into which they might enter and be satisfied. They had almost ceased to look for any help from literature. They would not sit down to the slow-moving, morality-laden narrative that related in five volumes the tears and triumphs of a sorely tried heroine ; even the novel of mystery and blood they found stereotyped and conventional and powerless to provide a thrill. They read Crabbe and Cowper, but with qualified enthusiasm ; such calm music could soothe, but not inspire. Walter Scott could stir their pulses, but he could not help them to deal with the puzzle of everyday life.

The trouble with regard to this public was that its members did not in any definite sense know what it was they wanted. They could not say " Give us another *Cecilia*, or another *Essay on Man*, or another *Pamela*, or even another *King Lear*," because they had no real desire for any one of these. They could not ask help from any of the poets of their day, saying, " Make us a work after such and such a pattern," for they had no clear vision of the thing they were waiting for. When it came most of them recognized it at once, though there were some who allowed themselves to be misled by reviewers whose spiritual necessities were entirely different from theirs. Only very slowly and quietly the power of the book found out first one and then another and brought him forth from the mass of his uncomprehending fellows to make him a member of the growing band of true Wordsworthians.

The emergence of these Wordsworthians began almost as soon as the *Lyrical Ballads* was published. The few copies sold out of the first edition sought and found several of the band. One copy came into the hands of a scholarly, precocious, sickly boy of thirteen, Thomas De Quincey, the son of a Lancashire merchant, then living with his widowed mother at Bath. He read it with rapture. " I found in those poems," he said, "an absolute revelation of untrodden worlds teeming with power and beauty as yet unsuspected among men." He never rested until he had made the acquaintance of both the poets, and through all his wayward, opium-clouded life he was their loyal and staunch admirer. Another copy travelled to Glasgow, where another schoolboy, about the same age as De Quincey, but very unlike him, fell upon it with delight. This boy was tall and strong and athletic and full of high spirits, and became later the robustious John Wilson of *The Edinburgh Review*. To him also the *Lyrical Ballads* opened a new world, and he wrote a long and exultant letter to Wordsworth, telling him that he valued the book only less than the Bible.

Poor Charles Lamb, sitting heavy-hearted in his shabby Pentonville lodging, read the poems and straightway forgot his troubles ; forgot the tragedy that lay two years behind him, forgot his childish, dying father, forgot even the sister who was separated from him by a terrible affliction. The *Lines composed a Few Miles above Tintern Abbey* and *The Mad Mother* moved him strongly, but strongest of all was the spell cast by *The Ancient Mariner*. " I was never," he said, " so affected by any human tale. After first reading it I was totally possessed by it for many days." He talked over the poem with a friend, Charles Lloyd, to whom Coleridge had lately introduced him. But Lloyd, instead of being carried away by *The Ancient Mariner*, dealt critically with it. " Lloyd does not like it," Lamb wrote to Robert Southey, " his head is too metaphysical." " And your taste is too correct," he added, for Southey had called the poem " a Dutch attempt at imagination." " I should call it," went on Lamb, valiant in defence of his own opinion, " a right English attempt, and a successful one, to dethrone German sublimity."

William Hazlitt was at this time just twenty—a moody, handsome, untidy youth, who had lately left the Unitarian college at Hackney, having given up the idea of becoming a Unitarian minister like his father, and not having made up his mind to any other calling. He was hanging discontentedly about his father's house at Wem, near Shrewsbury, when the *Lyrical Ballads* came out, and he read them

40

eagerly. Some time later he paid a visit to his elder brother at Bury St Edmunds. John Hazlitt was an artist and was executing commissions for miniatures of various people in the town, where he had made a good many acquaintances. He knew Thomas Clarkson, who had come to Bury, which was his wife Catherine's native place, to recover from a breakdown in health brought on by his labours in the cause of the emancipation of slaves. The Clarksons introduced John Hazlitt to the Robinsons, a well-known trading family of the town, and William Hazlitt, when he came, made friends with the eldest son, who was studying law in London and spending his vacations with his family. Henry Crabb Robinson was three years older than William Hazlitt, but he seems to have recognized at once that the awkward, badly dressed boy was his superior in literary taste, and allowed him to direct his reading. Hazlitt showed him the *Lyrical Ballads,* and Crabb Robinson became at once and for life a wholehearted and enthusiastic Wordsworthian. Before this time, he says, the four poems he had read oftenest were Pope's *Rape of the Lock,* Milton's *Comus,* Thomson's *Castle of Indolence,* and Goldsmith's *Traveller,* but the *Lyrical Ballads* caused " a little revolution " in his taste and made him " a passionate lover " of all Wordsworth's writings.

The two young men did their best to spread the fame of Wordsworth in Bury, and they gained at least one enthusiastic convert—Mrs Clarkson. Later on they met in London. An uncle had left Crabb Robinson a hundred pounds a year, so that he was able to live comfortably in " small and neat rooms " in Sherrard Street while he was waiting for advancement in his profession. Hazlitt had by this time made the acquaintance of Coleridge, and through him of Lamb and Southey, and he introduced Crabb Robinson in his turn ; and to the ardent, hero-worshipping young lawyer it seemed as if a new world had opened before him.

Very different from the members of this brilliant little society, where matters literary were the common topics of conversation, was Thomas Poole, of Nether Stowey, in Somersetshire. His father was the owner of a large tanyard, and had apprenticed his son to the business upon his leaving school. There was a small clan of Pooles settled in the neighbourhood—uncles and aunts and cousins—and there was much pleasant social intercourse and family visiting. They were prosperous, well-to-do people, living the comfortable, unpretentious life that such people did live in the country districts at the end of the eighteenth century, and not much interested in books, or ideas, or new movements of any kind. Thomas was the only one who cared for these things, and he was consequently misunderstood and a little despised. He would have liked opportunities for study and self-improvement, but he took his father's decision that he must go to the tanyard very quietly, and he worked there hard and successfully. He was intensely interested in the condition of the poor, and especially of the men his father employed. He established a book club in Nether Stowey in 1793, and the list of the first set of books he ordered for it shows how much he must have done in the way of self-education. There is a story that he and Coleridge first became acquainted when Coleridge was in the uniform of the dragoon regiment in which he had, while he was an undergraduate at Cambridge, enlisted, and when Poole was wearing the clothes in which he worked at the tanyard, and that they made friends in the course of a conversation on social matters as between a private soldier and a working man. But it is more likely that they met when, in 1795, Coleridge was travelling through the district round about Bristol trying to gain subscribers to his periodical, *The Watchman*. Poole became a great admirer of Coleridge's work, and proved himself a staunch friend to the poet all through his troubled life. He took great interest in the publication and sale of the *Lyrical Ballads*, and, in a quiet way, was always an ardent Wordsworthian.

It is a little surprising to find that there was a copy of *Lyrical Ballads* on the select bookshelves of Miss Hannah More, but there it was, and there it was found ten years later by a small boy, Thomas Macaulay, her godson, who took it down and read *The Ancient Mariner* with great delight. It was not there because the ladies of Cowslip Green were in any sense Wordsworthians. De Quincey, whose mother was one of their intimate friends, says that Miss Hannah More, taking no interest in the Lake Poets, for several years cautiously avoided mentioning their names in his presence. The explanation probably is that Joseph Cottle, the Bristol bookseller, who sometimes took tea with the Misses More, had induced them to purchase a copy. The booksellers did what they could to push the sale of the unfortunate book. It was probably Longmans who put it in the parcel addressed to Captain Arthur Donnithorne, The Chase, Hayslope, in June 1799, " along with a bundle of pamphlets on Antinomianism and Evangelicalism." The Captain brought the book to his godmother, stately old Mrs Irvine. " I know you are fond of queer, wizard-like stories," he said. " It's a volume of poems, *Lyrical Ballads* ; most of them seem to be twaddling stuff, but the first is in a different style—*The Ancient Mariner* is the title. I can hardly make head or tail of it as a story, but it's a strange, striking thing."

Mrs Barbauld did not approve of *The Ancient Mariner*. She acknowledged its " queer, wizard-like " quality, but she complained, characteristically, that it had no moral. Coleridge's reply to this criticism was equally characteristic : " Madam, the fault of the poem is that it has too much moral."

So far it would seem that *The Ancient Mariner* had proved the chief attraction—where any attraction was felt —of the little book. It was, as Arthur Donnithorne said, " a strange, striking thing " and caught the attention at a first glance. But *Lines composed a Few Miles above Tintern Abbey, Simon Lee, We are Seven, The Mad Mother,* and *The Idiot Boy* were by some readers better loved, especially on a second or a third reading. Although it had been so much ridiculed and abused, and although so few copies had been sold, the book had in some strange way managed to make a name and a place for itself. Everybody knew of it, everybody talked about it. The witty were devastatingly brilliant concerning it ; the dull derided it more coarsely ; and all these things proved that the life was still in it in spite of its rough treatment.

Wordsworth, who then as always had strong faith in his

own work, quietly prepared a new edition. He had settled in the beautiful valley of Grasmere, which was to be his home for the rest of his life. Coleridge, though he was living quite near, took no part in the work. Wordsworth added a good many more poems, including *The Reverie of Poor Susan*, *The Old Cumberland Beggar*, *The Brothers*, *Michael*, *Ruth*, *Hart-leap Well*, and the Lucy poems. In spite of the failure of the 1798 issue, Longmans agreed to pay a hundred pounds for the copyright, and in 1800 the new edition appeared, in two small volumes, price six shillings.

The clamour of ridicule and condemnation was louder even than it had been in 1798. The critics poured out torrents of abuse. " Idiot boys, mad mothers, wandering Jews, visitations of ague, and phrensied mariners who are fated to accost us with tales that almost make our faculties topple over " was one derisive criticism of the book. Fashionable literary society hastened to show the correctness of its taste by pointing out the absurdities it had discovered in the poems. It was a popular form of amusement in drawing-rooms to see who could make the wittiest jests about them, and Mrs Transome, in *Felix Holt*, when she was a handsome young lady, at the beginning of the century, gained some reputation in this way. But the little band of admirers was active in propaganda, and one by one new adherents came in. William Laidlaw, the lad whom Walter Scott took later from his father's farm in the Vale of Ettrick to be head man at Abbotsford, became a zealous Wordsworthian through some verses he had read in a newspaper —probably quoted in connexion with a derisive review. Scott himself delighted in some of the poems, though he confessed " the aberration from ordinary usage " in others got beyond him ; but he paid later a fine tribute to *The Fountain* in *The Antiquary*, where he made Jonathan Oldbuck quote, with much feeling, the beautiful lines :

> My eyes are dim with childish tears,
>   My heart is idly stirred,
> For the same sound is in my ears
>   Which in those days I heard.

DOVE COTTAGE, GRASMERE
Inhabited by Wordsworth for seven years, and afterward by De Quincey.
From a pencil sketch by E. T. Miller

44

WORDSWORTHIANS

Thus fares it still in our decay ;
And yet the wiser mind
Mourns less for what time takes away,
Than what he leaves behind.

Mrs Clarkson was an enthusiastic advocate of the new edition. " You must buy Wordsworth's two volumes of *Lyrical Ballads* and tell me what you think of them," she wrote to Mr R. E. Garnham, Fellow of Trinity College, in February 1801.

> We have not got them yet. I am fully convinced that Wordsworth's genius is equal to the production of something very great, and I have no doubt but he will produce " something that Posterity will not willingly let die " if he lives ten or twenty years longer. . . . *The Brothers, Lucy Gray, Poor Susan, Timothy*, and the poem in which Bewick is praised are all that I have seen of the second volume. . . . *Lucy Gray* is, I think, inimitable.

Henry Crabb Robinson was trying, and, as it appeared later, successfully, to bring his brother Thomas over to the Wordsworthians. " There are a few ballads in these exquisite volumes," he wrote to him in June 1802, " *The Thorn, The Idiot Boy, Goody Blake and Harry Gill*, etc., which will rank with the first-rate compositions in the language."

A few people of weight in the literary world were beginning to temper their criticism with praise. Samuel Rogers, a wealthy banker and author of *The Pleasures of Memory*, was then held to be the finest poet of the age ; and by his strong personality and the delightful entertainments he gave at his house in St James's Street, overlooking the Green Park, he had made himself also a leader of fashionable society. He read the *Lyrical Ballads* and admired it, though not unreservedly. He visited Wordsworth at Grasmere, and when the poet came to London in 1802 he introduced him to Charles James Fox, the patron of Crabbe. This great man was kind enough to say that his favourites among the poems in *Lyrical Ballads* were *Goody Blake and Harry Gill, The Mad Mother, We are Seven*, and *The Idiot Boy*. He did not care for *The Brothers* or *Michael*, because he disliked blank verse for subjects that were to be treated with simplicity.

So with some people buying the book for the satisfaction of deep spiritual needs, and others because they must be in the fashion and know all about what was being quizzed in a hundred drawing-rooms, the 1800 edition of the *Lyrical Ballads* was sold out. There was another edition in 1802 and a fourth in 1805. None of them probably were very large editions, for Messrs Longmans would not be likely to run too great risks. The success, however, was great enough to encourage Wordsworth to prepare a collected edition of his poems. He added a good many that had been written since 1800, and the book was issued in 1807.

There was now a new enemy in the field. In 1802 *The Edinburgh Review* had been established, and had taken to itself the office of supreme judge in all literary matters. It set itself to the work of crushing the Lake Poets—under which title it banded together most uncritically Wordsworth, Coleridge, and Southey. Jeffrey, one of the founders of the *Edinburgh*, wrote an article on Wordsworth's volume, which became at once, and has remained, famous—more famous than in after years its author appreciated. " This author," he said,

> is known to belong to a certain brotherhood of poets who have haunted for some years about the lakes of Cumberland ; and is generally looked upon, we believe, as the purest model of the excellences and peculiarities of the school which they have been labouring to establish.

He acknowledged that

> the Lyrical ballads were unquestionably popular, and we have no hesitation in saying, deservedly popular ; for in spite of occasional vulgarity, affectation and silliness, they were undoubtedly characterized by a strong spirit of originality, of pathos, and of natural feeling.

But, he went on to say, the admirers of Mr Wordsworth had praised him for these very vulgarities, affectations, and sillinesses, and had thus " begot a certain admiration of defects." Therefore, said Jeffrey, he felt it his duty to try to open the eyes of the public as to what were the beauties and what the defects in this new volume. He found it, on examination, much more marked with the peculiarities of its school than the first edition of the *Lyrical Ballads* had been, and he waited confidently for the popular verdict to be given against it. Its diction had nowhere any pretence to elegance or dignity, and scarcely ever condescended to give the grace of correctness or melody. This choice of words was not accidental, but deliberate, and was enough to render the poems ridiculous. The most lofty, tender, and impassioned conceptions were connected with objects and incidents low, silly, and uninteresting. He then proceeded to criticize individual poems. The last three lines of *The Redbreast chasing the Butterfly* were " downright raving"; *The Small Celandine* was namby-pamby. In the *Ode to Duty* a lofty vein had been very unsuccessfully attempted, and the last two lines were utterly without meaning. *Beggars* was a very paragon of silliness and affectation. As to *Alice Fell,* " if the printing of such trash as this be not felt as an insult on public taste, we are afraid it cannot be insulted." The climax of the review came when the great ode *Intimations of Immortality* was characterized as " beyond all doubt the most illegible and unintelligible part of the publication. We can pretend to give no analysis or explanation of it—our readers must make what they can of the following extracts." Some praise was given to the song of the minstrel of Lord Clifford, and the review concluded : " We venture to hope that there is now an end of this folly, and that, like other follies, it will be found to have cured itself by the extravagance resulting from its unbridled indulgence."

All those people who disliked Wordsworth's poems and made any claim to literary taste hastened to put themselves on the side of the oracle. The chorus of abuse grew louder and more violent than ever. " Surely Wordsworth must be mad as was ever the poet Lee," wrote Miss Seward to Dr Darwin.

> Those volumes of his which you were so good as to give me have excited by turns my tenderest and warmest admiration, and my contemptuous astonishment and disgust. The two latter rose to their utmost height while I read about his dancing daffodils, ten thousand as he says in high dance in the breeze

beside the river whose waves danced with them, and the poet's heart we are told danced too. Then he proceeds to say that in the hours of pensive or of pained contemplation these same capering flowers flash on his memory, and his heart, losing its cares, dances with them again. Surely if his worst foe had chosen to caricature the egotistic manufacturer of metaphysical importance on trivial themes he could not have done it more effectually.

Even kindly Walter Scott was only half-hearted in his championship. " Wordsworth is harshly treated in *The Edinburgh Review*," he wrote,

> but Jeffrey gives the sonnets as much praise as he does to anybody. I made him admire the song of Lord Clifford's minstrel, which I like exceedingly myself. But many of Wordsworth's lesser poems are *caviare* not only to the multitude, but to all who judge of poetry by the established rules of criticism.

Coleridge tried in vain to make the family of his friend, Thomas Wedgwood, appreciate the beauty of the thought which underlay some of the homely passages of the poems. He read aloud to them the verses on the leech-gatherer, and when he came to the lines (omitted in later editions) about his skin being so old and dry the leeches would not stick to it, Fanny Wedgwood, who was not quite twenty, burst out laughing. Coleridge grew angry, but Fanny only laughed the more. Coleridge very stiffly asked pardon for having read the poem, saying that to a person who had not genius it might seem absurd. By this time Fanny was in a fit of uncontrollable laughter, and even her father, who was a true admirer of Wordsworth, smiled as he said : " Well, Coleridge, one must confess that it is not quite a subject for a poem."

In Wordsworth's own neighbourhood of Grasmere he had a few scattered admirers. There were the two boys— Thomas De Quincey and John Wilson—who had received the *Lyrical Ballads* with rapture in 1798. De Quincey was settled, with his books for his sole companions, at Dove Cottage. John Wilson was living a jovial life at his fine house, Elleray. There was Charles Lloyd, the friend of Lamb, long since converted to the Wordsworthian faith, married, and with five or six children, at Low Brathey. There was Thomas Wilkinson, of Yanwath, a Quaker of whom Wordsworth said his tastes were " too pure to be refined," living in a cottage near the great castle of the Lowthers. But for the rest, " The neighbouring people in every degree," De Quincey tells us, " gentle or simple, literary or half-educated, who had heard of Wordsworth agreed in despising him." There were two ladies, daughters of Dr Cullen, a famous physician, who lived at the little hamlet of Clappergate. They were poor, but well educated and of literary tastes, but they completely ignored Wordsworth and his works ; " and," says De Quincey,

> in their total ignorance of everything either done or attempted by the Lake poets these amiable women persisted in one uniform tone of courteous forbearance, as often as any question arose to implicate the names either of Wordsworth or Coleridge ; any question about them, their books, their families, or anything that was theirs. They thought it strange indeed (for so much I heard from a circuitous route) that promising and intellectual young men—men educated at great universities, such as Mr Wilson of Elleray or myself or a few others who had paid us visits—should possess so deep a veneration for these writers ; but evidently this was an infatuation—a craze, originating perhaps in personal connections ; and as the craze of valued friends to be treated with tenderness. For us therefore—for our sakes—they took a religious care to suppress all allusion to these disreputable names.

In 1808 every one was reading *Marmion,* and Wordsworth and his poems, as far as the general public was concerned, were almost forgotten. Next year came another attack, even more savage than that made by the *Edinburgh,* but not nearly as damaging ; and in this case the Wordsworthians could take some comfort to themselves by reflecting that their idol suffered in company with most of the other poets of the day. Lord Byron, aged twenty, had been infuriated by a scathing attack in the *Edinburgh* on his volume of youthful poems called *Hours in Idleness.* In his rage he hit back hard and indiscriminately, trying, it would appear, to show that there were few people except himself who had any poetic or any critical faculty. He wrote *English*

D

Bards and Scotch Reviewers in a white heat of fury, and Wordsworth was mauled with the rest.

> Yet let them not to vulgar Wordsworth stoop,
> The meanest object of the lowly group,
> Whose verse, of all but childish prattle void,
> Seems blessed harmony to Lamb and Lloyd.

There is much more of the same kind, but though the blows were heavy little harm was done, and Byron and his anger retired to the Continent.

Still, amid this rough tempest of abuse, the little band of Wordsworthians remained staunch ; and still, by ones and twos, the new recruits came in. " The book is greatly extolled and liked by all who have seen it," declared Lamb in June 1809, which meant that his own particular circle, now extended to include Hazlitt, Crabb Robinson, Godwin, Dyer, Talfourd, and others, was unanimous in its praise. Coleridge sent a copy of the *Lyrical Ballads* and one of the 1807 *Poems* to his nephew, John Taylor Coleridge, aged sixteen, an undergraduate of Corpus Christi College, Oxford, who was later to become an eminent lawyer and a judge of the King's Bench. Young Coleridge read the poems with delight and showed them to his chosen friend, Thomas Arnold, the future famous headmaster of Rugby. These two and a few others among the undergraduates soon formed an enthusiastic body of Wordsworthians. " We were proof, I am glad to say," wrote Mr Justice Coleridge more than thirty years afterward, " against the criticism, if so it might be called, of *The Edinburgh Review*. We felt their truth and became zealous disciples of Wordsworth's philosophy."

In 1814 came *The Excursion* and another opportunity for the critics. The Byron fever, induced by the publication of *Childe Harold* in 1812, was still raging violently, and Byron from the triumphant height of his popularity renewed his taunts.

> A drowsy, frowsy poem called *The Excursion*
> Writ in a manner which is my aversion.

Jeffrey wrote his famous article in the *Edinburgh*, beginning with the magisterial pronouncement, " This will never do," at which many later critics have jeered ; but Southey's

comment, made in the December of the same year, remains
the most apt reply :

> Jeffrey, I hear, has written what his admirers call a *crushing*
> review of *The Excursion*. He might as well seat himself upon
> Skiddaw and fancy that he crushed the mountain.

Hazlitt gave his usual mixture of praise and jeers :

> The plan raised expectations that were not fulfilled, and the
> effect was like being ushered into a stately hall and invited to
> sit down to a splendid banquet in the company of clowns, and
> with nothing but successive courses of apple dumplings served up.

Master Thomas Macaulay, aged fourteen, in a letter to
Hannah More, telling her all about the new books that had
recently appeared, described *The Excursion* as " almost as
long as it is dull," but kindly added " not but that there are
many striking and beautiful passages interspersed."

Crabb Robinson was on a visit to Norwich, and found a
copy of the new book in a friend's drawing-room. He
glanced hastily through it, and was full of hopes and fears
for its success. He is afraid " it is too mystical to be
popular," but trusts that it will strengthen the zeal of
Wordsworth's few friends. " It may bring upon him the
imputation of dulness, but it will put an end to the sneers
of those who consider, or affect to consider, him puerile."
He longed to read it, but when he did so it afforded him less
intense pleasure on the whole than he expected. On a
second reading he liked it better, and he set to work to make
his friends share his appreciation. On December 10, 1814,
he noted in his diary :

> Took tea with the Flaxmans [the family of John Flaxman,
> the artist]. Read to them *Christabel* and passages from *The
> Excursion*. Flaxman took umbrage at some mystical expres-
> sions in the Preface, where Wordsworth speaks of seeing
> Jehovah unalarmed. " If my brother had written that," said
> Flaxman, " I should say, Burn it." I was unable, and still am,
> to explain the passage.

Robinson was scarcely more successful with another friend
to whom he read the poem, a Mrs Pattison, of Witham.
" She objected to Wordsworth's want of sensibility or rather
of passion, and even maintained that the reason I admired

him was that I never was in love." " Perhaps, after all," he sums up, a little dejectedly, " *The Excursion* will leave Mr Wordsworth's admirers and contemners where they were."

Next year came a new edition of the 1807 volume, with a few fresh poems added. There was the same outcry by the critics, the same mustering for defence of the little band of Wordsworthians, the same emergence of a few converts. " This, we think, has the merit of being the very worst poem we ever saw imprinted in a quarto volume," wrote Jeffrey of *The White Doe of Rylstone* ; and he lamented that a poet who had shown some few gleams of poetic genius now appeared to be sinking into a state of maudlin imbecility. Charles Lamb rejoiced, in what was, for him, quite a savage mood, that Wordsworth had refrained from making any alterations in his poems in an attempt to propitiate his critics.

> I am glad you have not sacrificed a verse to those scoundrels. I would not have had you offer up the poorest rag that lingered upon the stript shoulders of little Alice Fell to have atoned all their malice. I would not have given 'em a red cloak to save their souls. . . . Damn 'em if you give 'em an inch.

The 1815 edition sold very slowly. Shelley and his wife Mary had it, and Leigh Hunt, who had long ago recanted his youthful heresies regarding the *Lyrical Ballads*, though he was still critical of them, showed Wordsworth the volume, standing next to the works of Milton on his shelves, when the poet paid him a visit at Hampstead. Miss Mitford read it, and wrote to her friend, Sir William Elford, with whom she carried on a literary correspondence :

> Are you, my dear friend, of the Wordsworth school ? I think not ; so I may venture to say that I do not like that either. There is such waste of talent—such imagination buried alive in that vast, wordy wilderness.

There is some justice in Miss Mitford's criticism, but she did not see what was clear enough to readers of finer poetic sympathies, that the imagination of *The Excursion* was strong enough to inform and keep alive the whole mass. Like the *Lyrical Ballads*, it found readers even among those who thoroughly disliked it. Wordsworth's complaint to Crabb Robinson, that he has " not seen any one new thing whatever except abuse of myself and sometimes praise that persons mostly unknown to me are officious enough to forward," is testimony of a sort to an increase in the number of his readers.

There was one distinction of hostile criticism that Wordsworth had so far missed—the distinction of being caricatured in one of the novels of Thomas Love Peacock, where most eminent men of the day appeared sooner or later. But he attained to this in *Melincourt*, published in 1817, where he figured as Mr Paperstamp, " chiefly remarkable for an affected, infantine lisp in his speech, and for wearing waistcoats of duffel gray." Wordsworth's character as well as his poetry was attacked. The name ' Paperstamp ' was a sneer at his office of Distributor of Stamps for Westmorland, to which he had been appointed in 1813. He is represented as living at Mainchance Villa, and as being ruled in all his actions by the desire for money.

By 1818 there was a party of Wordsworthians at Cambridge as well as at Oxford. The two Coleridges—Derwent the son and Henry Nelson the nephew of the poet—were at Cambridge, and they had gathered round them a group of young men—Charles and Hyde Villiers, Sidney Walker, Moultrie, Praed, and others, all well known in their later careers—who were ardent admirers of both Wordsworth and Coleridge. Thomas Macaulay, who was not a Wordsworthian, but who knew Wordsworth's poetry as well as, or perhaps better than, most of the band, was now at Trinity, and there were endless arguments, which were the delight of their undergraduate audience, between him and the Coleridges.

Yet in spite of the increase in the number of readers the sale of the poems was not large enough to give much encouragement to the poet or his friends. There was a collected edition of his works in 1820 ; and in 1822 Dorothy Wordsworth wrote sadly to Crabb Robinson :

> He is giving his mind to poetry again, but I do not think that he will ever in his lifetime *publish* any more poems, for they

hang on hand—never selling—the *Sketches* and the *Memorials* have not, I daresay, sold half.

But a turn of the tide must have come during the next two years, for in 1825 she wrote : " He will soon be sending out a new edition of his poems, in six volumes, *The Excursion* included." From time to time after this Robinson wrote reporting favourable remarks by publishers and booksellers regarding the sale of the book ; yet that the abuse still continued is evident from an outbreak in his diary in October 1827. " Yes ! though a swinish rabble of readers unite in one unanimous grunt of censure, I must still think Wordsworth the greatest poet that ever lived." Perhaps Robinson had heard the jokes of some of the students of Trinity College, Cambridge, who about this time, as Edward Fitz-Gerald reports, began to call Wordsworth " the mee-serable poet," inspired thereto by the pronunciation, "mee-serable sinners," affected by Christopher Wordsworth, Master of Trinity and youngest brother of the poet, when he read the Litany in the college chapel. FitzGerald did not much care for Wordsworth or his poetry. He saw the merits of the poems, but they aroused in him no enthusiasm.

In 1828 there came to join the Wordsworthians a most notable convert. John Stuart Mill was the son of the eminent philosopher James Mill. He had been brought up by his father on a strictly logical and ordered plan, the aim of which was to bring all his powers to the highest attainable development by eliminating as far as possible all waste of time and energy. To a very large extent the plan had succeeded. At twenty-one the young man was a fine scholar, remarkable for his highly trained reasoning powers even among the school of philosophers to which his father belonged, and who were known from their leader, Jeremy Bentham, as Benthamites. He wrote brilliant, logical papers in support of their great governing principle, " the greatest happiness of the greatest number," but he failed to find happiness for himself. In his autobiography he tells of the terrible depression that attacked him in his twenty-second year. He had attained the objects which the ambitious plan of his childhood had set before him, but he

54

found no satisfaction in his success. Nothing seemed worth while, nothing repaid any of his efforts. The day's necessary tasks were a weariness, the leisure hours a burden. The future was as grey as the present, life had no good thing to offer. In the autumn of 1828 in a mood of languid curiosity he looked into the 1815 edition of Wordsworth's poems, without any expectation of gaining mental relief from it, " though I had," he says,

> resorted to poetry before in that hope. In the worst period of my depression I had read through the whole of Byron (then new to me) to try whether a poet whose peculiar department was supposed to be that of the intenser feelings, could rouse any feeling in me. As might be expected I got no good from this reading, but, the reverse. The poet's state of mind was too like my own. His was the lament of a man who had worn out all pleasures, and who seemed to think that life, to all who possess the good things of it, must necessarily be the vapid, uninteresting thing I found it. His Harold and Manfred had the same burden on them which I had ; and I was not in a frame of mind to derive any comfort from the vehement sensual passion of his Giaours or the sullenness of his Laras. But while Byron was exactly what did not suit my condition, Wordsworth was exactly what did. I had looked into *The Excursion* two or three years before, and found little in it ; and I should probably have found as little had I read it at this time. But the miscellaneous poems in the two-volume edition of 1815 . . . proved to be the precise thing for my mental wants at this juncture. . . . They expressed not mere outward beauty, but states of feeling, and of thought coloured by feeling under the excitement of beauty. . . . Compared with the greatest poets he may be said to be the poet of unpoetical natures, possessed of quiet and contemplative tastes. But unpoetical natures are precisely those which require poetic cultivation.

Side by side with these words, though in point of time it should come later, we will place the account given by another youth of his first reading of Wordsworth's poems. His name was William Hale White, and his upbringing had been strikingly different from that of the son of the stern intellectual agnostic James Mill. His father, a rigid Calvinistic Independent, was a well-to-do bookseller and printer in the small country town of Bedford. His education was of the narrowest, his society limited to the congregation of the chapel he attended with his parents. At seventeen he was sent to a theological college that he might be trained as a Dissenting minister, but he found there no mental or spiritual enlightenment. He was disillusioned and disgusted by the glib phrases, the smooth platitudes, the sentimental insincerities, that passed for religion. He was fast sinking into a state of miserable apathy when the miracle happened. " One day in my third year," he says,

> a day I remember as well as Paul must have remembered afterwards the day on which he went to Damascus, I happened to find among a parcel of books a volume of poems in paper boards. It was called *Lyrical Ballads*, and I read first one and then the whole book. It conveyed to me no new doctrine, and yet the change it wrought in me could only be compared with that which is said to have been wrought in Paul himself by the Divine Apparition. Looking over *Lyrical Ballads* again, as I have looked over it a dozen times since then, I can hardly see what it was which stirred me so powerfully. . . . It excited a movement of growth which went on till by degrees all the systems which enveloped me like a body gradually decayed from me and fell away into nothing.

Fine ladies and gentlemen, like those of Mrs Gore's *Manners of the Day*, might sneer at the Lake Poets as the " Holy Army of Martyrs " and the " Simplicitarians," but men and women spiritually sick recognized at once what Matthew Arnold later so finely eulogized—Wordsworth's special quality, his " healing power."

For more than thirty years after the publication of the *Lyrical Ballads* Wordsworth had gone on slowly, patiently, painfully seeking out his public, with many disappointments, yet on the whole with steadily increasing success. In the years between 1830 and 1837 the pace quickened ; readers came in by companies instead of by twos and threes. The *Edinburgh* did not recant, but it ceased its attacks. A new generation had grown up which was free from the prejudices of the old. The great mass of readers of " unpoetical natures, possessed of quiet and contemplative tastes " discovered that here was their poet. Charles Darwin, who was one of these, found out Wordsworth and took great delight in him. " I can boast," he said, " that I read *The Excursion* twice through." In 1832 there was a cheap edition of the poems in four volumes. Mrs Clarkson, writing to Crabb Robinson in October 1833, said : " It does seem to me that Wordsworth as a poet is becoming better appreciated, and as far as my limited observation goes, I think that party prejudices are giving way." In September 1834 Charles Greville recorded in his diary a conversation on literary subjects at one of the famous meetings at Holland House. " They held Wordsworth cheap," he said, but he added " except Spring Rice, who was enthusiastic about him." Soon volumes of Wordsworth's poems began to appear in Society drawing-rooms. Mrs Gore, in her novel *Mrs Armytage, or Female Domination*, published in 1836, makes an assembly of fashionable ladies " rave about the beauties of Wordsworth," and the heroine of *The Diary of a Désennuyée* sighs for " Wordsworth the inspired," who, she laments, " writes no more."

The climax came in 1839, when Oxford bestowed upon the poet, in company with other distinguished men, a doctor's degree. He was received with an enthusiasm which showed that the university as a body had gone over to his side. " I heard with great delight of your reception by the undergraduates of Oxford," wrote Crabb Robinson to Wordsworth, " a more significant symptom and sign of the times than the conferring of the degree itself " ; and Thomas Arnold, now headmaster of Rugby, was writing almost at the same time to the Rev. J. C. Cornish, who had been an undergraduate with him at Corpus Christi :

> I went up to Oxford to the Commemoration for the first time for twenty-one years, to see Wordsworth and Bunsen receive their degrees ; and to me, remembering how old Coleridge inoculated a little knot of us with the love of Wordsworth, when his name was in general a bye-word, it was striking to witness the thunders of applause, repeated over and over again, with which he was greeted in the theatre, by Undergraduates and Masters of Arts alike.

The Wordsworthians had triumphed.

57

CHAPTER IV

THE CLAPHAM SECT

THE label bearing the scornful inscription " the Clapham Sect " was attached to the 'Evangelicals' of the English Church by Sydney Smith. That portly, brilliant pillar of orthodoxy hated the Evangelicals almost as much as he hated the Methodists. He wrote against them and preached against them. Their religion, he said, was the " patent Christianity " manufactured at the " holy village " of Clapham, and was little better than no religion at all. The party, with all its works and all its ways, he included in one strong condemnation.

The Evangelicals, however, went calmly on their way, and grew strong and multiplied, in spite of scathing articles in the *Edinburgh* and witty denunciations in both public and private places. They submitted to be called—indeed, sometimes called themselves—" the Clapham Sect," with a sense of mild amusement, and Clapham remained their headquarters. One family followed another to this pleasant country village, until a little community, united by common beliefs and common aims, was established.

John Thornton, a wealthy banker and a friend of the Prime Minister, William Pitt, was the first comer. Thornton —in the words of Sir James Stephen, who was brought up a Claphamite, and has left us the best account we have of the small community's inner life—" became the owner of a spacious mansion on the confines of the villa-cinctured common of Clapham." For this mansion the great Pitt himself " dismissed for a moment his budgets and subsidies " for the amusement of planning an oval saloon "lofty and symmetrical and curiously wainscoted, with books on every side, except where it opened on a far-extended lawn, reposing beneath the giant arms of aged elms and massive tulip-trees." This room became the meeting-

58

CLAPHAM COMMON IN 1802
J. M. W. Turner

58

place of the Evangelical brotherhood, and the centre of a toilsome, but wholesome and happy life. The men who met there concerned themselves with family as well as with national affairs ; with the welfare of the children who played in the pleasant gardens and on the breezy common at Clapham, and with the welfare of toiling, ill-used slaves on the farther shores of great oceans ; with questions of morality and questions of politics; with schemes for sending out missionaries to heathen lands and schemes for supplying their work-people and their servants with the literature best suited for the reading of professing Christians.

" On the bright evening of a day which had run its course some thirty or forty summers ago," said Sir James Stephen, writing in 1844 (his style was surely formed in those early days at Clapham),

> the usual group had formed themselves in this library. Address-ing a nearer circle might be heard above the unbusy hum the voice of the Prelector investigating the character of Seneca's morality perhaps, or, not improbably, the seizure of the Danish fleet, or it might be the various gradations of sanity as exhibited by Robert Hall or Joanna Southcote, when all pastimes were suspended, all speculations put to flight, to welcome the ap-proach of what seemed a dramatic procession emerging from the deep foliage by which the further slopes of the now chequered lawn were overhung.

In advance came two noisy urchins and a tall, shaggy dog. A slight figure followed.

> Limbs, scarcely stouter than that of Asmodeus, sustaining a torso as unlike as possible to that of Theseus, carried him along with the agility of an antelope, though under the weight of two coat pockets protuberant as the bags by which some learned brother of the coif announces and secures his rank as leader of his circuit. Grasping a pocket volume in one hand, he wielded in the other a spud caught up in his progress through the garden. At one instant a staff, on which he leant and listened to the projector at his elbow developing his plan for the better coppering of ships' bottoms, at the next it became a wand pointing out to a portly constituent from the Cloth Hall at Leeds some rich effect of the sunset ; then a truncheon beating time to the poetical reminiscences of a gentleman of the Wesleyan persuasion, looking painfully conscious of his best clothes and of his best behaviour, and ere the sacred

59

cadence had reached its close a cutlass raised in mimic mutiny against the robust form of William Smith, who as Commodore of this ill-assorted squadron was endeavouring to convoy it to port.

This was William Wilberforce, Member of Parliament for Hull, and "the very sun of the Claphamite system." He lived, with his wife and his two young sons, in a house "whose demesne was co-terminus with that of Mr Thornton," and in the closest intimacy with him and with the other Evangelical families of the Common. He was small and sickly, but he had a marvellous voice, that made its way to all hearts, and a personality that charmed even his stiffest opponents. Dullness, we are told, fled at his approach. He had also a tremendous capacity for hard work—a quality. which was common to all the leading members of the Clapham group. It was a quality which had done much toward gaining for them the position which they held ; and, added to the strictness of their principles, it might have made them hard taskmasters to the younger generation had it not been tempered with a large measure of loving-kindness.

Zachary Macaulay, formerly governor of Sierra Leone, another prominent Claphamite, lived in the High Street. His house was not a mansion, but it was roomy and comfortable, with a small, pleasant garden. He came to it in 1802, with his wife and his eldest son, Thomas Babington, who was then two years old, and by 1807 four more children —three daughters and one son—had been born to him. They were a lively, high-spirited company, and as they grew up their serious-minded father was often troubled to see them developing tastes and habits so different from his own. But he was indulgent in small matters, and the strong respect and affection they felt for him kept them from doing anything which would really outrage the proprieties of the community.

On the outskirts of Clapham, or, as Sir James Stephen puts it, "At the distance of a few bowshots from the house of Henry Thornton " (who had succeeded his father, John Thornton) " was the happy home in which dwelt Granville Sharp and his family." He was the grandson of an arch-

60

LORD MACAULAY'S SCHOOL AT CLAPHAM
Photo M. L. Harry

bishop and the son of an archdeacon, but he himself in his youth had been apprenticed to a linen-draper on Tower Hill. He had afterward obtained a post as clerk in the Ordnance Department, and while there circumstances had led him to come forward as a strong advocate of the African negroes. He had spent all his leisure in studying the law as regards slavery, until he was recognized as the greatest authority on the subject, and when the Society for the Abolition of Slavery was formed he was made its President.

Other members of the Clapham community were Lord Teignmouth, at whose house, at the corner of the Common, the Bible Society was founded; Mr Stephen, a barrister, who had married a sister of Mr Wilberforce, and several of whose descendants were to become famous; and Mr Grant, Director of the East India Company. There were others, dwelling outside the bounds, who were such frequent visitors as to be almost reckoned as members— Dean Isaac Milner and Charles Simeon from Cambridge; Thomas Gisborne from the banks of the Trent; and Thomas Clarkson, the originator of the abolition of slavery movement, from Cumberland. " Alas ! " says Sir James Stephen,

> it is not given to anyone, not even to Thomas Clarkson, to enjoy glory complete and unalloyed. Far be it from us to pluck one leaf from the crown that rests on that triumphant head. But with truth there can be no compromise, and truth wrings from us the acknowledgment that Thomas Clarkson never lived at Clapham.

All these men were Churchmen, but the Evangelicals, in their struggle for reform, were only too glad to work with those Dissenters whose aims were the same as their own. William Smith, the Unitarian Member of Parliament for Clapham, and John Mills the Quaker were among the most honoured of their company. Macaulay said that Thackeray, in the opening chapters of *The Newcomes*, unduly stressed the importance of the Dissenting element in Clapham; but he did not deny that the picture given was, in essentials, a true one. Thackeray settles the heiress of the wealthy house of Hobson Brothers, who married Thomas Newcome, in Clapham. At her mansion, called the Hermitage, the most eloquent expounders, the most gifted missionaries, the most interesting converts from foreign islands were to be found at her sumptuous table, spread with the produce of her magnificent gardens. It was a serious paradise. As you entered at the gate gravity fell upon you, and decorum wrapped you in a garment of starch. . . . The rooks in the elms cawed sermons at morning and evening, the peacocks walked demurely on the terraces, the guinea fowls looked more Quaker-like than those savoury birds usually do. The lodge-keeper was serious and a clerk at a neighbouring chapel. . . . The head gardener was a Scotch Calvinist after the strictest order, only occupying himself with the melons and pines provisionally until the end of the world, which event, he could prove by infallible calculations, was to come off in two or three years, at farthest. . . . On a Sunday the household marched away in separate couples or groups to at least half a dozen of religious edifices, each to sit under his or her favourite minister, the only man who went to Church being Thomas Newcome, accompanied by Tommy, his little son, and Sarah his nurse. . . . Tommy was taught hymns very soon after he could speak, appropriate to his tender age, pointing out to him the inevitable fate of wicked children, and giving him the earliest possible warning and description of the punishment of little sinners. He repeated these poems to his stepmother after dinner, before a great shining mahogany table covered with grapes, pine-apples, plum-cake, port wine and Madeira, and surrounded by stout men in black with baggy white neckcloths, who took the little man between their knees and questioned him as to his right understanding of the place whither naughty boys were bound.

There was no taint of hypocrisy in all this, though such open profession of godliness tended to encourage hypocrites. The Chadbands and the Stigginses and the Brocklehursts were not members of the Clapham Sect; they were its degenerate descendants. Mrs Thomas Newcome was a woman of sincere piety, untiring in charitable works. When she died, at a good old age, "her funeral," says one of the clerks in her house of business, who knew her well,

was one of the most imposing sights ever witnessed in Clapham. There was such a crowd you might have thought it was a Derby day. . . . And besides the empty carriages at the funeral, and the parson in black, and the mutes and feathers, and that, there were hundreds and hundreds of people who wore no black, and who weren't present, and who wept for their benefactress, I can tell you. She had her faults, and many of 'em; but the amount of that woman's charities are unheard of, Sir—unheard of—and they are put to the credit side of her account up yonder.

In spite, however, of all Mrs Newcome's virtues, life at the Hermitage was undeniably dull. Her stepson Tommy found it unbearable. Sir James Stephen admits that Clapham was, as a whole, " a serious Paradise." The Claphamites had a heavy hand in social matters. " Their festivities were not exhilarating. New faces, new topics, and a less liberal expenditure of wisdom immediately after dinner would have improved them." The Claphamites never went to the theatre, except by stealth as Brian and Hobson Newcome sometimes did on Saturday nights; their mother knew nothing of it, and they took care to be ready to go to chapel with her next morning. Mrs Barbauld reports, in 1813, that " Mrs Siddons's readings are much patronised by the Evangelical people, as they are called, of fashion, who will not enter the doors of a theatre." Mrs Warren, the fervently Evangelical wife of a Norwich barrister, had " strong objections to some papers in *The Spectator* as having a direct tendency to recommend the Theatre and the Ball-room." Thomas Babington Macaulay was eighteen, an undergraduate of Trinity College, when he saw his first play. It was performed at the local theatre by a company of travelling players, who came to Cambridge during the Long Vacation. Macaulay's companions were astonished when he told them he had never before seen a play. "What!" said one of them. " Did you then never go to the play as a boy ? " " No," replied Macaulay, " after the straitest sect of our religion, I was bred a Pharisee."

On Sundays—or, rather, the Sabbath—Clapham was at its dullest. Light and frivolous conversation was considered unseemly, and only the most serious books were approved. Walking for walking's sake was never allowed. The family went to church twice, and in the afternoon and again at evening prayers a sermon was read aloud to the assembled household. At an early hour everybody went to bed.

Such was Sydney Smith's " holy village " ; but, as Sir James Stephen says, the Clapham Sect did not end with

Clapham. It had sent its messengers throughout England, and in many towns and villages small communities were forming, during the last years of the eighteenth century and the early years of the nineteenth, whose members held the same beliefs and followed the same practices as the parent society, though sometimes with a less enlightened enthusiasm.

Scarcely less famous than Clapham itself was Cowslip Green, near Bristol, the Evangelical stronghold in the West. Here lived Miss Hannah More—fashionable Blue-stocking, stout Churchwoman, and active philanthropist—with her four sisters, Miss Mary, Miss Betty, Miss Sallie, and Miss Patty. They were intimate friends of Henry Thornton, Zachary Macaulay, and William Wilberforce, and many visits were exchanged between the Evangelicals of Clapham and the Evangelicals of Bristol. Many famous people came to Cowslip Green—bishops and statesmen, and well-known authors, both men and women. Thomas De Quincey says that one of his reasons for keeping up his annual visits to Somersetshire was that he might call on Miss Hannah More, where he was almost sure to meet some person interesting by rank, station, political or literary eminence. The mother of De Quincey had, in her earlier days, when the family lived at Bath, been a great friend of Miss Hannah's, and a strict Evangelical.

At Bristol, as at Clapham, there was a close alliance between the Evangelicals and the various Dissenting bodies. Mr Mills, the Quaker bookseller, was their staunch friend. His pretty daughter Selina, who had been a favourite pupil of the Misses More in the days when they kept a select school for young ladies, had married Zachary Macaulay and gone to live at Clapham.

From Bristol the tenets of the Clapham Sect had been carried through the neighbouring counties. Clarissa Trant, daughter of General Sir Nicholas Trant, who had served with distinction in the Peninsular War, describes in her diary a round of visits which she made among certain Evangelical families in the West, and complains that she found them very dull. At Stowey Mead, the house of Lord Sandford, the entry made in her diary says :

64

THE CLAPHAM SECT

Twice to church, two sermons at home, then Sunday School, then religious reading, then lunch, and then a walk, then a Bible Class for the village people. No one speaks of anything but Evangelical people and books.

In the north the city of York, which was the home of the Wilberforce family, and which William Wilberforce later represented in Parliament, was the chief Claphamite outpost. In the *Papers and Diaries of a York Family*, lately published, we read how William Gray and Faith his wife bought in 1788 the Great House in the Minster Yard, to the north-east of the Cathedral. Here they lived and brought up their family on strict Evangelical principles, and were succeeded by their children and their children's children. They loved and revered Wilberforce, who often visited them, and they were intimate also with Joseph Milner, John Newton, Lindley Murray, and a number of other well-known Evangelicals. The account given in Faith Gray's diary of her life and her friends at York shows a society as sober and devout in its manner of living as the society at Clapham, and with a serenity and simplicity which is almost Quaker-like, and which gives them what the Evangelicals sometimes lacked—a true dignity of life.

George Eliot, who was brought up in an Evangelical community, and who in her girlhood held its tenets as devoutly as any Claphamite, has shown us what Evangelicalism was like in some of the small country towns where the clergy were not of the highest type, where the people were uneducated, and where a coarse and bitter opposition had to be encountered. Mr Tyke and the Bulstrodes and the Plymdales at Middlemarch, the Reverend Amos Barton at Shepperton, and Mr Tryan and his devoted followers at Milby were in many ways different from the Wilberforces and the Macaulays, the Mores and the Grays. They were narrower, sourer, more sanctimonious, apter to confuse non-essentials and essentials. But the root of the matter was in them, and they were of the brotherhood ; even Miss Rebecca Linnet, of *Janet's Repentance*, had her claim to be considered as a member of the Clapham group.

One thing that tended strongly to maintain this unity

E

was that they all read the same books. They possessed a distinct and characteristic literature, manufactured by members of their own body, and specially adapted to their aims and beliefs. It was not a great or a very interesting literature, and few but Claphamites cared to read it. Among them it was devoutly studied. The more educated members of the body also read, and read widely, books that lay outside its boundaries, but even they did not neglect it. The less educated—that is, the great mass of Evangelicals—read nothing else.

One of the most remarkable examples of this literature was a small book called *The Dairyman's Daughter*, written by Legh Richmond, a Bedfordshire clergyman who had been converted by Wilberforce's *Practical View of Christianity*. It told the story of an unnaturally pious girl who converted first her frivolous younger sister, and then her father, the dairyman, and her mother. The sister died, and the minister of the parish, Mr Legh Richmond himself, was called upon to bury her. He thus became acquainted with the family and showed such interest in the elder daughter, who was rapidly wasting with the same disease that had brought her sister to her death, that she was encouraged to write to him a series of long letters. In these she set out in detail her religious experiences, telling of her trials and temptations and how she had overcome them, exhorting him to greater fervour in spiritual matters, and expressing an ardent belief in all the articles of the Evangelical faith. Finally she died in the most edifying manner, making long deathbed speeches and bestowing parting blessings on her family and her friends.

Of this work two million copies were sold, and from every side came reports of the good influence it had exerted and the converts it had brought in. A second book of Mr Richmond's, *Domestic Portraiture*, which was an account of his own family life and the training of his sons and daughters, was almost as successful. Charlotte Brontë, who was an Evangelical of the sterner type, read it, and wrote to her friend Ellen Nussey saying that it "strongly attracted and strangely fascinated my attention. Beg, borrow, or steal it without delay." When Mr Legh Richmond died, his life was written by his son-in-law, and this book too became a favourite with the Claphamites. It was among the volumes lying on Mrs Linnet's parlour table on the summer afternoon on which George Eliot introduces us to that pleasant apartment. A group of ladies sat round the table busy with black canvas and scissors and paste and green labels preparing the books for the Paddiford Lending Library ; and as they worked they talked of Mr Tryan, the new Evangelical curate, and the wonders he had worked in Paddiford. " Upon my word," said Miss Pratt,

> it is a most admirable selection of works for popular reading, this that our excellent Mr Tryan has made. I do not know whether, if the task had been confided to me, I could have made a selection, combining in a higher degree religious instruction and edification with a due admixture of the purer species of amusement.

The other ladies could not express themselves with the fluency and authority of Miss Pratt, for she was " the one blue-stocking of Milby, possessing, she said, no less than five hundred volumes " ; but they all had something to say about the books and about the curate.

> " That's a book I'm very fond of—the *Life of Legh Richmond*," said Mrs Linnet. " He found out all about that woman at Tutbury as pretended to live without eating. Stuff and nonsense ! "
>
> Mrs Linnet had become a reader of religious books since Mr Tryan's advent, and as she was in the habit of confining her perusal to the purely secular portions, which bore a very small proportion to the whole, she could make rapid progress through a large number of volumes. On taking up the biography of a celebrated preacher, she immediately turned to the end to see what disease he died of ; and if his legs swelled, as her own occasionally did, she felt a stronger interest in ascertaining any earlier facts in the history of the dropsical divine—whether he had ever fallen off a stage-coach, whether he had married more than one wife, and, in general, any adventures or repartees recorded of him previous to the epoch of his conversion. She then glanced over the letters and diary, and wherever there was a predominance of Zion, the River of Life, and notes of exclamation, she turned over to the next page ; but any passage in which she saw such promising nouns as "smallpox," "pony," or "boots and shoes," at once arrested her.

THE ENGLISHMAN AND HIS BOOKS

It is possible that other readers among the Evangelicals adopted Mrs Linnet's captivatingly simple and time-saving method of reading religious biography ; which might account for the extreme popularity of that form of literature. *The Memories of Felix Neff* and *The Life of Father Clement* were also among the books that were in Mrs Linnet's parlour, the latter being admitted as a cautionary story, being, as Miss Pratt described it, " a library in itself on the errors of Romanism." Clarissa Trant read it in 1824.

The Evangelical literature of the poorer classes consisted almost entirely of tracts. Hannah More had been the first tract-provider, with her *Village Politics* and " Cheap Repository Tracts," which were short sketches, homely, interesting, and moderately well written, of scenes in the life of the poor. They were sold for a penny, or sometimes a halfpenny, and had an enormous circulation. Popular numbers, like *The Shepherd of Salisbury Plain*, sold by thousands. Susan Sibbald tells in her memoirs how this tract first gave her the taste for Sunday reading. The Gray family knew them well, but were not blindly admiring. Jonathan Gray, Faith's son, aged sixteen, wrote to his mother while he was away on a visit : " We admire very much the history of the two farmers, Braywell and Worthy, in the Church Repository. It seems superior to anything Hannah More can do." This particular tract was written by Mrs Trimmer.

The great success of these publications led to the Religious Tract Society being formed in 1799, and then the vogue of tracts began. Zealous Evangelical clergymen sent the ladies of their congregation " tracking "—as the Reverend Amos Barton, curate of Shepperton, tried to do, but with only partial success. " There's that Track Society as Mr Barton has begun," said Mrs Hackit, wife to one of the most prosperous farmers in the parish. " I've seen more o' the poor people with going tracking than all the time I've lived in the parish before." But Mrs Patten, the rich widow of the owner of Cross Farm, representing the older and more orthodox faction, would have nobody tracking out of her house.

> I've hear'd of no good from interfering with one's neighbours, poor or rich, and I hate the sight o' women going about,

trapesing from house to house, in all weathers, wet or dry, and coming in with their petticoats dagged and their shoes all over mud.

Sydney Smith was on the side of Mrs Patten, and held up to ridicule a proposal that had been made by one enthusiastic ' tracker ' that travellers, for every pound they spent on the road, should fling one shillingsworth of tracts out of the window of their chaise. But in spite of these scoffers the belief in the efficacy of tracts grew into an article of faith staunchly held by all good Evangelicals. By 1807 upward of four million had been issued by the Religious Tract Society, and the demand was still increasing. Zachary Macaulay, reproving his son for unflattering criticisms made by him on the people of Shelford, where he was at school, wrote :

> Now instead of railing at the people of Shelford, I think the best thing that you and your schoolfellows could do would be to try to reform them. You can buy and distribute useful and striking tracts, as well as Testaments among such as can read. The Cheap Repository and Religious Tract Society will furnish tracts suited to all descriptions of persons.

The misguided zeal of some perfervid Evangelicals gave great occasion to the scoffers and helped to bring about the decline of this branch of their literature. Writers eager for the joys of authorship, but with little ability, sprang up on every side. There was a certain bookseller named Vine Hall who wrote a tract called *The Sinner's Friend*, and who spent a large part of his time in distributing copies of it throughout the country. He visited prisons and gave copies of it to the prisoners ; he handed it to passers-by and to his fellow-passengers in omnibuses ; and occasionally he dropped a few numbers upon the pavement. Altogether three million copies of it were printed, and it was translated into thirty languages. Pious and eloquent ladies aspired to be known as tract-writers ; others, as pious and scarcely less eloquent, sought fame as tract-distributors. The current religious phraseology of the sect degenerated into a sanctimonious formula which, as used by many shallow and voluble persons, might reasonably be termed " cant." Crude attempts to impress and to move the sinner led to absurdities which the enemy was quick to exploit. Thackeray exhibited Lady Emily Sheepshanks, a mature spinster who wrote those sweet tracts *The Washerwoman of Finchley Common* and *The Sailor's True Binnacle* ; with her noble parent, the Countess of Southdown, who favoured such soul-stirring efforts as *A Voice from the Flames, A Trumpet Warning to Jericho, Fleshpots Broken, or The Converted Cannibal,* and was always ready to put up a little parcel of such soothing literature for the sick or the afflicted. For the servants' hall these ladies had a special selection, with such appropriate titles as *Crumbs from the Pantry, The Frying Pan and the Fire,* and *The Livery of Sin.*

Dickens created Mrs Pardiggle to immortalize those determined ladies who insisted on forcing tracts upon disgusted recipients who would certainly never read them. " Have I read the little book wot you left ? " said the brickmaker. " No, I an't read the little book wot you left. There an't nobody here as knows how to read it ; and if there wos, it wouldn't be suitable to me. It's a book fit for a babby, and I'm not a babby." " As to the little book," goes on the teller of the story, " we acquired a knowledge of it afterwards ; and Mr Jarndyce said he doubted if Robinson Crusoe could have read it, though he had no other on his desolate island."

Wilkie Collins followed with *The Moonstone,* in which Miss Drusilla Clack, " Reader and Visitor under not less, first and last, than fourteen beloved clerical friends," presents the female tract-distributor in her most relentless and ubiquitous form. She called at a relative's house and offered a tract to " the person " who answered the door. It " was one of a series addressed to young women on the sinfulness of dress. In style it was devoutly familiar. Its title was, *A Word with you on your Cap-ribbons.*" The " young castaway " rejected it in a contumelious speech.

> She handed me back the tract, and opened the door. We must sow the good seed somehow. I waited till the door was shut on me, and slipped the tract in the letter-box. When I had dropped another tract through the area railings, I felt relieved, in some small degree, of a heavy responsibility towards others.

The Good School-Mistress.

On another occasion she " committed the prodigality of taking a cab."

> I paid the cabman exactly his fare. He received it with an oath ; upon which I instantly gave him a tract. If I had presented a pistol at his head, this abandoned wretch could hardly have exhibited greater consternation. He jumped up on his box, and, with profane exclamations of dismay, drove off furiously. Quite useless, I am happy to say ! I sowed the good seed, in spite of him, by throwing a second tract in at the window of the cab.

She endeavoured to speak a word in season, in a stormy domestic scene, to an elderly gentleman in a towering passion. He answered violently.

> It is impossible for me to write the awful word which is here represented by a blank. I shrieked as it passed his lips ; I flew to my little bag on the side table ; I shook out all my tracts ; I seized the one particular tract on profane swearing, entitled, *Hush, for Heaven's Sake* ; I handed it to him with an expression of agonized entreaty. He tore it in two and threw it back at me across the table.

But the era of the Pardiggles and the Clacks came nearly fifty years after those early Clapham days when Miss Hobson presented her future stepson with " A tract in one syllable suited to his infant understanding." Evangelicalism had lost its hold on the mass of the people, and dishonour had fallen upon it through many who adopted its outward form, but knew nothing of its spirit. Ridicule went far toward destroying the popularity of the tract, though Lord Rayleigh says that as late as 1887 Lady Ashburton, whose views were strongly Evangelical, had

> a touching belief in the efficacy of tracts. I remember that we were invited to use the billiard table whenever we wished, but this was more easily said than done, as it was covered with a layer of this kind of literature a foot or more in depth. When our kind hostess took us for a drive a pile of edifying pamphlets were placed on the seat beside her, and they were flung out to any passer-by. If no one was in sight the good seed would often be sown on the roadside.

The leading members of the Evangelical party did not confine themselves to their own peculiar literature, but read widely, like the scholars and cultured gentlemen that they were. Although they held that reading should be for edification, not for amusement, they were no domestic tyrants, and a certain amount of light reading, especially among the younger members, was tolerated, if not approved. But ' solid ' books formed the basis of their collections. Sir James Stephen says that in his father's library " drawn up in deep files were the works and biographies of Puritan divines from Thomas Cartwright to Matthew Pool. This veteran battalion was flanked by a company of lighter works, drafted from the polite literature of a more frivolous age." Macaulay speaks of his father's " very sullen library," and of a certain book containing translations of some Spanish comedies as one of its " few bright specks." If we could have looked round the many shelves of that oval saloon designed by William Pitt we should have found a marvellous collection of works—historical, political, legal, philosophical—bearing on the reforms for which this little group of earnest men was striving. Memoirs, pamphlets, dispatches, Blue Books—everything that could throw light on debatable questions concerning them was there, and all were in constant use. Zachary Macaulay was noted among the band for the variety as well as the depth of his reading.

> It was difficult to understand when he had time to pick up his knowledge ; or how he made room for it in a mind so crammed with facts and statistics relating to questions of the day, that when Wilberforce was at a loss for a piece of information he used to say, " Let us look it out in Macaulay."

Some of the religious works favoured by the Evangelicals were almost alarmingly weighty and portentous. " I have fagged hard at good old Bishop Reynolds," wrote Hannah More,

> a fat folio of near twelve hundred pages, which I have almost got through. Such solid Christianity ! Such deep views of sinful man ! And as to tediousness, I rather like it. I never can pick up any sustenance out of your short, scanty books.

Every one read Paley's *Natural Theology* and *Evidences of Christianity*, though Wilberforce did not entirely approve of the views expressed, and Hannah More agreed with him. Lady Wharncliffe thought very highly of the work. Wilberforce's *Practical View of Christianity* was in every library, and so was Dean Milner's *Ecclesiastical History,* and there were rows of sermons and religious biographies. The Gray family read Taylor's *Life of Christ,* Milton's poems, *The Life of Colonel Gardiner, Mason on the Sacraments, The Pilgrim's Progress,* homilies by Mr Richardson—*On the Misery of Man,* etc.—*The Life of Whitfield, The Whole Duty of Man,* Law's *Serious Call, The Life of Johnson,* Hannah More's works, and Thomas Gisborne's *Sermons.* Several times in the early days before her marriage Faith records that her reading is " a strange mixture of history and morality," and once she adds " and Novels," but it is evident that she early overcame this leaning toward frivolous literature, for in the sermon preached at her death it was stated: " The Bible and religious authors were her chief study, and the meagre romantic trash that forms the delight of many female minds had no charms for her." Mr Wilberforce guided and advised the Grays in their choice of literature, and on one occasion at least he sent a present of books to Faith's children—Hannah More's works in ten volumes for Margaret Gray, Wither's poems in nine volumes for Lucy Gray, and Gregory's *Economy of Nature* in three handsome volumes for Jonathan Gray.

Clarissa Trant's list of books read in 1824 includes *Memoirs of Cowper, Patriarchal Piety,* Hannah More's *Moral Sketches,* William Scott's *Essays,* Cunningham's *Morning Thoughts,* and Paley's *Evidences,* and in 1827 *Mason on Self-knowledge, Impressions of the Heart with Respect to Religion, Guide of Young Disciples,* Doddridge's *Rise and Progress,* and Watts' *Improvement of the Mind.* Even the dairyman's daughter had Doddridge's *Rise and Progress,* Romaine's *Life, Walk, and Triumph of Faith, The Pilgrim's Progress,* and Baxter's *Saints' Rest.* Miss Clack had " a little library of works . . . all calculated to arouse, convince, prepare, enlighten, and fortify." One of these was called *The Serpent at Home,* and contained such arousing chapters as " Satan in the Hair Brush," " Satan behind the Looking-glass," " Satan under the Tea-table," and " Satan out of the Window." Miss Clack had a ' serious ' friend at Brighton, a single lady like herself, who had a library "composed throughout of precious publications," of which the most precious of all seems to have been the *Life, Letters and Labours of Miss Jane Ann Stamper.*

As for the children in the Clapham houses, they, from their earliest years, read the Bible daily or listened while it was read to them ; they learned hymns and studied tracts specially written for their edification. They read also *The Pilgrim's Progress* and such religious stories as Mrs Trimmer's *History of the Robins* and Mrs Sherwood's *The Fairchild Family,* and in some of the more liberal families they read the ordinary nursery classics and fairy-tales. It is related that Miss Hannah More, then a sedate lady of nearly sixty, called on the afternoon of a day in 1804 at the house of Mr Zachary Macaulay. She was received with great politeness by her godson Thomas, a bright-eyed, fair-haired boy of four years old, to whom she was then unknown. He explained that his parents were not at home, but that if she would step into the drawing-room he would bring her a glass of old spirits. The offer took away the good lady's breath almost as completely as the old spirits would have done; but it appeared upon inquiry that it had been meant merely as a polite attention, prompted by the recollection that Robinson Crusoe had often indulged in and greatly appreciated such refreshment. Little Tom Macaulay at four years old evidently knew his *Robinson Crusoe* as well as he knew his Watts' *Catechisms.* During the next ten years Miss Hannah More delighted to foster his taste for reading, to give him books and advise him in choosing others for himself. He stayed with her often at Barley Wood, near Bristol, to which she and her sisters had removed in 1802, and read as many as she would allow of her large collection of books, which was certainly less "sullen" than that of his father. He read her *Lyrical Ballads,* and her *Don Quixote* in four volumes, which Mrs Carter, one of the Bluestockings, had left to her. He read everything he could get hold of, histories, poetry, even sectarian theological treatises.

Thomas Macaulay is, however, in this matter of reading scarcely a fair example of the Claphamite children, for he was from his babyhood one of those mortals who must and

THE
SHEPHERD
OF
SALISBURY-PLAIN.

Sold by S. HAZARD,
(PRINTER to the CHEAP REPOSITORY for Religious and
Moral Tracts,) at BATH;

By J. MARSHALL,
At the CHEAP REPOSITORIES, No. 17, Queen-Street,
Cheap-Side, and No. 4, Aldermary Church Yard; and R. WHITE,
Piccadilly, LONDON; and by all Bookfellers, Newfmen, and
Hawkers, in Town and Country.

☞ Great Allowance to Shopkeepers and Hawkers.
Price 1d. or 4s. 6d. per 100. 2s. 6d. for 50. 1s. Cd. for 25.

[Entered at Stationers Hall.]

COVER OF ONE OF HANNAH MORE'S "CHEAP REPOSITORY TRACTS"

will read in whatever circumstances they find themselves. Margaret Gray, granddaughter of Faith, is probably more typical. " As soon as she was able to speak," we are told, " she was taught to commit to memory Dr Watts' *Divine Songs for Children* ; at the age of four she could read the Bible and repeat the Church Catechism ; and from that period for some years she regularly committed to memory the Gospel for the day." At twelve she read *Paradise Lost,* and was much impressed with its pictures of Satan and of hell. At seventeen she made out a plan for her daily reading. In the morning she was to read Prideaux's *Connection* for an hour ; in the evening and at other convenient times Watts' *Improvement of the Mind* aloud to her mother ; for miscellaneous reading Jowett's *Researches in Syria* ; for religion Chalmers and Thomas à Kempis. " For ornamental reading one has always time and inclination," she adds, but does not tell us to what books her inclination leads her, which is tantalizing.

As the children grew up difficulties multiplied. The godly, devoted elders, working with single-hearted zeal for causes which were to them the greatest things in life, felt uneasy and distressed when they saw their sons and daughters desirous of giving so much precious time to idle reading. The delight his children took in such reading was, Hannah Macaulay says, a thorn in the flesh of her father. Of novel-reading he entirely disapproved, yet he was too kind-hearted to insist on his family giving up what they enjoyed so highly. He only stipulated that there should be no reading of novels or poetry in the mornings, and except during the holidays this rule was kept. The evenings were usually given to reading aloud, especially when Tom was at home. " His notion of perfect happiness," his sister says,

> was to see us all working round him while he read aloud. . . . Among the books selected I can recall Clarendon, Burnet, Shakespeare (a great treat when my mother took the volume), Miss Edgeworth, Mackenzie's *Lounger* and *Mirror*, and, as a standing dish, *The Edinburgh* and *The Quarterly Reviews.* Poets, too, especially Scott and Crabbe, were constantly chosen.

They read, too, Pepys, Addison, Horace Walpole, and

Dr Johnson, and all the standard novels, such as those of Richardson, Miss Burney, Miss Austen, and Lord Lytton, as well as piles of trashy, sensational novels from the circulating library.

There are several novels on Clarissa Trant's list, including Disraeli's *Vivian Grey* and Lister's *Granby* ; but her father was not an Evangelical, and allowed her to please herself in her choice of books. Susan Sibbald's father would not allow his daughters to read any of the romances or novels in his collection, so they secretly subscribed to a circulating library and read the books in their room at night, after their maid had been dismissed. They shivered with delicious terror over Mrs Radcliffe's " most horrible romance of *The Mysteries of Udolpho*," and took care " to leave off reading before the dreaded hour of twelve when ghosts might be expected to make their appearance." Jonathan Gray too read *The Mysteries of Udolpho*, and Faith, as we have seen, read some novels ; probably, too, they formed part of Margaret's " ornamental reading."

When the Waverley Novels began to appear all except the very strictest of the Evangelicals admitted them for family reading. But before that time an attempt had been made to satisfy the deplorable but apparently determined demand of the younger generation for novels by supplying an article which cunningly took on the outward shape of this worldly invention, but within was pure Evangelicalism. Hannah More once again, as in the case of the tracts, stepped gallantly into the breach. She wrote a book called *Cœlebs in Search of a Wife*, which was published in December 1809 —just in time for Christmas presents. The second edition was sold out before Christmas, and we can picture all the Clapham people sitting down to it for their holiday reading. The elders doubtless saw in it a shining example of the way in which base things can be transmuted by religion and genius. The feelings of the younger are probably expressed in the words of Sara Coleridge : " To read Mrs More's new book was a sort of good work which made the reader feel satisfied with him or herself when performed."

Some people outside the Clapham Sect read *Cœlebs*.

Cassandra Austen did, and recommended it to her sister Jane ; and Jane wrote in reply : " You have by no means roused my curiosity after *Cœlebs*. My disinclination for it before was affected, but now it is real. I do not like the Evangelicals. Of course I shall be delighted when I read it, like other people, but till I do, I dislike it." Susan Sibbald and her sisters read it, but do not record their opinions ; only when a young relative of theirs came to pay them a visit, " with the idea of picking up a cousin," they called him jestingly " Cœlebs in Search of a Wife."

Hannah More told Clarissa Trant an anecdote concerning the book which proves that it had some readers among university students. Some friends of hers overheard the following conversation : Said one Oxford undergraduate, " Well, have you read *Cœlebs in Search of a Wife*? " " Yes," replied the other. " What do you think of it ? " " Think ? Why, I think it is a great bore. But that fellow has one good quality. He drives a curricle."

A friend of Charles Lamb's bought *Cœlebs*—" a very careful, neat lady "—and Lamb borrowed it from her. Its overmuch piety aroused in him that ribaldry to attacks of which he was lamentably subject. " It has reached eight editions in so many weeks," he wrote, " yet literally it is one of the very poorest sort of common novels, with the drawback of dull religion in it. Had the religion been high and flavoured it would have been something." He returned the lady her book with this verse written on the opening page :

> If ever I marry a wife,
> I'll marry a landlord's daughter,
> For then I may sit in the bar,
> And drink cold brandy and water.

Where is that copy now ? And where are all the other thousands of copies of *Cœlebs* that were in existence a hundred years or so ago ? Where the two million copies of *The Dairyman's Daughter* ? How many people have read either of these truly remarkable works ? They have gone, except a few preserved in libraries, and no one would dream of reprinting them. When the Clapham Sect died out its literature died with it.

CHAPTER V

THE SCHOOLROOM

YOUNG ladies in the schoolroom were, during the
first half of the nineteenth century, a company
cloistered and set apart, not to be mistaken by any
instructed person for their emancipated sisters who had
' come out.' " The distinction," said Miss Crawford, of
Mansfield Park, enlightening an ignorant male audience,
" is so broad. Manners as well as appearance are generally
speaking so totally different. A girl not out has always
the same sort of dress—a close bonnet, for instance—looks
very demure and never says a word." For social purposes
the young lady in the schoolroom did not exist. She was
not included in any invitations, and visitors, if by chance
she came in their way, were not required to take any special
notice of her.

At the age of seven or eight the girls of that period
definitely left the nursery and passed under schoolroom
rule, and there they remained usually for about ten years,
though the period varied in different families. Lady
Leonora MacDougall, of *Midnight Weddings*, came out on
her sixteenth birthday. The Misses Bertram, of *Mansfield
Park*, looked forward to seventeen as the age of their release.
Miss Eliza Coke, daughter of the great Mr Coke, of Norfolk,
remained in the schoolroom until she was eighteen. Lady
Catherine de Burgh, of *Pride and Prejudice*, was shocked to
hear that the five Misses Bennet, of ages varying from
fifteen to twenty-three, were all out at once. " The younger
ones out before the elder are married ! " she exclaimed,
and Elizabeth Bennet acknowledged that fifteen was " full
young to see much company." " But really, ma'am," she
went on coolly, while Lady Catherine was stiff with dis-
approval, " I think it would be very hard on younger sisters
that they should not have their share of society and amuse-

78

ment because the elder may not have the means, or inclination, to marry early." Yet that is what did happen in a great many families, and consequently the young ladies in the schoolroom took a keen interest in the love affairs of their elders and were nearly all sworn allies of an eligible suitor. Mrs Gore in her *Manners of the Day* tells of the delight felt by the young ladies of the family, " who were still incarcerated in the schoolroom of which the backboards and inclined planes afforded specimens of torture," when Lord Willersdale began to pay his addresses to their sister Helen, aged eighteen, who had just come out, and was regarded by them as " an enfranchised dove, rescued from the dreary monotony of their ark."

The schoolroom in which the rites of those early years were performed was in some cases that of a very select boarding-school—day-schools for the daughters of gentlemen were almost unknown. Jane Austen and Mary Butt (afterward Mrs Sherwood, author of *The History of the Fairchild Family*) went to the Abbey School, Reading. Mary Russell Mitford and Lady Caroline Lamb went to the same school after it had been removed to Hans Place, London. Shelley's sisters and Harriet Westbrook went to Mrs Fenning's school on Clapham Common ; Amelia Sedley and Miss Swartz were pupils at Miss Pinkerton's academy for young ladies on Chiswick Mall ; Rosamond Vincy was the flower of Mrs Lemon's school near Middlemarch, where the teaching " included all that was demanded in the accomplished female." All these schools were very exclusive and very dear, and all of them held as their first article of faith that young ladies must be secluded from the world, and especially from the eyes of possibly admiring males.

But in the very best families—the families where birth and breeding were most highly considered—the daughters were usually educated at home. Their schoolroom was, wherever possible, out of the way of the rooms in which the social life of the rest of the household was carried on, and seems to have been in most cases a sufficiently dingy apartment. The educational value of a plentiful supply of light and air, and of bright and beautiful surroundings, was

79

scarcely thought of in those days. The young ladies must be content with windows without extensive views, with odds and ends of furniture too shabby or too unfashionable for the rest of the house, with ink-stained tables and chairs, with maps for pictures, and for ornaments the indispensable globes, celestial and terrestrial. The greater part of their indoor waking life was spent in these surroundings. They were allowed in the other parts of the house by favour, not by right. The schoolroom alone was their acknowledged domain.

The other inhabitant of the schoolroom was the governess, and she, more completely and permanently than her pupils, belonged to a dedicated band. " Governesses," observed Miss Hardman, of Charlotte Brontë's *Shirley*, " must ever be kept in a sort of isolation. It is the only means of maintaining that distance which the reserve of English manners and the decorum of English families exact." In that far-off time almost the only way in which a gently born woman could earn her living was by teaching. Poor clergymen's daughters, widows, orphans, dependants of ruined men who had once been rich, all turned to the schoolroom as to their natural refuge. It was, indeed, as Miss Hardman went on to point out, not only inevitable, but providential that they should be driven to seek it. " *We*," explained this admirable young lady,

> need the imprudences, extravagances, mistakes and crimes of a certain number of fathers to sow the seed from which *we* reap the harvest of governesses. The daughters of tradespeople, however well educated, must necessarily be underbred, and as such unfit to be inmates of *our* dwellings, and guardians of *our* children's minds and persons. *We* shall ever prefer to place those about *our* children who have been born and bred with somewhat of the same refinement as *ourselves*.

In fulfilment of this convincingly demonstrated law of supply and demand, the poor gentlewomen prepared for their work. If they had a little capital they set up a small boarding-school as the Brontë sisters so pathetically tried to do, and as Mrs Teachum, of Mrs Sherwood's *The Governess, or The Little Female Academy*, did with such remarkable
80

"Don't tease me Henry" said Lucy
"don't you see I am reading." *Page 47*

ILLUSTRATION FROM "THE HISTORY OF THE
FAIRCHILD FAMILY"

success. If they had none, they advertised, or asked influential friends to recommend them, for a post as private governess.

Some of these ladies had an imposing list of accomplishments—imposing, at least, on paper. There were Miss Pinkerton's two pupils, whom she recommended to Mrs Bute Crawley in the year 1814: Miss Tuffin, aged eighteen, of " exceedingly pleasing personal appearance," and Miss Hawky, aged twenty-nine, with a face " much pitted with the small-pox," and with " a halt in her gait, red hair, and a trifling obliquity of vision."

> Either of these young ladies is *perfectly qualified* to instruct in Greek, Latin, and the rudiments of Hebrew ; in mathematics and history ; in Spanish, French, Italian, and geography ; in music, vocal and instrumental ; in dancing, without the aid of a master ; and in the elements of natural sciences. In the use of the globes both are proficients. In addition to these, Miss Tuffin, who is the daughter of the late Reverend Thomas Tuffin (Fellow of Corpus College, Cambridge), can instruct in the Syriac language, and the elements of Constitutional law. . . . Both ladies are endowed with *every moral and religious virtue*.

Thackeray's presentment doubtless has a touch, or more than a touch, of caricature ; but Anne Brontë wrote in sad and sober earnest. Her Agnes Grey, the eighteen-year-old daughter of a country clergyman, though less alarmingly proficient than Miss Pinkerton's pupils, offered music, singing, and drawing, French, Latin, and German. The Brontës—Charlotte, Emily, and Anne—all at different times held situations as private governesses, and they had a more meagre list of accomplishments, which scarcely extended beyond the ordinary English subjects.

In addition to other qualifications, employers demanded " unimpeachable morality, a mild and cheerful temper, and an obliging disposition." The obliging disposition usually led to nursemaid's and needlewoman's tasks being laid upon the overworked but unprotesting governess ; and for all this fifty pounds was considered a really generous salary. Many a governess received far less. It is no wonder that there were members of this oppressed company who, like

Miss Morgan in *Middlemarch*, looked " brown, dull, and resigned," and, as Mrs Vincy comfortably said, " just the sort of person for a governess."

Some, however, were of a less submissive type. There was Mrs Fenwick, one of the Lambs' circle, who thought extremely well of herself, and managed to impose her estimate on her employers, so that they did their best to propitiate so valuable an inmate of their house. There was Mrs Garth, whom it is impossible to imagine as submitting to oppression from anyone ; and there was clever Becky Sharp, who managed so adroitly to get the upper hand wherever she went.

In the families of the smaller gentlefolk whose incomes were not large enough to admit of the expense of a resident governess the mother or an elder sister presided over the schoolroom. Schoolroom law was then less rigid, and schoolroom isolation less complete. Harriet Martineau relates how in her home at Norwich the eldest brother taught the rest Latin, the next eldest taught writing and arithmetic, and the sister Rachael French and reading. The experiment was not a success, and after a time the girls were sent to school. Priscilla and Tryphosa Broad, children of the Reverend John Broad, of Tanner's Lane Chapel, Cowfold, were taught by their mother, because there was only one school in Cowfold, and Mrs Broad, who prided herself on her descent from a genteel family and gave herself airs, objected to the ' mixture ' that was to be found there.

Governess and pupils being assembled in the schoolroom, the work of acquiring solid knowledge and elegant accomplishments began. The accomplishments took by far the more important place ; the solid knowledge was of the kind then held to be specially suitable to the female sex—a little history, ancient and modern, a smattering of geography, a little ladylike botany, a vast amount of curious lore known as " general knowledge," and the use of the globes. " Young ladies," pronounced Mrs Barbauld, " ought only to have such a general tincture of knowledge as to make them agreeable companions for a man of sense, and to enable them to find rational entertainment for a solitary hour."

This being the generally accepted view, it is difficult to understand why so much stress was laid upon the necessity of high attainments in a governess, or how it was possible for her to acquire them. The wonder is increased when we examine the lesson books in use in almost every schoolroom. These were generally in the form of question and answer ; the governess read the question, and listened while the pupil repeated the answer, which had been learned by heart. It would not, one would imagine, require the erudition of a Miss Tuffin or a Miss Hawky to do this successfully ; but it would have required all the learning of these ladies, and possibly more, to produce the books which thus lightened schoolroom labours.

These books were the descendants of the dialogues that were popular throughout the Middle Ages and Renaissance period ; Ælfric's *Colloquy*, written in the year 992, was the first English example, and the Church Catechism remains as a model of what can be done by the use of this form. But these early treatises confined themselves to one subject, or one aspect of life, whereas the question books of the early nineteenth century, like Lord Bacon, took all knowledge to be their province. The most famous was Mangnall's *Historical and Miscellaneous Questions for the Use of Young People*, published in 1800. These questions were compiled by Miss Richmal Mangnall, a Yorkshire schoolmistress, and were, as stated on the title-page, " intended to awaken a laudable spirit of curiosity in young minds." To a later generation they seem specially designed to quench such a spirit, for the lumps of miscellaneous information which they ruthlessly tumbled out must have loaded and choked up any young mind and made forgetting the only profitable mental exercise. Turning over the leaves of this dumpy little school-book, one picks up at random such precious items of information as the characteristic traits of the ancient Scottish Highlanders, where nutmegs grow, the duties of Justices of the Peace, how to make candles, the opinions, employments, and manner of living of the ancient

Brahmins, the great examples of mutual friendship, the place and period in which iron passed as current coin, and the way in which ducks give notice of coming rain by preening their feathers. It was certainly out of Mangnall's *Questions* that Maria and Julia Bertram, of *Mansfield Park*, learned before they were twelve years old " the chronological order of the kings of England with the dates of their accessions and most of the principal events of their reigns, the Roman Emperors as low as Severus, besides a great deal of the heathen mythology, all the metals, semi-metals, planets, and distinguished philosophers." For at least half a century this book was in use in almost every schoolroom. Mary Russell Mitford and her schoolfellows used it at Hans Place, and so did Fanny Kemble when she did her lessons at home with her Aunt Dall. Mrs Garth regarded familiarity with it as a necessary part of a good education. Mrs Carlyle tells of little Miss Adam Hunter, " that preposterous child," who came in December 1842 from her Kensington boarding-school to pay a visit in Cheyne Row. Mr Carlyle began to cross-question her

> about something she called her Mangnall's *Questions*, and turning to me with a look knowing enough for fifty [she] said, " Ah, I perceive Mr Carlyle is a dreadful quiz. Now aren't you, Sir, a great quiz ? " And, remember, this creature is not struck ten yet.

Miss Hunter was clearly an example of the forcing power of Mangnall's *Questions*.

No young lady who had been brought up on this remarkable work could be at a loss when called upon to supply a fact or a date in general conversation. " Captain Cook, as you justly observe, dear Miss, quoting out of your Mangnall's *Questions*," says Thackeray, " was murdered by the natives of Owhyee *anno* 1779."

There were many followers in Miss Richmal Mangnall's footsteps. Isabella, a schoolroom young lady whom we meet in Miss Edgeworth's *The Good French Governess*, talked of " our Gray's *Memoriatechnica*," which gave the names and dates of the kings and Roman emperors and remarkable events such as the making of paper and the introduction of printing. Lady Wharncliffe wrote to her mother in 1810 telling her of a new book she had got for the children which she liked very much, " a Catechism by Blair of all the common sort of things that ought to be early known " ; and Mrs Fenwick used the same book, Blair's *Preceptor on the Arts and Sciences*, in the schoolroom where she taught the three Misses Honnor and their small brother. Charles Butler's *Guide to Useful Knowledge* rivalled even Mangnall's *Questions* in the amazing range and variety of the information it conveyed. From less than two pages of this work the pupil can learn all about the mechanism of a barrel organ, and when cannon were first used, with the principles and construction of the telescope, the bude light, and the oxy-hydrogen microscope.

About 1820 a certain Mr Pinnock issued a series of catechisms on a large variety of subjects, which he sold at ninepence each. They were so successful that he enlarged the series until it included eighty-three volumes, and after a time he took over various other works, among them Mangnall's *Questions*. Pinnock's *Catechisms* became a general title for all these works. Miss Letitia Elizabeth Landon, better known as ' L. E. L.,' tells us in her novel *Lady Anne Granard* that Pinnock's *Catechisms* were lying on the table of the dingy schoolroom in which her ladyship's daughters and their governess spent their days ; and the heroine of Mrs Gore's *Diary of a Désennuyée*, when she comes back to London at the age of twenty-five, says, " And though I may revisit Hatchard's shop it will not be to procure a series of Pinnock's *Catechisms* cased in strong calf, for the use and *abuse* of the schoolroom." Perhaps this lady had shared her governess's instructions with a small brother who, like the naughty boy in *Carols of Cockayne*,

> When they taught him how to spell, he showed his wicked whims
> By mutilating Pinnock and mislaying Watts's hymns.

Books in the form of " conversations " were also very popular in the schoolroom. In these the pupil asked inspired questions, which the instructress answered at length. Mrs Jane Marcet, the learned wife of a doctor, was famous for her *Conversations* on various branches of science. Her

Conversations on Political Economy led Harriet Martineau to write her celebrated tales. Fanny Kemble's niece, known as A. (in the *Record of a Girlhood*), who seems to have been a delightful young lady, heartily detested Mrs Marcet's *Conversations on Natural Philosophy*. She persisted in calling it " Nat. Phil." and was, as her aunt says, so rabid against it that when a daughter of its learned author was expected to pay a visit to the Kemble family Miss Kemble took A. with her to the theatre, fearing the consequences if the two should meet.

A very short time spent in reading " Nat. Phil." is enough to arouse a good deal of sympathy with naughty A.'s feeling toward it. There is a Mrs B. (who appears in all Mrs Marcet's *Conversations*) who seems to be versed in every science except mathematics, of which she confesses her entire ignorance ; a knowledge of mathematics was not, in those days, considered quite ladylike. To Mrs B. comes one of those governess-sisters of whom we have spoken, Emily, aged twelve. " I must request your assistance, my dear Mrs B.," says Emily, " in a charge which I have lately undertaken. It is that of instructing my younger sister, a work which I find more difficult than I had first imagined." The little sister, it appears, has asked what it is that supports the world in space, and Emily has found herself unequal to supplying a satisfactory explanation. Mrs B. gladly undertakes to enlighten her, and they discourse on the properties of matter. At the next lesson Emily brings with her another sister, Caroline, and says, " I have related to my sister Caroline all that you have taught me of natural philosophy, and she has been so much delighted with it that she hopes you will have the goodness to admit her to your lessons." Caroline apparently bears the character of being apt to show less deference to her elders than becomes a young lady in the schoolroom. " I fear that I shall not find you so tractable a scholar as Emily," says Mrs B. " I know that you are much biassed in favour of your own opinions." " Then you will have the greater merit in reforming them," replies Caroline, and this idea seems to appeal to Mrs B., who forthwith accepts her as a pupil. The way is now open for the conversations.

THE LION.

CHARACTERISTIC QUALITIES.

Courage, Strength, Activity.

This animal is produced in Africa, and the hottest parts of Asia. It is found in the greatest numbers in the Torrid Zone. In these desart regions, from whence mankind are driven by the rigorous heat of the climate, this animal reigns sole master: its disposition seems to partake of the ardour of its native soil. Inflamed by the influence of a burning sun, its rage is most tremendous, and its courage undaunted.

The form of the Lion is strikingly bold and

ILLUSTRATION FROM MARY TRIMMER'S "A NATURAL HISTORY OF QUADRUPEDS, ADAPTED TO THE CAPACITIES OF YOUTH" (1803)

The illustrations were by T. Bewick.

THE SCHOOLROOM

Emily asks questions marvellously apt for a young lady of her age ; Caroline dissents and argues ; Mrs B. brings forth her stores of knowledge, and replies to both.

A special and dignified place in the school curriculum was given to " the use of the globes." It was a subject, we are led to understand, peculiarly suited to young ladies, as distinguished from young persons. No well-bred female's education was complete without a knowledge of its mysteries. Florence Nightingale and her sister Parthenope learned the use of the globes, and so did Queen Victoria ; so did Priscilla and Tryphosa Broad in the small parlour of their home in Tanner's Lane. Mr Cecil Torr, in his *Small Talk at Wreyland*, says that few people realize how wide the subject was ; and he quotes some questions from Butler's *Exercises on the Globes* in illustration : What is whalebone ? Who were the Sirens ? What are the properties of dogs ? What is the difference of latitude between the places where Burns was born and Lazarus raised from the dead ?

In 1831, when Princess Victoria was twelve years old, the Duchess of Kent summoned the Bishops of London and Lincoln to examine the royal pupil in the subjects she had been studying with her governess.[1]

Another book to be seen in every schoolroom was Lindley Murray's *English Grammar*. Mr Murray was a devout Evangelical ; he lived at York, and was a close friend of the Grays. In 1793 some of his friends established at York a school " for the guarded education of young females." Exactly what this means we do not know, but probably the " young females " were not " young ladies." Some of the younger teachers in this school were very inexperienced and found much difficulty in teaching English grammar. They entreated Mr Murray to help them, and it was in response to this request that he wrote his book.

[1] Their lordships reported that " in answering a great variety of questions proposed to her the princess displayed an accurate knowledge of the more important features of Holy Scriptures, and of the leading truths of the Christian religion," as well as " an acquaintance with the chronology and principal facts of English history remarkable in so young a person. To questions on Geography, the Use of the Globes, Arithmetic and the Latin Grammar the answers which the princess returned were equally satisfactory." Did the bishops, we wonder, question the royal pupil out of Butler's *Exercises* ?

87

It was published in 1795, and quickly became the accepted standard in propriety and correctness of language. It contained a large number of illustrative passages, and Mr Murray was praised as much for the moral and pious sentiments that these contained as for the grammatical instruction the book provided. The grammar closed with "a sensible, affectionate, and truly Christian address to young students on the proper application of their literary attainments and the happiness they would find in a pious and virtuous course of life."

The Evangelicals, as was natural, lauded the work as a shining and perfect example of what a schoolroom book should be, and the praise that came from people outside the community was nearly as enthusiastic. All over England there were governesses who, like Mrs Garth, "in a general wreck of society would have tried to hold their *Lindley Murrays* above the waves"; and all over England there were pupils who, like hers, were imbibing right views on such subjects as the concord of verbs and pronouns with "nouns of multitude or signifying many" by laboriously committing to memory nicely turned phrases like "not without regard to the import of the word as conveying unity or plurality of idea." Lindley Murray's book had an enormous influence on the teaching of grammar during the hundred years that followed its publication. It guided and directed that teaching, and brought it at length to the point where wholesale and drastic reform became a necessity.

History was learned in most schoolrooms from Oliver Goldsmith's *History of England* in four volumes, one of his many compilations. It is a delightful work, charmingly written, and full of picturesque detail. It does not claim to be original in its matter; it was designed, its author said, to instruct beginners and refresh the minds of the aged, and "not to add to the historical knowledge, but to contract it." Jane Austen used it, and there are various comments in the margin of her copy showing that she did not agree with the author's views on the character and fate of Charles I and Mary Queen of Scots. The book was abridged by the industrious Mr Pinnock in 1825.

Goldsmith's *History of the Earth and Animated Nature* was

another schoolroom favourite. This is a huge compilation from many sources, and fills eight volumes. Goldsmith knew very little of natural history and accepted in perfect good faith the current old wives' tales and legends. He believed that horses would go mad if a tub of blood were placed in their stable, and he described gravely how monkeys caught crabs by baiting their tails and drawing their prey out of the water with a violent jerk. But in spite of its lack of scientific truth the book makes delightful reading. Mary Russell Mitford read it at the age of fourteen, while she was at school in Hans Place. " It is quite a lady's natural history and extremely entertaining," she wrote to her father after she had finished the first volume. It was admitted, as being a serious scientific work, to the library at Edgeworthstown, and the little Edgeworths must have fallen upon it with delight after their surfeit of strictly utilitarian literature. Maria Edgeworth makes the children of her *Moral Tales* read it and profit greatly by its learning.

Literature was studied in ' selections ' or in editions of standard works specially prepared for the use of young ladies. Few governesses or mothers could have been found who would have agreed with Charles Lamb's dictum that the best education for a girl was to turn her loose in a good library. The views of the majority were far more nearly represented by those of Mr Podsnap, as described in *Our Mutual Friend*. " A certain institution in Mr Podsnap's mind, which he called ' the young person,' may be considered to have been embodied in Miss Podsnap his daughter " (Georgina Podsnap was almost eighteen). " The question about everything was would it bring a blush to the cheek of the young person, and the inconvenience of the young person was . . . she seemed always liable to burst into blushes when there was no need at all." Dr Bowdler had expurgated Shakespeare and Gibbon with the avowed purpose of keeping the cheeks of his readers free from these painful suffusions, and, following him, other strict moralists had ' bowdlerized ' various classics. Mr Lindley Murray published in 1800 *The English Reader, or Elegant Selections in Prose and Poetry* : "designed to improve the highest class of learners in reading, to establish a taste for just and accurate composition, and to promote the interests of piety and virtue." Its contents, as *The Gentleman's Magazine* said in its notice of the book,

> are drawn from the most correct and elegant writers, and in the selection all due attention has been paid by the compiler to preserve untainted the morals at the same time that he agreeably amuses the minds of the rising generation. We are glad to perceive that in his search after material for the poetical department of the volume Mr Murray has blended with the productions of Young, Thomson, etc., a few flowers from Cowper, Williams, and Crabbe, and has not wholly overlooked the pious, poetical, and too much neglected poems of Ogilvie.

The most popular volumes of selections were *Elegant Extracts in Prose and Verse* by Vicesimus Knox and *The Speaker* of Dr Enfield. These were read by almost everybody both in the schoolroom and outside it. Miss Austen's Emma Woodhouse read *Elegant Extracts* with her governess ; Nonconformist families were in most cases brought up on Enfield's *Speaker*. Goldsmith's *Poems for Young Ladies* was moderately popular, but his *Beauties of English Poesy* was condemned as containing two poems by Prior which were not fit for the reading of the young.

When lessons were over the young ladies were allowed certain books for recreation, but these were strictly overlooked by governess or parent. The inmates of the schoolroom might, on their rare visits to their mother's drawingroom, look longingly on the pile of Minerva novels lying on a side-table, but until the day of their emancipation came these alluring volumes were not for them. " Novel-reading you have been told by your governess as I was by mine," said Lady Delacour to Belinda Portman, in Miss Edgeworth's *Belinda*, " novel-reading for young ladies is most dangerous." They were not supposed to read Byron, but many of them did. Walter Scott was open to them, and Fanny Kemble tells how, before she was twelve, she read with rapture *Marmion* and *The Lay of the Last Minstrel*. When she went to school in France—it was the same school as Mary Russell Mitford had attended in Hans Place, transferred now to the Rue d'Angoulême in Paris, and with Miss Rowden, formerly the assistant, as headmistress—her supply of literature was

MISCELLANEOUS

STORIES FOR CHILDREN.

COLLECTED BY

JANE TRIMMER.

—o—

With many Fine Cuts.

LONDON;

EDWARD LACEY, 76, ST. PAUL'S CHURCH-YARD;

HENRY LACEY, 64, BOLD STREET, LIVERPOOL;

AND ALL BOOKSELLERS.

—o—

Title-page to "Miscellaneous Stories for Children"
(1820?)

cut off, and she had to listen to such books as "l'Abbé Mellot's *Universal History* of blessed, boring memory" read aloud at meal-times. "At length," she says, "I undertook to write out *The Lay of the Last Minstrel* and *Marmion*, so as not absolutely to lose my possession of them." A little later she read a short passage from Byron's poems in a book belonging to a parlour boarder, and it impressed her imagination so powerfully that she could not get it out of her head. When she came back to England, at the age of thirteen, her education was continued at home, and no very strict check was kept upon her reading. Some of her time was spent at a farm in Hertfordshire, and there she read in the hours allowed her for recreation the works of Lord Byron and of Jeremy Taylor. "I read them on alternate days," she says, "sitting on the mossy-cushioned lawn, with a cabbage leaf full of fresh-gathered strawberries, and a handful of fresh-blown roses beside me, which Epicurean accompaniments to my studies appeared to me equally adapted to the wicked poet and the wise divine." Diplomatic Becky Sharp read secretly with her pupil, Miss Rose Crawley, "many delightful French and English works, among which may be mentioned those of the learned Dr Smollett, of the ingenious Mr Henry Fielding, of the graceful and fantastic Monsieur Crébillon the younger, . . . and of the universal Monsieur de Voltaire"; and she satisfied the solemn Mr Pitt Crawley, who was scandalized at seeing his sister one day with a volume of French plays in her hand, by assuring him that such reading was only for the purpose of acquiring the French idiom in conversation.

But there was, in these early years of the nineteenth century, a really good store of interesting and entertaining books for younger children freely admitted to the schoolroom by even the strictest of parents. When Thomas Day, in 1783, published his *Sandford and Merton* he stated in the preface that he had written it because he had observed a great lack of proper books for children's reading. "The least exceptionable I could find for this purpose," he said, "were Plutarch's *Lives* and Xenophon's *History of the Institution of Cyrus* in English translations, with some part of *Robinson Crusoe* and a few passages in the first volume of Mr Brooke's *Fool of Quality* and *Mary and Florence, or Grave and Gay*, by Miss Frazer Tytler." In the twenty years that followed all this was changed. Miss Edgeworth published her *Parent's Assistant, Moral Tales*, and *Popular Tales*, where children, from seven to seventeen, might find real, interesting stories, suited to their varying tastes. Mrs Sherwood's *The Fairchild Family, Little Henry and his Bearer*, and *The Governess, or The Little Female Academy* were also most deservedly popular. To readers of to-day they seem overweighted with their moral, but that was in the fashion of their time ; and they still have interest as stories. The little ones loved them ; the elders who had read them and grown tired of them found consolation in thinking how near they were to that border-line over which they must step to ' come out,' and of what stores of fascinating literature awaited them on the other side.

CHAPTER VI

THE MINERVA PRESS

THE English public suffered its first attack of the novel-reading fever in 1743, when Richardson published his *Pamela*; and during the fifty years that followed the complaint spread until it became epidemic. Mrs Radcliffe's *Romance of the Forest*, which appeared in 1791, started a new and peculiarly violent form of the malady; the temperature of the patients rose rapidly as a stream of similar tales—blood-curdling romances full of mystery and horror and ill-fated love—poured from the press. During the closing years of the century the fever raged widely. As in the days of Miss Polly Honeycombe and Miss Lydia Languish, it attacked with especial violence young lady members of the community who had little to do and not much to think about, but these were by no means its only victims. Everybody read the ' horrid ' novels, even those people who disapproved of them. Thomas Poole bought a copy of *The Romance of the Forest* for his Nether Stowey Book Society, where it figured rather strangely among the serious historical and political works that made up most of the collection. The Edgeworths, while on a visit to Clifton, allowed themselves to be drawn into reading the fashionable novel of which every one round them was talking. Maria found it interesting, and the horrible parts well worked up, " but," she said, " it is very difficult to keep Horror breathless with his mouth wide open through three volumes." Henry Crabb Robinson sat up all night reading it, Jane Austen and her family delighted in both the works of Mrs Radcliffe and those of her imitators. Shelley as a small boy at school gloated over *The Mysterious Hand, or Subterranean Horrors, The Demon of Sicily*, and other stories with equally attractive titles. Macaulay and his sisters talked of the heroes and heroines of these romances

93

as familiarly as they talked of their friends at Clapham. Even Jonathan Gray, one of the strictest of the Evangelicals, betrayed his backsliding in this matter when he wrote to his wife: " Your description of the approach of Ockbrook reminded me of *The Mysteries of Udolpho.*"

To maintain this fever at the height to which it had risen became the aim of publishers and writers, and they worked with an ever increasing activity. Somewhere about 1790 a certain William Lane had set up in Leadenhall Street a printing-press which, with a fine sense of fitness, he called the Minerva Press, and from this press he sent out a full and unceasing stream of works of fiction which had a very small share of either the wisdom or the strength with which its patron is credited. In connexion with this press Mr Lane opened a circulating library on a larger scale than any that had yet been established. Very soon the Minerva novels, each in three or more indifferently printed volumes, with mottled covers, were to be found in most of the drawing-rooms and parlours of genteel London.

Early in the new century Mr Lane and his fellows, keeping an interested eye upon the patients and their symptoms, noticed some falling off in the consumption of ' horrid ' novels, with a corresponding decrease of fever in the consumers. It was very slight, but serious enough to give cause for anxiety. The ladies and gentlemen who supplied the Minerva Press with stories ranged far and wide in search of new terrors to stimulate what was clearly a jaded appetite, but without success. It remained to seek out the cause. The natural reaction against a too highly flavoured diet accounted for a good deal ; but Sir Walter Scott's diagnosis probably came very near the truth when he declared that what was amiss with these tales of terror was, paradoxical as it might seem, their monotony. The occasion of this pronouncement was a review, written by him for the *Quarterly* in 1810, of one of the most conspicuous examples of the type, *The Fatal Revenge*, by Maturin. The review was intended, its author said, to provide " one of those light and airy articles which a young lady might read while her hair was papering," but he found the subject a heavier one than he had anticipated. He sent to his publisher for an assortment of the newest and most fashionable novels. They arrived in a good-sized hamper, and he sat down conscientiously to read them. He found it a dreary task.

> We strolled through a variety of castles, each of which was regularly called Il Castello ; met with as many captains of *condottieri* ; heard various ejaculations of Santa Maria or Diavolo ; read by a decaying lamp in a tapestried chamber dozens of legends as stupid as the main history ; examined such suites of deserted apartments as might fit up a reasonable barrack ; and saw as many glimmering lights as would make a respectable illumination.

It is small wonder that he came to the conclusion that " spirits and patience may be as completely exhausted in perusing trifles as in following algebraical calculations."

Mrs Mary Meeke, one of the most industrious of the Minerva authoresses, seems to have had some glimmering of a change in, or an extension of, the public taste in novel-reading when she wrote in the preface to her *Midnight Weddings*, published in 1802, that in her opinion subscribers to circulating libraries were favouring " either the quiet romance teeming with ghosts and spectres, or the satirical adventures of a political Quixote replete with wit and judgment or else the more simple narrative founded on events within the bounds of probability." Romantic love-tales, she said, were very generally discounted. This statement that " simple narratives " were finding some degree of favour is suggestive, especially as Mrs Meeke followed it up by saying that her own story was of the new variety. She complained that in this type of fiction it was difficult for authors to think of new and interesting plots, and announced that she had conceived the original idea of beginning her novel at the point where most works of the kind left off—the marriage of the hero and heroine. But in spite of this brilliant inspiration, fate, or habit, was too strong for her, and we have the inevitable wedding at the end of the book also. It is arranged by the young man's father, who expresses himself gratified at finding his son " willing to oblige " him and take a bride he has never seen on a parent's recommendation, but owns to a fear that the bridegroom may "recant at the altar." "Your having made choice of this young lady is alone sufficient to prevent my committing so gross a solecism in politeness," answers this correct young man. "I am prepared to esteem her, and after I have plighted my faith, I will endeavour to love her, because I am convinced she possesses many estimable qualities." A son after Sir Anthony Absolute's own heart, but scarcely, one would have thought, to the taste of the nineteenth-century Lydia Languishes who patronized the circulating libraries! But perhaps they forgave him because they were in the secret that the bride his father had chosen for him was really the mysterious damsel whom he secretly and hopelessly loved, and because his whole career had been so thoroughly romantic, beginning with an interrupted wedding and the discovery that he was a nameless foundling instead of an English nobleman as he had believed, and going on through a series of thrilling episodes to the discovery of his real parentage.

Midnight Weddings was a great success, and Mrs Meeke was encouraged to go on producing "simple narratives founded on events within the bounds of probability." Many other writers followed her example and filled up with their inanities the capacious bookshelves of Mr Lane's library in Leadenhall Street, where they stood side by side with the lurid, breathless efforts of the latest terror-mongers. The new style of novel grew month by month more popular, and the purveyors of fiction discovered that it was not really necessary to try by new devices to increase the feverishness of the patient's condition. The appetite appeared to be as good, or even better, when a low diet was supplied—milk-and-water dishes, well sweetened and mildly flavoured, with here and there a lump of quite ordinary bread, disguised, but unmistakable.

Customers flocked to the library in Leadenhall Street. Fashionable ladies drove up to the door, and their gorgeous footmen carried in a pile of books and came out bearing a fresh supply. Young bucks lounged in and picked out the latest publications from the shelves. Smart lady's-maids brought their mistress's lists, looking with interest at the titles, for they intended to begin on Volume I themselves as soon as my lady passed to Volume II. Misses from boarding-schools, milliners' girls, young lawyers from the Temple, stout, elderly gentlemen, prim maiden ladies, schoolboys, pages, matrons, clergymen, passed into the abode of this new Minerva, and came out carrying her gift of books. Some of them came so often that they must have been on quite intimate terms with the goddess. Leigh Hunt visited her first when he was a handsome, high-spirited schoolboy, in blue gown and yellow stockings, at Christ's Hospital ; and he came again and again, through the next twenty years, eager always for a renewal of her favours. He had none of the superior person's affected disdain of novels. He enjoyed them thoroughly, and said so with great frankness. " Except where they repel me at the outset with excessive wordiness," he wrote in his *Autobiography,*

> I can read their three-volume enormities to this day without skipping a syllable ; though I guess pretty nearly all that is going to happen from the mysterious gentleman who opens the work, in the dress of a particular century, down to the distribution of punishments and the drying of tears in the last chapter. I think the authors wonderfully clever people, especially those who write most, and I should like the most contemptuous of their critics to try their hand at anything half so engaging.

Another old Christ's Hospital schoolboy, nine years older than Leigh Hunt, came often to the library—not on his own behalf, for he had no liking for novels—narrative teased him, he said. He came with his sister Mary, who could not get on without her regular supply of fiction, and was willing to take a Minerva novel when nothing better offered. She would stand serene and cheerful, unmoved by her brother's kindly gibes, and make her choice carefully ; then the two would trudge happily home to their lodgings, and after supper would settle down in their low-ceilinged, tobacco-smoked room with its old-fashioned furniture and its bright fire. Charles would bring out his beloved old volumes—Sir Philip Sidney, Donne, Beaumont and Fletcher, or some other of the Elizabethans—and Mary would produce her Minerva novel ; evening would pass into night and find them both still absorbed in their books.   Charles Lamb says in one of his essays that their common reading-table was " daily fed with assiduously fresh supplies " of modern tales for Mary's reading.   If this is to be taken literally she outdid those " young ladies from the boarding school and milliners' girls " who Hazlitt scornfully declared were the only people who read all the new novels that came out. She outdid that aristocratic spinster Lady Betty St Clair, of Miss Ferrier's *The Inheritance*, who read " all the novels and romances which it is presumed are published for the exclusive benefit of superannuated old women and silly young ones," such as *The Enchanted Head, The Invisible Hand, The Miraculous Nuptials, Bewildered Affections, or All is not Lost*, and *Midnight Weddings*.   She outdid even Mary Russell Mitford, whose book-lists show that she read about twenty-four books per month—nearly all of them novels.   Plump little Miss Mitford left Miss Rowden's school in 1802 with a high reputation as the prize pupil in English literature and composition, and went to live at the grand new house at Grasely, about three miles from Reading, which her father had built with part of the twenty thousand pounds she had won in a lottery when she was ten years old. There was a circulating library at Reading from which the Minerva novels could be obtained, so we can only think of her as visiting the Leadenhall Street establishment during the brief visits she paid to London.   She was an insatiable reader of novels.   She read the works of Miss Edgeworth, Joanna Baillie, and Mrs Opie, and considered those authors " three such women as have seldom adorned one age and one country."   Her list of books read in January 1806 includes many novels little known even in their own day and now quite forgotten—the trash of the libraries—with a few of a slightly higher type.   There is *Clarentine*, by a sister of Fanny Burney, Miss Edgeworth's *Leonora*, Mrs Meeke's *Midnight Weddings*—eighteen novels altogether, out of a total of twenty-four books.

There was another Hampshire family, the Austens of

Steventon, who were, as Jane said, " great novel-readers, and not ashamed of being so." The family was made up of father and mother, four sons and two daughters—Jane, the youngest, being twelve years older than Mary Mitford. The Austens had begun their novel-reading career as far back as the days of Fanny Burney. They had welcomed the advent of the Radcliffian Tale of Terror, and when that had begun to pall had turned with equal delight to the ' simple narratives ' of the school of Mrs Meeke. It is probable that while Jane was on one of her long visits to her married brother in London she went to the Leadenhall Street library, and revelled in the ample choice it offered her ; at other times she obtained her supplies from the local purveyor of Minerva novels. " We are reading *Clarentine*," she wrote to her sister Cassandra in 1807,

> and are surprised to find how foolish it is. I remember liking it much less on a second reading than at the first, and it does not bear a third at all. It is full of unnatural conduct and forced difficulties, and without striking merit of any kind.

In January 1809 the family were reading *Woman, or Ida of Athens*, by Miss Owenson. " We have only read the preface yet," wrote Jane, " but her *Irish Girl* does not make one expect very much. If the warmth of her language could affect the body it might be worth reading this cold weather." She did not much care for Mary Brunton's *Self-control*—a novel highly thought of at that time by most people. " I am looking over *Self-control* again, and my opinion is confirmed of its being an excellently meant, elegantly written work, without anything of nature or probability in it."

Self-control is the work in which appears Miss Julia Dawkins, whom we have already met in her mother's parlour above the hosier's shop in Holborn, attempting to model her behaviour on that of Madame D'Arblay's admired heroine Camilla, whose story she had lately read. Each novel she obtained from the circulating library stimulated her to similar efforts.

> After reading *Evelina* she sat with her mouth extended in a perpetual smile, and was so very timid that she would not for the world have looked at a stranger. . . . After perusing *The*

Gossip's Story she, in imitation of the rational Louisa, suddenly waxed very wise, spoke in sentences, despised romance, sewed shifts, and read sermons.

When she was reading *Tom Jones* she outraged the fine feelings of her mother's lodger, Miss Laura Montreville, by becoming exceedingly lively and arch, and inclined to profess a disregard for nice points of morality. " Don't you love Tom Jones ? " she inquired of Miss Laura, but that well-bred young lady replied, " I prefer the hero of Miss Porter's new publication, *Thaddeus of Warsaw.*" Nearly all the young ladies of that day adored Thaddeus of Warsaw. He was the model of a Minerva Press hero—handsome, eloquent, sentimental, and unhappy. It was of Thaddeus and his like that Miss Medora Trevilian was thinking when she wrote entreating her bosom friend, Miss Araminta Vavasour, not to accept the lover her parents had selected for her unless he resembled these romantic heroes :

If he's only an excellent person—
My own Araminta, say " No ! "

Remember the thrilling romances
We read on the bank in the glen ;
Remember the suitors our fancies
Would picture for both of us then.
They wore the red cross on their shoulder,
They had vanquished and pardoned their foe—
Sweet friend, are you wiser or colder ?
My own Araminta, say " No ! "

Miss Rebecca Linnet's method of demonstrating her susceptibility to the charms of the various heroines of whom she read differed slightly from that adopted by Miss Julia Dawkins. Before Mr Tryan, the Evangelical curate, had come to Milby Miss Rebecca had been a great reader of Minerva novels.

Nothing but an acquaintance with the course of her studies could afford a clue to the rapid transitions in her dress, which were suggested by the style of beauty, whether sentimental, sprightly, or severe, possessed by the heroine of the three volumes actually in perusal. A piece of lace, which drooped round the edge of her white bonnet one week, had been rejected by the next ; and her cheeks, which, on Whitsunday, loomed through a Turnerian haze of network, were, on Trinity Sunday, seen reposing in distinct red outline on her shelving bust, like the sun on a fog bank. The black velvet meeting with a crystal clasp, which on one evening encircled her head, had on another descended to her neck, and on a third to her wrist, suggesting to an active imagination either a magical contraction of the ornament, or fearful ratio of expansion in Miss Rebecca's person.

When she became an Evangelical all this was changed ; she remained faithful to a grey gingham dress and white collar, and the circulating library lost a subscriber.

About the year 1815 the Leadenhall Street library first saw a short, thickset, fair-haired youth, who from that time was to be one of its most constant and generous patrons. This was Hannah More's godson—Thomas Babington Macaulay, from Clapham. Like Leigh Hunt, he could read and enjoy anything in the shape of a novel. He knew some of the works of Mrs Meeke almost by heart, though he quite agreed when his sister Hannah complained that one of them was just like another, " turning on the fortunes of some young man in a very low rank who eventually proves to be the son of a Duke." Another favourite author was Mrs Kitty Cuthbertson, who wrote *Santo Sebastiano, or The Young Protector, The Forest of Montalbano, The Romance of the Pyrenees*, and *Adelaide, or The Countercharm*. Years later, while he was in India, a copy of *Santo Sebastiano* was sold by auction, and he and Miss Emily Eden, sister of the Governor-General, both of them moved by fond recollections of past delights, bid against each other, until at last the book was knocked down, at a fabulous price, to Macaulay. " As an indication of the thoroughness with which this literary treasure has been studied," says his sister Hannah,

> there appears on the last page an elaborate computation of the number of fainting fits that occur in the course of the five volumes :
>
> | | |
> |---|---|
> | Julia de Clifford | 11 |
> | Lady Delamore | 4 |
> | Lady Theodosia | 4 |
> | Lord Glenbrook | 2 |
> | Lord Delamore | 2 |
> | Lady Enderfield | 1 |

THE ENGLISHMAN AND HIS BOOKS

Lord Ashgrove   1
Lord St Orville   1
Henry Mildmay   1

A single passage selected for no other reason than because it is the shortest will serve as a specimen of these catastrophes. " One of the sweetest smiles that ever animated the face of mortal now diffused itself over the face of Lord St Orville, as he fell at the feet of Julia in a deathlike swoon."

Macaulay's letters to his sisters are full of lively comments and questions on the novels he has been reading or has heard talked about. " What novel have you commenced ? Or rather how many dozen have you finished ? " he wrote in 1831. " Recommend me one. What say you to *Destiny* ? Is *The Young Duke* worth reading ? And what do you think of *Laurie Todd* ? " And again in 1833 :

> But why plague ourselves about politics when we have so much pleasanter things to talk of ? *The Parson's Daughter*; don't you like *The Parson's Daughter* ? What a wretch Harbottle was ! And Lady Frances, what a sad worldly woman ! But Mrs Harbottle, dear suffering angel ! and Emma Lovell, all excellence ! Dr MacGopus you doubtless like, but you probably do not admire the Duchess and Lady Catherine. . . . But if you will have my opinion I think it is Theodore Hook's worst performance, far inferior to *The Surgeon's Daughter*.

Miss Eden could have told him all about Susan Ferrier's novel, *Destiny*, for she had read it before the end of 1829, when she wrote to her sister : " What curious creatures we are, as that old Machy in *Destiny* (have you read it ?) keeps on observing." That Miss Eden was given to novel-reading we gather from a remark in one of her letters : " I am quite glad to find that when I cannot get novels I can read other books just as well." She was a great admirer of Jane Austen, and most of us will agree delightedly with her estimate of Mr Collins. " I never met with such an instance of politeness in my life, as the immortal Collins observes— not the Professor Collins, but the far greater *Pride and Prejudice* Collins."

Miss Austen was not a Minerva Press novelist, and there were readers to be found who placed her works below its fascinating productions. Katharine, Lady Pechell, wife of

102

THE MINERVA PRESS

Admiral Sir George Pechell, thought the characters of *Mansfield Park* " unnatural and absurd " and the book altogether " very nonsensical." Lady Harriet Duncan, of *Granby*, was equally disapproving. She was " a sickly, but rather pretty looking woman," priding herself on her literary tastes —a " light Blue." " But do tell me your favourite novels," she began volubly to a young man who had just been introduced to her.

> I hope you like nothing of Miss Edgeworth's or Miss Austen's. They are full of commonplace people that one recognizes at once. You cannot think how I was disappointed in *Northanger Abbey* and *Castle Rackrent*, for the titles really did promise something. Have you a taste for romance ? You have ? I am glad of it. Do you like *Melmoth* ? It is a harrowing book. Dear Mrs Radcliffe ! Very lovely things, but they are so old !

Lady Harriet's reading-table was covered with the newest books from the circulating library, in regard to which she certainly could not make the complaint that they were "full of commonplace people that one recognizes at once."

Fanny Kemble, the actress, read *Destiny* and liked it very much. " Besides being very clever," she said, " it leaves a pleasant taste in one's mind's mouth." Miss Kemble is to be numbered among the professed novel-readers ; she enjoyed the absurdities of the Minerva Press as keenly as did Macaulay. One evening at a party her father was introduced to a lady whose name he did not catch, and after a few slight, conventional remarks he allowed the conversation to be broken off. When he discovered that the lady was a duchess whom he ought to have recognized, his annoyance was extreme. " I feared," wrote his daughter in her diary,

> my poor father would go home and remain awake all night, sobbing softly to himself, like the eldest of the nine Miss Simmonses in the ridiculous novel, because in her nervous flurry at a great dinner party she had refused instead of accepting a gentleman's offer to drink wine with her.

It would be pleasant to make the acquaintance of this afflicted Miss Simmons and her eight sisters, but Miss Kemble tells us nothing that will guide us to the ridiculous novel in which they are to be found. There were so many ridiculous novels. Dorothy Wordsworth, writing to Henry Crabb Robinson in 1825, said: " Novels from our Lady Friends have poured in upon us so fast that we are muddled among them, and can never attempt to get through all " ; and a little later the heroine of Mrs Gore's *Diary of a Désennuyée*—a wealthy, beautiful widow of twenty-five—gave her opinion of these productions. She sent, she said— doubtless to Leadenhall Street—for a supply of novels by lady writers. " What an ocean of milk and water ! False sentiment, tawdry style, and a total absence of sense or sensibility. When will a Goldsmith or an Inchbald cheat us of genuine tears." Strong-minded Mrs Fenwick, the friend of Charles and Mary Lamb, would have entirely agreed with this summing up. She complained that the family in which she was employed as a governess subscribed to a library " which, I imagine, is a very bad one, for the novels of character we have sent for are never to be had, and the generality of the Minerva Press compositions I cannot, however fond of a story, read."

Some readers, however, found these compositions moving enough. Lady Louisa Percy read *The False Step* and *The Sisters* and cried over the latter all the morning. Miss Julia Dawkins was in the habit of paying " watery tributes " to the sorrows of sorely tried heroes and heroines. Young ladies of that day expected to cry over their novels. All the Minerva heroines were constantly bursting into tears or having their slight forms shaken by sobs, and their readers followed their example. They did not even shrink from exhibiting the unbecoming after-effects of such captivating sensibility. Lovers were constantly discerning the marks of tears upon their adored one's fair countenance ; and no one seems to have minded coming down to the drawing-room " with a headache, a sideache, a heartache, and swollen red eyes "—as Fanny Kemble did after she had read *The Borderers*. Such traces of emotion only made a pretty young lady more ' interesting.'

Thackeray knew all about the Minerva novels : quite a number of his characters are readers of these fascinating productions. Miss Briggs, we feel sure, brought the parcels of library books that she carried to lively old Miss Crawley, at her house in Park Lane, from Leadenhall Street. We suspect, too, that Mrs Brian Newcome's footman, gorgeous in his " scarlet plush integuments," was not unknown there, for, in spite of that lady's avowed devotion to literature of the higher sort, we are inclined to believe that there were one or two Minerva novels among the library books scattered over the back seat of her fine barouche. As for Lady Anne Newcome, she had obviously sent that invaluable " foring cove," who was courier, footman, and valet all in one, for the large and varied store she took with her to Brighton. *Ralph the Resurrectionist*, by Miss Pennafer, which the Reverend Charles Honeyman glanced over at his club, as a relaxation from severe parish duties, was certainly from the Minerva Press. No one but William Lane would have ventured to publish a ' startling ' novel written by a young lady who was " actually in the nursery."

Dickens also knew the famous library. It was undoubtedly from Leadenhall Street that Alphonse the page brought *The Lady Flabella* which Kate Nickleby read to her employer, Mrs Wititterly. Mrs Wititterly was a lady of such exquisite sensibility that any excitement was likely to prove fatal to her, and *The Lady Flabella* was " a production admirably suited to a lady labouring under Mrs Wititterly's complaint, seeing that there was not a line in it, from beginning to end, which could by the remotest contingency awaken the smallest excitement in any person breathing." Kate was reading the passage in which a page, dropping on one knee, presented to his lovely mistress a golden salver, gorgeously chased, on which lay a scented *billet*.

> " ' The Lady Flabella, with an agitation she could not repress, hastily tore off the envelope, and broke the scented seal. It *was* from Befillaire—the young, the slim, the low-voiced—*her own* Befillaire.' "
>
> Mrs Wititterly was deeply affected by this moving passage.
>
> " Oh ! charming ! " she exclaimed. " Poetic, really. Read that description again, Miss Nickleby."
>
> Kate complied.

"Sweet indeed !" said Mrs Wititterly with a sigh. "So voluptuous, is it not ? So soft !"

"Yes, I think it is," replied Kate, gently, "very soft."

"Close the book, Miss Nickleby," said Mrs Wititterly, "I can bear nothing more to-day. I should be sorry to disturb the impression of that sweet description. Close the book."

Kate complied, not unwillingly.

The sole defect of Mr Lane's library, considered as a national institution, seems to have been that its freedom was bestowed only upon payment of a subscription proportionate to the benefits conferred ; and consequently there were many readers who could not hope to enter its doors, or the doors of any of its branch establishments. These unlucky people were not, however, entirely neglected. For them there were many humbler establishments with a small collection of well-thumbed second-hand novels, and with subscriptions sometimes as low as a penny for each volume lent. There was the little library near Holborn where Thomas Noon Talfourd, the young law student, found a copy of Charles Lamb's *Rosamund Gray* "exhibiting proper marks of due appreciation," and the library combined with a milliner's shop at a certain country watering-place where Hazlitt met the young lady who found Scott's novels so dry she could scarcely get through them, and recommended *Agnes*. There was Miss Flinders' library in the neighbourhood of Walpole Street. Miss Flinders took in dressmaking for the servants of the great houses round about, sold Sunday newspapers to the footmen and lollipops to their sons. She had also a stock of novels for the ladies of the upper servants' table. Here John James Ridley, son of Mr Samuel Ridley, butler and confidential valet to the Right Honourable Baron Todmorden, spent many hours. He was a sickly, almost deformed child, of whom "there was no making nothink," as his father pathetically lamented. He would sit on the floor behind Miss Flinders' counter forgetting everything but the story he was reading out of one of her torn and dirty books. When he went away he would ask leave to take one with him, and carry it home joyfully under his pinafore. He read *Manfroni, or*

The One-handed Monk, Abellino, the Terrific Bravo of Venice, and *Rinaldo Rinaldini, Captain of Robbers.* He read *Thaddeus of Warsaw* and *The Scottish Chiefs,* and made pictures of these heroes in all their warlike attire. Another library of the same kind was that kept by Miss Minifer in Newcastle Street, Strand. She ran it in conjunction with a school for young ladies and a small millinery and brandy-ball business. From this establishment pretty Fanny Bolton, who had been a pupil in Miss Minifer's school, borrowed the very much the worse for wear Minerva Press novels which turned her silly little head, and prepared her to fall in love with the first " young gentleman " she met in real life.

It is small wonder that Mr Lane made a handsome fortune, and was seen riding about London, as Samuel Rogers tells us he was, in a splendid carriage, attended by footmen with cockades and gold-headed canes. All over England people were contributing to the fund which made him rich. Even the Waverley Novels did not drive his publications out of the field, though they dealt them some hard blows. The Minerva novels remained in favour until public taste changed and they went out of fashion. Readers of to-day would be dismayed if they were set down, say, to the seven volumes of Mrs Bennett's *The Beggar Girl and her Benefactors,* of which, we are told, two thousand copies at thirty-six shillings a copy were sold on the day of publication. The light reading of one generation is the heavy reading of another.

CHAPTER VII

YOUNG GENTLEMEN AT THE UNIVERSITY

WHILE the young ladies of genteel families were immured in the schoolroom their brothers were enjoying the freer life of Eton or Harrow or some other scholastic establishment ; and at sixteen to eighteen, the age when their sisters ' came out,' the young gentlemen went to the university, which in those days meant Oxford or Cambridge. The young ladies looked forward to two or three years of parties, admiration, strict chaperonage, and Minerva novels, to be followed by a handsome bridegroom, a fashionable wedding, and an adequate establishment. The young gentlemen saw before them a pleasant life in a community, without the restrictions of school, freedom and independence, as much study as they chose, and a chance of gaining distinction through the high degree which they (most of them) meant to take at the end of their course.

They came up to the university very hopefully, a troop of emancipated schoolboys entering with zest on a new life. The young noblemen among them put on the gold-tasselled cap and handsome silk gown of the gentleman commoner, and prepared in all things to claim and uphold the rights and privileges of their order. The sons of country squires and lawyers and doctors and parsons were content to be robed in the stuff gown of the ordinary undergraduate ; and there were a few eager scholars, whose parents were not able to afford the university fees, who were willing to wear the sizar's badge and serve their fellows in menial tasks.

Very soon they settled down and formed themselves into little groups and began to read hard or play hard or idle away their time according to their several tastes and dispositions ; and before very long personalities began to emerge, and those who were going to make a mark in the

108

university and leave memories behind them showed themselves a little more distinctly than the others against the general background. There was a handsome, blue-eyed, smiling youth named Henry Temple who came up to St John's College, Cambridge, in 1803 from the fine Hampshire mansion of his father, Viscount Palmerston. He had had two years in Edinburgh with Professor Dugald Stewart, and was considered to have in him the making of a model university student. Very easily and happily he proceeded to fulfil his friends' expectations. He read diligently, though he gave his parties like the others, and presently wrote home asking that six dozen of port, two dozen of sherry, and two dozen of Madeira might be sent to him. " No one is ever pressed to drink more than they chuse," he said, but it was necessary that a gentleman commoner should have wine of the best to offer. St John's was a college where tassels and silk gowns were common, and young Temple found many friends of his own order. His brother joined him the next year, and the two read together and drilled together with the Cambridge volunteers. He passed his examinations as they came, easily and without undue agitation, and was placed each time in the first class ; but he observed with grave candour that though he valued the habit of mind acquired by preparing for these examinations he had no high opinion of the system, since knowledge thus acquired of details at Cambridge was worth nothing, because it evaporated soon after the examination was over.

The Johnians were rather haughty and exclusive young gentlemen and had little to do with undergraduates outside their own society, and it is probable that they never noticed a pale-faced youth who came up in October 1805 and occupied a sizar's room in their college. He was the son of a butcher of Nottingham, and for two years before he came to Cambridge he had worked as a clerk in an attorney's office. But he had a passion for learning, and he spent every moment of his time at home in study. His family scarcely saw him, for he even took his meals alone in his own room so that he need not be separated from his books. At length Mr Simeon, Vicar of Trinity Church, Cambridge, and one of the leading lights among the Evangelicals, heard of him, of his talents and his piety—for this youth, Henry Kirke White, was also a fervent Evangelical. A sizarship at St John's was procured for him, and he joined the young gentlemen at the university. The butcher's son was as good a scholar as any of the prize pupils from Eton or Harrow, and he took his work far more seriously than they did. All through the days that the others found so joyous, and far into the night, he read and wrote the pious poems that expressed his fervent Evangelical faith ; and, fading quietly away, in October 1806 he died. The elegant Johnians learned with surprise when, during the next year, the *Remains of Henry Kirke White* was edited, with an account of his life, by Robert Southey that they had harboured a poet in their midst and had not known him.

There was another youth, who came up to Trinity College, Cambridge, from Harrow in 1805, when Henry Temple was reading hard for his final examination, who very soon thrust himself upon the notice of everybody in the university. He was a dark, handsome boy, with an arrogant turn of the head, a scornful twist of the lip, and a lame foot. He was seventeen years old, and a present and actual lord, not merely heir to a peerage, as most of the gentlemen commoners were, and his name was George Gordon Byron. He began at once to make himself more notorious in the university than his looks, his peerage, and his name had made him already. He gave uproarious wine-parties, he sat up until four o'clock in the morning playing hazard, he got drunk, he consorted with all sorts of disreputable and unsavoury characters. Swimming and riding were the only two bodily exercises that his lame foot permitted, but in both those he excelled. Through all his dissipations he read, not for his degree—he had no intention of troubling himself about that—but for pleasure. The list of books that he had read before he was twenty—history, philosophy, poetry, and " novels by the thousand "—is an amazing one. When Thomas Moore's new volume of verse came out in 1806 he and his friend, Edward Noel Young, bought a copy and spent several evenings reading it together ; and he

"The Rake's Progress at the University," No. 5

"Convened for wearing gaiters, sad offence:
Expelled—nor e'en permitted a defence."

One of a series of satires on university life by James Gillray.

even found time to prepare for the press a small volume of his own poetry. When Henry Temple, who was Viscount Palmerston now through the death of his father, finished his blameless university career by taking a First Class in 1807 Byron was notorious all over Cambridge. He kept a tame bear and several bulldogs and named them after some of the masters and tutors. He paid no attention to college rules and lived with reckless extravagance. " My life here," he wrote to a cousin, in July 1807, " has been one continual round of dissipation—out at different places every day and engaged to more dinners, etc., than my stay would permit me to fulfil. Sorry to say I have been drunk every day and not quite sober yet." In October he wrote: "This evening a large assortment of jockeys, gamblers, boxers, authors, parsons and poets sup with me." It is small wonder that he left the university without a degree and ten thousand pounds in debt.

One of Byron's schoolfellows at Harrow had been a tall, yellow-haired, blue-eyed boy named Robert Peel, the son of a rich Lancashire cotton-manufacturer. Though the two lads were very unlike they had been on friendly terms during most of their time at Harrow, but when they left school they parted. Robert Peel went up to Christ Church, Oxford, at the same time as Byron went to Cambridge. He was reserved in temper, and his manners were shy and stiff, so that he was slow in making new friends, but there were a good many of his Harrow schoolfellows at Oxford, and they formed a little company of their own. He read diligently—Homer, Cicero, Quintilian ; his brother said that no one ever read harder than Robert for the two or three terms before his examination.

He did not belong to the athletic set, and though he must certainly have heard a great deal about a certain gentleman commoner of Magdalen, John Wilson, we do not know that the two ever met. John Wilson at this time was a fair-haired young giant of twenty, whose feats of strength and agility were the talk of the university. His long jump in Christ Church meadow, when he cleared the Cherwell at a flying leap—twenty-three feet on a dead level—was remembered through generations of undergraduates. He was hot-tempered, though he was not quarrelsome, and was always joyously ready to defend his opinions with his fists. There was a certain shoemaker in the town whose ambition it was to beat Wilson in a man-to-man battle, and the two fought several times amidst the intense excitement of their supporters, but each time the undergraduate was victorious, and the shoemaker's ambition remained unattained.

Yet this noisy, robustious, restless youth was a fine scholar, who loved books as fervently as he loved bodily exercise and read with as much energy as he ran and jumped. He read classics, law, history, and philosophy, and he passed the examination for his bachelor's degree in a way that his tutor described as " glorious." He had read the *Lyrical Ballads* when he was a schoolboy, and ever since he had seized on the poems of Wordsworth and Coleridge as they appeared and read them until he knew them by heart. He loved all poetry and romances and everything in literature that was stirring and impassioned. He talked freely and enthusiastically to his fellows about the books he read, but few of them cared very much to listen, and he did not know that in one of the rooms in Worcester College there lived a youth with a large head, a small, frail body, and the face of a beautiful child who was as ardent a Wordsworthian as he was himself. This youth, whose name was Thomas De Quincey, lived, in the midst of the university world, the life of a recluse. He belonged to a good Manchester family, but his father was dead, and he had only a small allowance to cover his university expenses ; and most of this he spent on books. He took no part in the social life of Oxford ; he neither gave nor accepted invitations ; sometimes for days together he scarcely spoke to anyone, though when, as happened occasionally, he was drawn into an argument on Wordsworth's poetry, or any other subject that greatly moved him, his eloquence bore down all his opponents. Such undergraduates as noticed him in his shabby, almost threadbare clothes walking round the quadrangle with a book in his hand thought him a rather comical figure, wondered for a moment who he was and what he was doing, and troubled no more about him. He himself was happiest when he was shut up in his room in Worcester, reading one of the many volumes of classics, philosophy, history, and poetry with which it was littered, though he regretted in later years when he and John Wilson had become friends that, though their time at the university exactly coincided, they never met.

There was quite a large sporting and drinking set at Oxford, who did their best to make it appear that betting and getting drunk were the main university activities. Miss Austen's John Thorpe, of *Northanger Abbey*, had gone down some years before, but his successors remained. Undergraduates still boasted that the guests at their wine-parties drank five pints a head, which was a pint above the average, but " Mine is famous good stuff, to be sure " ; and they were still ready to bet any number of guineas that they would drive their curricle any distance in less time than some-body else could drive his. These young gentlemen read very little—*Tom Jones*, or a novel or two of the Mrs Radcliffe type, and, in the case of those to whom a degree was of importance, just so much of the books set for their examina-tion as would enable them, they hoped, to scramble through. Sometimes they miscalculated, and were plucked, as was the unhappy fate of handsome young James Crawley, of *Vanity Fair*, and his friend Bob Ringwood, son of Lord Cinqbars, who found that a too exclusive attention given to such champions as the Rottingdean Fibber and the Tutbury Pet led to disaster.

No such disaster overtook Robert Peel, though as his final examination drew near panic seized upon him, and he wrote home to say that he could not go up as he was sure he would fail. But he did go up, and passed brilliantly, making a sensation in the university by taking a double First. " The crowd that went to hear him," wrote his friend Dawson, " resembled more the assembly of a public theatre than that attending a scholastic examination." Divinity was taken first ; then Aristotle. One flowing, comprehen-sive answer was enough on that. " In his construing of Sophocles, Æschylus, Pindar, and Lucretius it seemed as if the whole assembly was actuated with one sentiment of applause."

Meanwhile an interesting group was gathering at Corpus Christi. In 1806 came fourteen-year-old John Keble from his father's Gloucestershire vicarage, with a scholarship won in competition with boys three or four years older than himself. John Taylor Coleridge, nephew of the poet, came in 1809, George Cornish, afterward a famous missionary, in 1810, and Thomas Arnold, the future headmaster of Rugby, in 1811. Corpus Christi was one of the smallest of the colleges, and there were no undergraduates except holders of scholarships or exhibitions. "We lived on the most familiar terms with each other," said John Taylor Coleridge, writing an account of his university days thirty years later, when he was one of her Majesty's judges.

> We might be, indeed we were, somewhat boyish in manner and in the liberties we took with each other ; but our interest in literature, ancient and modern, and in all the stirring matters of that stirring time was not boyish ; we debated the romantic and classic question ; we discussed poetry and history, logic and philosophy ; or we fought over the Peninsular battles and the Continental campaigns with the energy of disputants personally concerned in them. Our habits were inexpensive and temperate ; one break-up party was held in the junior common room at the end of each term, in which we indulged our genius more freely, and our merriment, to say the truth, was somewhat exuberant and noisy, but the authorities wisely forbore too strict an enquiry into this.

Like John Wilson and Thomas De Quincey, these young undergraduates of Corpus loved the *Lyrical Ballads* and were enthusiasts for Wordsworth and Coleridge. Each of them kept a book which he called a " Silva," and in which he wrote down passages that he specially admired from the works of various poets, and sometimes verses written by himself or by one of his friends.

There were no university games in those days, and undergraduates who could not afford to keep horses took their exercise by swimming and walking. The Corpus Christi group loved making what they called a ' skirmish ' across country. They left the road, climbed fences, waded streams, leaped ditches, or fell into them, letting no obstacle prevent them from going on their way. Sometimes they met two other youths whom they knew by sight as undergraduates of University College. One of them was a dark, strongly built young man, a little older than the general run of freshmen. The other was a tall, slight boy with a beautiful face, eyes that looked as if they saw visions, and a mass of brown hair that stood out round his small head. He stooped a little and moved awkwardly, and he looked shabby because, although he wore expensive, well-cut clothes, they were tumbled and unbrushed. Sometimes he had a book in his hand, and read eagerly as he walked beside his friend ; sometimes he talked, in a high-pitched voice that Hogg declared was " excruciating," and with ungraceful, impassioned gestures. At times he would stop, pin a card to a tree, and fire at it with a pistol that he carried in his pocket ; or he would kneel down by a wayside pool, make a boat out of some scrap of paper, and watch with absorbed interest, though a keen east wind was blowing and Hogg was impatiently urging him to come on, while it tried its fortune on the tiny waves.

The Corpus Christi group, although they often had to put on a desperate spurt for the last mile or so, usually managed to get back in time for the five o'clock college dinner ; but Hogg and Shelley purposely loitered, for Shelley hated to take his food with the others, and preferred a meal of bread and cheese and fruit, with beer or wine, eaten in his own room or in Hogg's. When this meal was over Hogg would get out the books and history that he had to read for his degree, and study for several hours. Shelley would lie down on the hearthrug, with his head so placed that the fiercest heat of the fire fell upon it, and go to sleep. He always woke about ten o'clock, ready to drink large quantities of the tea that they made for themselves ; then he too got out his books and read until nearly two in the morning. They were not always, indeed not often, the books that he ought to have been reading for his university work. He hated mathematics and refused entirely to read the books on that subject set by his tutor, and the fact that Aristotle was one of the books to be prepared for the examination made him determine at once that he would not read it, though he felt a real interest in its subject matter. He read Plutarch and Euripides in translations, he revelled in stories of Eastern life, and he devoured immense quantities of poetry. Hogg declared that Shelley often had a book in his hand sixteen hours out of the twenty-four. He read at meal-times, in bed, and walking along the street. " If I were to read as long as you read, Shelley," said Hogg, " my hair and my teeth would be strewed about on the floor and my eyes would slip down my cheeks into my waistcoat pockets, or at least I should become so weary and nervous that I should not know whether it were so or not." But no such dire happenings came to warn the book-worshipping young man, and he took no heed of his friend's warnings. Shakespeare he loved and read over and over again, and he was fascinated by Landor's epic poem, *Gebir*. One morning Hogg went to his room eager to tell him some interesting piece of news, but Shelley had *Gebir* in his hand, and paid not the slightest attention to what his friend was saying. Hogg, in annoyance, snatched the book from the reader's hand and threw it out of the window into the quadrangle. Shelley looked up as if awakened from a dream, and remarked thoughtfully, " It is something for a man to have produced what could please one fellow-creature and offend another so much."

The subject in which at this time Shelley took the most eager interest was metaphysical speculation, and he and Hogg read together Locke's *Essay concerning Human Understanding*, Hume's *Essays*, and other works of the same kind, and often sat up discussing them until the early hours of the morning. As a result, Shelley, with his usual impetuosity, declared himself a convinced atheist ; and he proceeded to write, and to have printed, a little pamphlet of two pages which he called *The Necessity of Atheism*. Copies of this he distributed among his friends, and he also advertised them for sale in the *Oxford University and City Herald*. The pamphlet was brought to the notice of the college authorities, and Shelley was asked if he had written it ; he refused to reply, and was expelled from the university.

116

Hogg stood by him bravely. He denounced the injustice of the dons' methods ; he himself, he said, might as well be accused as Shelley, and if he were accused he would refuse to answer, just as his friend had done. When Shelley went off by the London coach, on the morning of March 26, 1811, Hogg went with him, and the university knew them no more.

For a time the expulsion of the son of Sir Timothy Shelley, of Field Place, Sussex, made some stir in Oxford and in the world outside. People talked about the dreadful atheistical books that the young gentlemen of the university *would* read, and asked why the proctors, or some one, did not put a stop to such practices. But the two young men had not had many friends at Oxford, and the affair was soon forgotten. Nobody seemed very anxious to read *The Necessity of Atheism*, and the few copies that had been sold soon disappeared.

Just at this time the young gentlemen had something to read that was far more interesting than a metaphysical pamphlet. Lord Byron, that wild, handsome, wicked youth, of whose college career thrilling tales were told in both universities, had written a poem which had taken the town by storm, and the young gentlemen were not going to be behind their fathers and mothers and sisters and brothers in giving their judgment on the new work. Up to that time Walter Scott had been the poet best beloved by the undergraduates, and there were many who still held staunchly by the old favourite, and these argued hotly with the other party, who declared that Byron had completely beaten Scott out of the field. There was a dark, keen-faced, good-looking undergraduate at Balliol, named John Gibson Lockhart, who had come up from a Scottish manse, and who was noted, and a little feared, among his fellows for his witty, caustic tongue. He was one of the upholders of Scott, and he tells how when *Rokeby* came out in December 1812 there was tremendous excitement. The bookshops were besieged by undergraduates clamouring for early copies, and when some lucky youth managed to obtain one he was followed to his rooms by a vociferous crowd, anxious to get a glimpse of the new poem and give their opinion as to its chances of success. They even made bets as to which of the two poets would win in the race for popularity, and were as fervent in enumerating the points of their favourite as were the members of the sporting set when they offered odds on Dutch Sam or Molyneux.

One of Lockhart's friends was William Hamilton, afterward professor of logic and metaphysics in Edinburgh, who complained that he was " so plagued by those foolish lectures of the college tutors " that he had little time for anything else. He was a great reader, and bought fascinating old books at a bookshop near St Giles, though he owned that the price was " wonderfully high." He bought also Crabbe's poems, Dr Reid's works in two volumes, and the works of Tacitus in four. He read many works on philosophy, and was apparently able to find some interest in " the most terrible philippic in defence of the existence of women's souls," sent him by his Aunt James.

Lockhart, a good many years after he had left Oxford, wrote a novel called *Reginald Dalton*, in which he gave a picture of university life. It is chiefly concerned with the dissipated set among the undergraduates and with the temptations that beset an inexperienced youth, such as the hero, coming up from a quiet country home.

In October 1818 Thomas Babington Macaulay left his private school in Hertfordshire and came up to Trinity College, Cambridge. He was now eighteen, and the chubby, boyish prettiness of his early days was all gone. The prodigy of Clapham was short, thickset, and ungraceful ; even his adoring sisters admitted that Tom's figure was bad and that his clothes did not sit well upon him. But his spirits were as quick and lively as ever, and at Cambridge, as elsewhere, few people, while they were in his company, had time or inclination to think about his looks. At first he lived in lodgings in Jesus Lane with Henry Sykes Thornton, eldest son of the Member for Southwark, who had come up with him from Clapham. Both had the same tutor, hoping by this arrangement that each might benefit by the instruction given to the other. But Thornton was reading mathematics, a subject that Macaulay hated ; only with groans and lamentations did he submit to being taught just so much of it as

Trinity College, Cambridge

Macaulay's rooms were on the left of the small door.

From a pencil sketch by E. T. Miller

Trinity College. Cambridge

was necessary for his examination. " Oh for words to express my abomination of that science, if a name sacred to the useful and embellishing arts may be applied to the perception and recollection of certain properties in numbers and figures ! " he wrote to his mother. " Oh that I had to learn astrology, or demonology, or school divinity ! Oh that I were to pore over Thomas Aquinas, and to adjust the relation of Entity with the two Predicaments, so that I were exempted from this miserable study ! " The hour with the tutor was usually taken up with arguments by which Macaulay tried to prove the worthlessness of the subject, and Thornton felt regretfully obliged to take his coachings by himself ; and a little later Macaulay moved into rooms in Trinity College.

Very soon he made friends with a number of freshmen whose tastes were similar to his own—that is, who loved books and discussion and talk without end, and cared little for bodily exercise or dissipation. Among these were the two Coleridges—Derwent, the son of the poet, and Henry Nelson, his nephew ; Charles Villiers and Hyde Villiers, of St John's, brothers of Lord Clarendon ; Winthrop Mackworth Praed, who had come up from Eton with a great reputation as a scholar and as the editor of the *Etonian*, which he had made unique among public school magazines ; and the gifted, charming Charles Austin, of Jesus, whose strong personality made him from the first the leader of the little band. Others joined them as the time went on—Strutt and Moultrie and John Romilly—and so was formed a brilliant band, every member of which was to make his name famous in the years that followed his university life.

The days were not long enough for the reading and the talking that these eager youths tried to cram into them, and they often sat up half the night, and parted unwillingly in the grey of the morning. The two Coleridges, as was their bounden duty, extolled the *Lyrical Ballads* and *Christabel* and *The Excursion*, and Macaulay opposed them with argument and ridicule, and apt illustrations with which his marvellous memory supplied him. Charles Austin, who was an ardent Utilitarian and a convinced Radical, quoted Bentham's *Principles of Morals and Legislation*, and the others assailed

119

THE ENGLISHMAN AND HIS BOOKS

him with quips and sarcasms on the Benthamite ideal of
" the greatest happiness of the greatest number " ; but
Austin valiantly held his own and succeeded in making a
Radical of the Tory Macaulay, whereat there was consternation at Clapham. Praed, his pale, almost cadaverous face
showing strangely in that boyish company, argued wittily on
historical subjects, but reserved his most brilliant efforts for
the Union debates, which were held in a large room at the
back of the Red Lion in Petty Cury. For a long period the
Union had not been allowed to debate on any subjects concerning which political arguments could be used, but in
1820 the Vice-Chancellor reluctantly consented to the discussion of public affairs previous to the nineteenth century.
This was quite enough for the quick-witted undergraduates.
At once a programme was made out including such motions
as, " That Catholic Emancipation should have been granted
in 1795," " That our commercial policy previous to 1800
should have been founded on the basis of Free Trade."
There followed an eager reading of contemporary authorities
to supply the would-be debater with arguments and the
heated discussion of those arguments before a crowded
assembly that cheered each carefully pre-dated reference to
the politics of the day with mischievous delight. When the
meeting was over they went to supper, and regaled themselves on cold roast turkey and milk punch, followed by
" floods of tea " and equally copious floods of conversation.

At the beginning of 1820 some officious friend informed
Zachary Macaulay that his son was known throughout
Cambridge as " the novel-reader," and Thomas Babington
had to defend himself against his father's grieved displeasure.
" Nothing that gives you disquietude can give me amuse-
ment," he wrote,

> otherwise I should be excessively diverted by the dialogue which
> you have reported with so much vivacity. . . . There are men
> here who are mere mathematical blocks ; who plod on their
> eight hours a day to the honours of the Senate House. . . . How
> often have I seen such men go forth into society for people to
> stare at them and ask each other how it comes that beings so
> stupid in conversation, so uninformed in every subject of history,
> of letters, and of taste, could gain such distinction at Cambridge.

YOUNG GENTLEMEN AT THE UNIVERSITY

> It is in such circles, which, I am happy to say, I hardly know but by report, that knowledge of modern language is called novel-reading : a commodious name, invented by ignorance and applied by envy.

He did not deny that he had read novels at the university. He had been among the most enthusiastic in welcoming *The Bride of Lammermoor*, *The Legend of Montrose*, and *Ivanhoe*, which had been published since he came up ; and he had probably borrowed from the Cambridge circulating library some of the works of his favourite Mrs Meeke and Mrs Cuthbertson. But he entirely denied that he deserved the title of " the novel-reader " and cited the opinion of several of his friends to bear him out.

In November of the next year he was in trouble at Clapham once more. It was the fashion among certain undergraduates to admire the mawkish, sentimental verses contributed to various magazines by such writers as the once famous L. E. L. (Letitia Elizabeth Landon), Mrs Hemans, and Lady Blessington. Macaulay wrote some verses which he called *The Tears of Sensibility* in imitation of these effusions and sent them to the *Morning Post*, which in all seriousness published them. At Cambridge it was well understood that the whole thing was a hoax, and the author was highly applauded ; but at Clapham it was taken seriously, and when Mrs Macaulay read the poem, which began

> No pearl of ocean is so sweet
> As that in my Zuleika's eye,
> No earthly jewel can compete
> With tears of sensibility,

she was moved to write a criticism of it to her son, who, greatly irritated, had to explain that " it was meant solely for a caricature on the style of the poetasters of newspapers and journals."

The ridicule of one of their number could not, however, kill the taste for this style of writing among the young gentlemen of Cambridge. Edward Bulwer, youngest son of General Bulwer, of Heydon Hall, Norfolk, came up to Trinity in the year that Macaulay left it. " There was always in the Reading Room of the Union," said this young gentleman, a rush every Saturday afternoon for *The Literary Gazette* ; and an impatient anxiety to hasten at once to that corner of the sheet which contained the magical letters L. E. L. And all of us praised the verse and all of us guessed at the author. We soon learned that it was a female, and our admiration was doubled and our conjectures tripled.

Thus did Miss Landon, pretty, charming, sentimental, and nineteen years old, become the idol of the youth of Cambridge, who knew of her not so much as her name. In many college rooms young gentlemen sat far into the night, their learned books pushed aside, racking their brains that they might pay her poetic homage in verses such as those which Edward Bulwer found among his papers long after he had left the university, and which began " Fair Spirit ! "

Edward Bulwer came up to Cambridge a languid, pampered young gentleman of nineteen, who believed himself to be misunderstood and unhappy. He was handsome and clever, with an aristocratic bearing of which he was proud and an effeminate manner of which he was unconscious. During his first term he made no friends or acquaintances. He began to read history, but found it dreary work ; the lectures did not interest him, but there was one among the undergraduates he saw there who did. " In our lecture room," he said, " one face instantly arrested my eye ; a face long, pale, worn, with large eyes and hollow cheeks, but not without a certain kind of beauty, and superior to all in that room for its expression of keen intelligence." This was Winthrop Mackworth Praed, and it was the attraction that Bulwer felt for him that drew the young freshman from his moody aloofness. Alexander Cockburn, a Scottish undergraduate who became Attorney-General, with whom he had formed a slight acquaintance, persuaded him to join the Union, of which Praed was honorary treasurer. At that time an attack was being made upon him for some alleged misdemeanour in that office. " The interest I felt in Praed," said Bulwer,

animated me to the effort to defend him, and I rose late one evening and spoke in public for the first time. My speech was short, but it was manly and simple, spoken in earnest, and was at once successful. At the close of the debate the leading men

MONSTROSITIES of 1821.—

A CARICATURE BY GEORGE CRUIKSHANK OF THE FASHIONS OF THE DAY

of the Union introduced themselves to me. I had become as it were suddenly one of their set. I had emerged from obscurity into that kind of fame which resembles success in the House of Commons.

After that he quickly formed a circle of friends, and the rest of his university life was passed very happily, with credit to himself, though without any really strenuous reading.

Soon after Bulwer left Cambridge a remarkable group of undergraduates began to gather at the university. In 1826 there came to Trinity Charles Buller, so full of fun and jokes that he shocked some of the graver minds ; in the next year he was joined by James Spedding, a youth mild and wise and unselfish to such a rare degree that his fellows revered as well as loved him, and Joseph Blakesley, dry and caustic of tongue. Then came the wonderful year of 1828. From a little Lincolnshire village arrived two brothers, Charles and Alfred Tennyson. Both of them were tall and dark, with waving hair, great domed foreheads, and strong features. Charles was twenty and Alfred nineteen. Arthur Hallam, a lad of seventeen, son of the famous historian, came also, and John Kemble, brother of Fanny. Monckton Milnes, afterward Lord Houghton, Richard Trench, the future Archbishop of Dublin, Henry Alford, who was to become Dean of Canterbury, and Charles Merivale the historian, who was to become Dean of Ely, were also members of the group.

They were a wonderful company, and they drew together naturally into happy comradeship. They read and talked together, they tramped all over the country, arguing and joking, with great bursts of laughter that sounded over the wide fields that Alfred Tennyson hated because they were so " disgustingly level." They joined the Cambridge Conversazione Society, which had been started in 1824, and very soon gained for themselves the title of " the Cambridge Apostles." The society met on Saturday evenings, and at each meeting a member read an essay on a given subject. The member whose turn it was to read entertained the others to coffee and anchovies on toast. Many subjects were discussed at these meetings—the poetry of Landor, Southey, Keats, Coleridge, and Wordsworth, the philosophy of

123

Niebuhr, Bentham, and John Stuart Mill, with many others of a less literary nature. "Ghosts" was the subject that fell to Alfred Tennyson, but he was not ready when the time came, and so was expelled from the society. He remained, however, an unofficial member, being probably in somewhat the same position as Charles Brookfield, who said, " I was an acting Apostle, though never rated as one on the ship's books."

Arthur Hallam especially distinguished himself in these debates. " I have a very deep respect for Hallam," said Monckton Milnes. " He really seems to know everything, from metaphysics to cookery." Every one of the Apostles delighted in these evenings and looked back on them afterward with keen regret for joys that were past. " Alas ! Alas ! " said Merivale,

> what reckless joyous evenings those were ! What solemn things were said, pipe in hand ; how much serious emotion was mingled with alternate bursts of laughter ; how every one hit his neighbour intellectually right and left, and was hit again, and no mark left on either side ; how much sentiment and how much humour !

Tennyson in *In Memoriam* wrote of the place :

> Where once we held debate, a band
> Of youthful friends, on mind and art,
> And labour, and the changing mart,
> And all the framework of the land.

There were at Trinity College at this time two undergraduates who were not included among the Apostles and were not intimate with any of them until several years after they had all left Cambridge. These were Edward Fitz-Gerald and William Makepeace Thackeray. FitzGerald was not given to company, preferring to spend his time lounging and reading in his own room, and not troubling himself very much about what was going on so long as he could get plenty of books. He loved *Don Quixote*, and Waller's poems, and the works of Sir Thomas Browne, and all sorts of out-of-the-way literature. Once his mother came to visit him in her grand yellow coach with the four black horses, and sent a manservant to bring her son out to greet her ; but he could not come, for he had only one pair of boots, and they were at the cobbler's being mended. Yet, though he did not join very freely in the life of the place, he loved Cambridge, and recorded in his notebook Roger Ascham's words: " He that is able to mayntain his liffe in learning at Cambridge knoweth not what a felycitie he hath."

Thackeray too loved books, but he was a little idle and pleasure-loving, like the hero of his *Pendennis*, and he could not bring himself to set to work on the books required for his examination. He went to sleep, he said, over Galt's *Life and Administration of Cardinal Wolsey*, but he read eagerly all the poetry and novels that came in his way. When he came up to Cambridge in 1829 a rage for Shelley's poetry had seized upon the university. Thackeray began to read *The Revolt of Islam*, and was enchanted with it. He wrote to his mother telling her of his delight, and saying he would bring the poem with him when he came home. " It is in my opinion a most wonderful poem, though the story is absurd and the republican sentiment conveyed in it, if possible, more absurd." He changed his mind later about taking *The Revolt of Islam* home to his mother; he decided that, in spite of the wonderful music of its lines, it was not exactly suitable for reading aloud in the family.

The Apostles also were enthusiastic in their admiration of Shelley, and discussed his poems eagerly at their meetings. They talked indignantly of the stupidity and blindness that Oxford had shown in turning away this marvellous youth from her gates ; and they doubted whether even now, when his genius had been so clearly proved, she appreciated him as he deserved. It was suggested that an attempt should be made to open the eyes of this dull sister-university, and out of this suggestion grew a project which was undertaken with the complete approbation of the authorities. Cambridge challenged Oxford to a discussion on the relative merits of Byron and Shelley, and the challenge was accepted. Three representatives were chosen—Sunderland, Arthur Hallam, and Monckton Milnes—and they started for Oxford early one morning, driving in a chaise and taking ten hours on the journey. They were hospitably entertained " by a young student by the name of Gladstone," who had been a school-

fellow of Arthur Hallam's at Eton, and then they all went to
the room where the discussion was to be held.

The motion was " That Shelley is a better poet than
Byron." " Sunderland spoke for it," said Milnes,

> then Hallam, then some Oxonians—and I succeeded. The
> contrast from our long, noisy, shuffling, scraping, talking,
> vulgar, ridiculous-looking kind of assembly to a neat little
> square room with eighty or ninety young gentlemen sprucely
> dressed was enough to unnerve a more confident person than
> myself. Sunderland was somewhat awed and became tauto-
> logical, and spoke what we should call an inferior speech, but
> which dazzled his hearers. Hallam, as being among old friends,
> was bold and spoke well. I was certainly nervous, but I think
> pleased my audience better than I pleased myself. The Oxonian
> speaking is wretched.

Doyle (afterward Sir Francis) was one of the principal
speakers for Oxford, and he took the side of Shelley. Manning
(the famous Cardinal) supported Byron. As the discussion
went on it became clear that few of the Oxonians had read
Shelley's poems ; it was, declared the shocked and disgusted
Cantabs, the first time they had heard of him. " We
cowered like birds and fled like sheep," said Manning ; but
when it came to voting the ayes were 33 and noes 90. Byron
had won by 57 votes.

The " young student by the name of Gladstone " was
William Ewart, afterward Prime Minister of England, but
his story belongs to the later chapter of university history
which tells of the Oxford Movement and the famous Tracts.

When the young gentlemen had finished their university
course they came home fully equipped for the distinguished
career that awaited them, and the young ladies regarded
them with awe and admiration, as Praed tells us was the case
with that " talented man " Mr Tully St Paul :

> He came up from Brazen Nose College,
>   Just caught, as they call it, this spring ;
> And his head, love, is stuffed full of knowledge
>   Of every conceivable thing.
> Of science and logic he chatters,
>   As fine and as fast as he can ;
> Though I am no judge of such matters,
>   I'm sure he's a talented man.

CHAPTER VIII

BOOKS AND POLITICS

I REMEMBER," said Mr Brooke, of *Middlemarch*, in 1831, he being then nearly sixty years old, " when we were all reading Adam Smith. *There* is a book now ! " It was while Mr Brooke was an undergraduate at Cambridge that Adam Smith's great work, *The Wealth of Nations*, began to be widely read in England. It had been published in 1776, and had at once made for itself a great name among that comparatively small public that was seriously and intelligently interested in the new science of political economy. Statesmen and scholars all over the world acclaimed its importance ; the English Government, it was said, was in several instances guided by its suggestions in the framing of the Budget. But the people in general took little interest in it. Revolution was in the air, and there was restlessness and excitement throughout Europe and America. Half the people were shocked and disgusted by the new ideas, and spent themselves in opposing them. The other half saw visions of a world made new, and believed that they possessed the formula that would change those visions to reality if only the power were in their hands. There was a great deal of vague thinking and impassioned talking, but very little inclination for the serious study of a closely argued thesis.

Then came July 14, 1789, and the fall of the Bastille ; and all England watched breathlessly while France put into practice the theories which, as many believed, must lead to national regeneration. The months and the years went by, and the Revolution passed from one stage to another ; and, very slowly and unwillingly, the most thoughtful of its supporters in England began to doubt whether, after all, the true and infallible principle of government had been found. Doubts of another kind came to those who had always held the Revolution in horror and who found their horror deepen every day. Facts which they had not known, or had ignored, were forced upon their notice, and they were roused to the poignant realization that the poorer classes really were suffering from evils which the Government of the country might, and should, remove.

In this mood of perplexity the public turned eagerly to books to see if they could find there any teaching as to the best means of bringing a state to a condition of general prosperity and happiness. There were books in plenty on the subject ; piles of tracts and pamphlets were coming out every week. Most of them were too wildly partisan to be of any use ; some were philosophical treatises on human nature and human conduct which did not attack the question with the plainness and directness that the readers demanded. It was then that *The Wealth of Nations* was discovered by the general reader and seized upon with eagerness. Men and women all over the country studied its arguments and discussed its conclusions. Intellectual young students like Mr Brooke ' went into ' it and approved. Mr Lovell Edgeworth read it with enthusiasm, and so did his dutiful daughter Maria. It turned Mrs Jane Marcet to the study of political economy, so that, later on, she wrote the work of which Macaulay said, " Every girl who has read Mrs Marcet's little *Conversations on Political Economy* could teach Walpole or Montagu many lessons in finance "; and Mrs Marcet in her turn inspired Harriet Martineau. Lady Wharncliffe obtained it from a circulating library—it was a sign of the times that such a book should be found there, among the Minerva novels—and though she said, " I fear it is beyond me," she added, " I am delighted with the beginning."

But readers as a whole did not find even *The Wealth of Nations* entirely satisfying. It set out, it is true, very clearly the sources of a nation's material well-being. " The annual labour of every nation," it said, " is the fund which originally supplies it with all the necessities and conveniences of life which it annually consumes."

> The natural effort of every individual to better his own condition, when suffered to exert itself with freedom and security, is so powerful a principle that it is alone, and without any assistance,

not only capable of carrying on the society to wealth and prosperity, but of surmounting a hundred impertinent obstructions with which the folly of human laws too often encumbers its operations.

All industrial restrictions, all attempts to regulate commerce, should be swept away, and then " the obvious and simple principle of natural liberty establishes itself of its own accord."

This, after all, only dealt with the material side, and the aroused national conscience demanded something more. True, if wealth could be more evenly distributed and poverty removed a great step would have been taken toward universal happiness. Yet what became of the promised brotherhood of man, and how would Adam Smith's scheme help the nations toward political freedom ? The people might still be oppressed, still be powerless, still be driven into unjust wars and made to serve the purposes of their rulers. It would be each man for himself, and the golden vision of universal brotherhood would disappear. It was this aspect of Adam Smith's teaching that made Ruskin declare in 1871 that the principle upon which *The Wealth of Nations* was founded was, " Thou shalt hate the Lord thy God, damn His laws, and covet thy neighbour's goods."

There was another book which had been published thirteen years after *The Wealth of Nations*, in the year of the outbreak of the French Revolution, and which dealt more directly with the subject the people had at heart. This was Jeremy Bentham's *Introduction to the Principles of Morals and Legislation*. It was not a popular book, for it was written in an unattractive style, and was full of technicalities and unfamiliar terms, some of them of the author's own invention. But it set out a very definite and very carefully reasoned system. "Nature," said Bentham, "has placed mankind under the governance of two sovereign masters, pain and pleasure. It is for them alone to point out what we ought to do, as well as to determine what we shall do." He went on to argue that things are good or evil according to the amount of pleasure or pain that they entail, and so to the enunciation of the principle upon which the whole of his system was built. " The test of the

I

rightness of any action is whether it will result in the greatest happiness of the greatest number."

The book at first had few readers, but these were nearly all men of proved ability. Chief among them were Samuel Romilly and Lord Sherborne, James Mill, author of a *History of British India*, and David Ricardo, himself a writer on political economy. This little group of thinkers took up the new system enthusiastically, and called its principle the principle of utility and themselves Utilitarians. Bentham himself afterward grew dissatisfied with this name, and preferred to talk of " the greatest happiness principle " ; " for," he said, " the word *utility* does not clearly point to the ideas of pleasure and pain as the words *happiness* and *felicity* do ; nor does it lead us to the consideration of the *number* of interests affected."

Bentham's book had not gained any general popularity when, in 1790, all England turned from every other kind of political literature and began eagerly to read Edmund Burke's *Reflections on the French Revolution*. Here was something very different from the detached reasoning of *The Wealth of Nations* and the *Principles of Morals and Legislation*. Burke was strongly opposed to the Revolution and all its works, and he had been roused to fiery wrath by the action of some English people who had joined to form a society which they called the Revolutionary Society and had sent a message of sympathy to the National Assembly which then governed France. His book was written hurriedly and in a passion of indignation, but there was no sign in it of haste or lack of care. It was full of splendid oratory and magnificent images ; it put the arguments against revolution with tremendous power, and showed conclusively to what end it must lead.

The Tories and all who hated revolutionary principles and dreaded their spread in England read Burke's *Reflections* with almost reverent thankfulness ; it seemed to them that this was a book which might save Europe. Mr Brooke and his like were captivated by its eloquence. " Burke, now ! " said Mr Brooke forty years later to a young writer whose style he greatly admired, " that avalanche and the thunder of yours, now, was really a little like Burke." Whig politicians such as the famous Thomas Coke, of Norfolk, read it with fury and denounced it as false and dangerous But thirty thousand copies of the book were quickly sold, and many readers who had been inclined to waver in their faith became once more staunch supporters of the King and the British Constitution.

The extreme party—those who supported the Friends of the People and similar revolutionary societies—were even more enraged by the book than were the Whigs. Thomas Paine wrote in answer to it his famous *Rights of Man*, but this was too crude and vociferous to have much influence with educated people, though it raised a tumult among the working classes. *Vindiciæ Gallicæ*, another reply, by the eminent philosopher Sir James Mackintosh, erred on the other side. It was too calm and judicial in tone to make a strong appeal to minds as highly excited as those of the Englishmen of that day.

Seventeen-ninety-one passed, and seventeen-ninety-two. In France they saw the flight and capture of the King and the royal family, the murder of prisoners, the September massacres, the deposition of the King, and the setting up of the Commune. In England there was some rioting and a great deal of revolutionary propaganda, but this could not keep back the strong side of anti-revolutionary feeling that was rising all over the country. Burke's great words of warning and of exhortation were still sounding in men's ears: " With or without right a revolution will be the very last resource of the thinking and the good." " By following those false lights France has bought undisguised calamities at a higher price than any nation has purchased the most unequivocal blessings." The chill of disillusionment spread, and the ardour of the revolutionaries began to cool. Was there no way but the old way, and was the bright promise of a world swiftly and wonderfully made new only a deceitful dream ?

Seventeen-ninety-three opened gloomily ; and before the first month was over England heard with shuddering horror that the King of France had been guillotined. Who now could cling to the revolutionary faith, or who hope that his country would follow the example of France? All except the most violent partisans now denounced her, and when, on February 1, 1793, France issued her declaration of war most Englishmen and Englishwomen felt that they were entering upon a struggle which had all the righteousness of a crusade. Mournfully and unwillingly those who had put their faith in Revolution resigned their hopes and looked for a new prophet.

He came quickly and unheralded, rising in their very midst. Before the first week of February was over there appeared in the bookshops *An Enquiry concerning Political Justice, and its Influence on General Virtue and Happiness.* It was written by William Godwin, a needy and hard-worked bookseller's hack, who had begun his career as a Dissenting minister and was now an atheist. The ideas of the writer were set forward with an apparently irresistible logic which delighted and intoxicated the eager seekers of a means of regenerating the world. It seemed so easy, so inevitable. Birth and heredity, said Godwin, have nothing to do with forming the character of man. Environment alone makes him what he becomes. Man has a natural tendency toward virtue; therefore, put all men in favourable circumstances and all men will be virtuous. That is the first part of the argument. The next is founded upon the premise that man's actions are guided solely by his reason. A virtuous man acting according to reason cannot but do what is wise and right. Therefore no outside constraints are necessary, no laws, no punishments, no formal marriages, no checks at all upon the freedom of the individual. A free society will be founded in which man will advance easily, happily, inevitably, toward that perfection which is his natural state.

To the younger generation *Political Justice* came with light and healing and invigorating hope. Southey borrowed it from the Bristol circulating library—" read, and almost worshipped." Coleridge wrote a sonnet in praise of its author. Henry Crabb Robinson at the age of twenty read it, and said afterward, " It gave a turn to my mind, and in

"Sansculottes feeding Europe with the Bread of Liberty"

Showing revolution in progress in Holland, Savoy, Germany, Italy, and England.
John Bull stands in the centre with Sheridan and Fox.

From a caricature by James Gillray, 1792

effect directed the whole course of my life." Wordsworth advised a young student to throw away his science books and read *Political Justice*. Shelley read it while he was a boy at school and conceived a passion of admiration for its author. Earnest and enthusiastic young men and women called Godwin " the Master " and themselves Godwinites or Godwinians ; and they wrote verses in praise of the great prophet who had opened their eyes to the truth.

Some readers took the other side, and denounced the new doctrine. Burke declared *Political Justice* to be " a thoroughly bad book," whose anti-moral paradoxes " deserve no refutation but that of the common hangman." Fox got it from his bookseller, read a few pages, did not like it, and sent it back. Samuel Newton considered that it was " peculiarly censurable." But no one denied that it had a tremendous influence, especially upon the young people of the day. " No work in our time gave such a blow to the philosophic mind of the country," said William Hazlitt. " Tom Paine was considered for a time a Tom Fool to him, Paley an old woman, Edmund Burke a flashy sophist."

James Ballantyne, the schoolfellow of Sir Walter Scott, was, at the time of the publication of *Political Justice*, a young solicitor of Kelso. In 1796 he visited London, and met there William Godwin and his friend Thomas Holcroft. " They were both," said Ballantyne,

> very full of triumphant confidence in the truth of their systems. They were as willing to speak, therefore, as I could be to hear, and as I put my questions with all the fearlessness of a very young man, the result was that I carried away copious and interesting stores of thought and information ; that the greater part of what I heard was full of error never entered into my contemplation. My delight and enthusiasm were boundless.

A little later Ballantyne met Walter Scott, whom he had not seen for some years, in the coach travelling from Kelso to Glasgow, and all through the journey the two young men talked fast and eagerly. Scott told his tales and legends, so that his companion was " more delighted with him than ever." " And then," said Ballantyne,

133

> I opened upon him my London budget collected from Holcroft and Godwin. Hour after hour passed away and found my borrowed eloquence still flowing, and my companion still hanging on my lips with unwearied interest.

Mr Brooke looked into *Political Justice* and found it well worth studying. " I took in all the new ideas at one time," he told the friends of his later years, " human perfectibility, now ! " It was at the Mr Brookes of his day that Thomas Love Peacock poked fun in his novel *Headlong Hall*, where Mr Foster, the perfectibilian, Mr Escot, the deteriorationist, and Mr Jenkinson, the *status quo*-ite, reduced to absurdity every subject discussed by their one-sided reasoning. Mr Foster declared that " everything we look on attests the progress of mankind in all the arts of life and demonstrates their gradual advancement towards a state of unlimited perfection." Mr Escot disagreed entirely.

> These improvements, as you call them, appear to me only so many links in the great chain of corruption which will soon fetter the human race in irreparable slavery and incurable wretchedness.

" There is not in the human race a tendency either to moral perfectibility or deterioration," declared Mr Jenkinson.

> The quantities of each are so exactly balanced by their reciprocal results, that the species, with respect to the sum of good and evil, knowledge and ignorance, happiness and misery, remains exactly and perpetually *in statu quo*.

This is a not unfair summary—though touched by caricature—of the endless fantastic arguments held by serious young people, who gathered in shabby lodgings and round frugal dinner-tables, in the college rooms of undergraduates and at West End clubs. The perfectibilians were in a large majority, and no one seems really to have grappled with the question as to why, if the law propounded by Godwin worked certainly and inevitably, mankind was still, in this nineteenth century, so very far from its promised perfection. No doubts troubled these ardent disciples, and their faith sustained them through the years that saw the Reign of Terror and the establishment of a military despotism in France, and poverty, distress, discontent, and rioting ever increasing in England. No one dreamed of the blow that was soon to be dealt it by an enemy who might almost be considered as within its gates.

There was a certain young Mr Thomas Malthus, a Fellow of Jesus College, Cambridge, who was not, as many of his fellows were, entirely carried away by Mr Godwin's great book. He inclined to the philosophy of the Benthamites, and he had a strictly logical and reasoning mind and was disposed to question a statement and examine it very closely before he accepted it. It seemed to him that there was probably a flaw in the reasoning on which was founded a doctrine so pleasant, so simple, and so opposed to all human experience, but he did not give it any serious consideration until one day he discussed the subject with his father, who was a convinced Godwinite. Then, as one argument after another was brought forward, the weakness of the whole theory of *Political Justice* grew apparent to him, and he found himself attacking it with a force and directness that was entirely convincing to himself, if not to his father. His interest was aroused, and he pursued, with careful study and investigation, the line of thought on which he had started; and in the year 1798 he published a book which he called *Essay on the Principle of Population*.

Malthus first stated what he believed to be a natural law in operation all over the world—that population increases in geometrical ratio, while productiveness of the earth increases only in arithmetical ratio; which is to say that the difference between increase of population and increase of productiveness is of the same order as the difference between compound interest and simple interest. From this he reasoned that the time would surely come when the earth would not be able to support the people who dwelt upon it, and he pictured the horrors of starvation, violence, and cannibalism that would follow. The more prosperous and happy were the peoples of the world, the sooner, if some check were not imposed, would this appalling state of things be reached. Vice and misery and injustice kept down the population, and therefore in a certain sense must be regarded, if not as blessings, at least as necessary evils.

The ideas which Malthus set forward were not entirely new. Other writers had touched on the subject, but never with the emphasis and directness necessary to stir the public mind. Now the whole country was roused. It was a grim and grisly picture which replaced the golden visions of the Godwinians. An alarmed and indignant England gazed on it with fascinated horror, even while they denounced the man who had set it before them. " Impious ! " " Blasphemous ! " they cried, and they quoted the old pious saying : " Where God sends mouths he sends bread to fill them." It was as much as to say, declared Southey, that God made men and women faster than He could feed them. Southey was married now and settled at Keswick, and he had renounced most of his revolutionary ideas, but not his large and active kindliness. He abhorred the doctrines of Mr Malthus, and lost no chance of saying so, and his word carried weight. So did the word of William Hazlitt, who was equally disapproving and outspoken.

The outcry against the book grew louder, and helped to spread the opinions of Mr Malthus from one end of England to the other. Here was a man, declared the outraged public, who defended smallpox, slavery, and child-murder ; who denounced soup-kitchens, early marriage, and parish allowances; who denied the fostering care of Providence; who would nip young love in the bud and take all the romance out of life. It followed, clearly, that he must approve of the French Revolution and all its excesses. He was a dangerous man, and his book ought to be suppressed. Harriet Martineau said that she had never met anyone who had read the *Essay*, though she had heard many people talk about it eloquently and forcibly. Everybody professed to know the contents of the book, but in most cases the knowledge had come through a garbled account made up of many flying rumours.

It was probably because so few people read the book, though many talked about it, that a new and amended edition of the *Essay*, published in 1803, did very little

136

toward changing the public conception of it. In the five years that had passed since it had appeared in its earlier form Mr Malthus had been going on vigorously with his investigations, and the results had caused him to modify many of the opinions he had previously expressed. The main thesis was the same, but he had, he said, " tried to soften some of the harshest conclusions of the first essay." As the years went on the violence of the opposition began to die down, and the Malthusians, as the followers of Malthus were called, increased in numbers. The Benthamites accepted his doctrines in their amended form. Thomas Noon Talfourd, the young law student from Reading, was an ardent upholder of them. Harriet Martineau, though she declared that before she was sixteen she was sick of the very name of Malthus, adopted his ideas with enthusiasm a few years later. Mrs Barbauld and her circle reverenced him as a great and good man.

In 1817 came his inevitable appearance in a novel by Thomas Love Peacock. He is Mr Fax, in *Melincourt*, " the champion of calm reason, the bearer of the torch of dispassionate truth that gives more light than warmth." So far he is like the other Benthamites ; but the torch which he carries is used first and foremost to throw a light on questions of population. " Bachelors and spinsters I decidedly venerate," said Mr Fax, " the world is over-stocked with featherless bipeds." " The cause of all the evils of human society," he declared, " is the tendency of population to increase beyond the means of existence." Once, when he was out walking with his friend, Mr Forester, Mr Fax passed a church where a rustic wedding was about to take place. He confronted the bride and bridegroom as they entered the churchyard, and addressed them in solemn tones. " I stand here," he said, " as the representative of general reason, to ask if you have duly weighed the consequences of your present proceeding." But the happy couple fail altogether to understand his argument. First they take " general reason " to be a military commander, and when Mr Fax assures them that this is not so, they conclude that he is a Methody preacher. They are entirely undismayed by the gentleman's dismal picture of the future that lies before them. When Mr Fax asks, " Do you realize that in all likelihood in the course of six years you will have as many children ? " the bridegroom replies, " The more the merrier, zur " ; and to the question, " How will you bring up your children ? " he answers with equal cheerfulness, " Why, in the fear of the Lord, to be zure." It was evidently a difficult matter to introduce Malthus's theory of population into the brains of the English rustic.

The subject became a popular one with people of fashion, and a reputation for cleverness could be cheaply gained by having ' ideas ' concerning Mr Malthus and his doctrines. " Lady Wigley has just written a pamphlet on ' Population,' " said Lady Harriet Duncan, of *Granby*, " a very clever thing, I'm told, but I don't pretend to understand the subject. But she has such a powerful mind—quite the highest order of intellect."

But although satirists jested and fashionable ladies posed, this question of population remained a very serious one for most people in the country. Malthus had raised two terrible spectres, Famine and Violence, and neither argument nor ridicule sufficed to lay them. For many years a shuddering people saw always those gaunt forms lurking threateningly in the background of national life. When prosperity came, rejoicing was stopped by the thought that the evil day was being hastened. In times of scarcity came the horrid fear that this was the beginning of the end. Tennyson did not exaggerate the fear which dwelt in men's minds when he wrote :

> Slowly comes a hungry people, as a lion creeping nigher,
> Glares at one that nods and winks beside a slowly dying fire.

Meantime, through Godwinian sunshine and Malthusian gloom, the disciples of Jeremy Bentham had been working hard to spread the doctrines of their master. Some of the most eminent among them had edited the *Introduction to the Principles of Morals and Legislation*, and had put it into a form that would be more acceptable to the general reader than the original version had been. Soon the cause began to make headway, and the Benthamites formed themselves into a political party which, as time went on, became strong enough to exercise a considerable influence on the affairs of the nation.

When the Continental war ended in 1815 England concentrated her attention on home affairs. For a long time discontent had been growing, especially with regard to the condition of the lower classes. The strong wave of anti-revolutionary feeling had spent itself, and the country was no longer held back by the fear that to advocate change of any sort was to take the first step toward revolution. The cry for reform became more and more urgent, and gradually it narrowed itself down to a demand for a change in the system of Parliamentary representation. That elusive vision of a perfect state which for ever floats before a nation's eyes seemed now, to a large proportion of Englishmen, to be attainable through Parliamentary reform. If only the people could choose their law-makers all would be well. Sydney Smith, with his genial common sense, put the point of view of the less-informed advocates of the measure fairly, though through examples that were openly and delightfully absurd, when he said :

> All young ladies expect that as soon as this bill is carried they will be instantly married ; schoolboys believe that gerunds and supines will be abolished, and that currant tarts must ultimately come down in price ; the corporal and sergeant are sure of double pay ; bad poets expect a demand for epics ; and fools will be disappointed as they always are.

The Benthamites took up with ardour the demand for Parliamentary reform. They began now to call themselves Philosophical Radicals instead of Utilitarians, and they applied their principle of " the greatest happiness of the greatest number " vigorously and uncompromisingly to all political questions. James Mill, who by the strength of his personality and his convictions made himself a leader in the party, was a democrat of the most bigoted type. He could see nothing good in monarchy or aristocracy. His scorn and hatred of the ruling classes amounted, we are told, to positive fanaticism. His interpretation of the doctrines of Bentham was rigid and logical in the extreme ; he allowed nothing for human weakness, human emotion, human inclination to this side or to that. When in 1817 he edited Bentham's *A Table of the Springs of Action* he touched it with his own narrow and unsympathetic views. Bentham himself said of James Mill that in advocating democracy he acted " less from love of the many than from hatred of the few."

Over the younger members of the Benthamite party Mill exercised a very complete domination. He had brought his own son up on the strictest Utilitarian principles, with the result, as we have seen, that the boy suffered later from spiritual starvation, from which the poetry of Wordsworth saved him. There was another young man, George Grote, the shy, clever, conscientious son of a rich banker, over whose development he had also had a great influence. " Mill the elder had seized him at the most enthusiastic time of life," said George Grote's wife, " and narrowed him under the idea that he was emancipating him."

Grote was one of a band of active, enthusiastic young men who attached themselves to the Philosophical Radicals and studied ardently the doctrines of Bentham as interpreted by Mill. Among these John Stuart Mill, son of James, was naturally prominent. At sixteen he was a youthful prodigy, a skilled logician brilliant in argument, and holding with fervour the views his father had taught him. About this time he read the *Introduction to the Principles of Morals and Legislation*, and this was, he said, one of the turning-points in his mental history. He went on to read eagerly other books which his father recommended to him, or which he himself thought would help him in his study of political economy, and he soon mastered Locke's *Essay concerning Human Understanding*, Hartley's *Observations on Man*, Brown's *Lectures*, as well as various works by Berkeley, Reed, and Dugald Stewart.

The other young Benthamites were all several years older than this precocious product of a remorseless system. The brilliant group of Cambridge undergraduates who had shone so brightly at the Union with Macaulay as their central star had left the university now, and many of them had come to join the Philosophical Radicals. There were John and Charles Austin, Hyde and Charles Villiers, Strutt, Charles Buller, and the younger Romilly. Macaulay had abjured the Radicals and become a Whig. Praed was a Tory, and wrote scoffing verses about his old companions:

> I find my Ovid very dry,
> My Petrarch quite a pill,
> Cut Fancy for Philosophy,
> Tom Moore for Mr Mill.

John Kemble's devotion to the Benthamite doctrines was alarming his family. " I sometimes fear that the passionate eagerness with which he pursues his pursuit, the sort of frenzy he has about politics and his constant excitement about political questions may actually injure his health," said his sister Fanny. " He is neither tory nor whig, but a radical, a utilitarian, an adorer of Bentham, a worshipper of Mill." Fanny declared that she too reverenced Jeremy Bentham, but she had doubts as to the value of his doctrines in practical politics. " His theories are so perfect that I think imperfection could never be brought to live under a scheme of government of his devising."

These enthusiastic young men formed themselves into a small society for the purpose of reading and discussing various books dealing with the subjects in which they were strongly interested. They met twice a week at George Grote's house in Threadneedle Street—" Threddle " his young wife had nicknamed it—adjoining the bank which he was now managing for his father. On Wednesdays and Saturdays, at half-past eight in the morning, twelve or more members arrived and " broke their fast on the latest emanation of the Mill brain " or some work equally satisfying and equally difficult of digestion. They read together Mill's *Elements of Political Economy*, Ricardo's *Principles of Political Economy and Taxation*, and Bailey's *Dissertations on Value*, and when they had had enough of political economy they read works on logic and psychology by Whately, Hobbes, Hartley, and Priestley.

The tall, handsome lady of the house made great fun of

these early morning guests, who were trying so earnestly to build up a new world on the foundation of pure reason. She nicknamed them " the Brangles," and mocked at their discussions on " the quantification of the predicate " and " the inconceivability of the opposite." She was as keen a politician as any of them, but with less of philosophy and more of humour and common sense. She herself read widely and seriously on political subjects, making careful notes of what she read. *A Letter to the Magistrates of England on the Increase of Crime* interested her strongly, and she studied as thoroughly as she could the jury system of the country. She was much more practical than the clever young Utilitarians who argued with such faultless logic, and her sympathies were warmer. George Grote, although he burnt with zeal to see all his fellow-creatures free and equal, could not talk to a common man of vulgar habits without disgust, but his wife, although she was an aristocrat by birth and breeding, had a robust kindliness and a fine sense of humour which made such intercourse easy and natural to her. " I like him," said Sydney Smith, " because he is so ladylike, and I like her because she is such a perfect gentleman."

Not all who read the *Introduction to the Principles of Morals and Legislation* became Benthamites. To many its teaching seemed narrow and joyless, offering no opportunities for generous self-sacrifice or high delight in pure loveliness. Hurrell Froude and the group of Oxford men who were to lead the Tractarian movement hated Bentham and his doctrines. Thomas Arnold, now headmaster of Rugby, spoke bitterly of " that godless Utilitarianism." Bulwer, in his *Ernest Maltravers*, put into the mouth of one of his characters a cynical profession of the Utilitarian creed: " I am a Benthamite, a benevolist, as a logician—but the moment I leave the closet for the world I lay aside speculation for others and act for myself. The greatest number to me is number one."

Disraeli, in his *The Young Duke*, tells how the Duke of St James's, riding in a coach to London, has for his fellow-passenger Mr MacMorragh, a Utilitarian and father of

142

Denis MacMorragh, who writes for the *Screw and Lever,* and has " subjected the universe to his critical analysis." This gentleman believed firmly in democracy and equality. " He demonstrated the inutility of all elevation and declared that the Andes were the aristocracy of the Globe. Rivers he rather patronised, but flowers he pulled to pieces, and proved them to be the most useless of existences." He informed the travellers in the coach that they were quite wrong in supposing themselves to be " the miracle of creation." On the contrary, he avowed that already there were various pieces of machinery of far more importance than man, and he had no doubt that in time a superior race, entirely machine-made, would be evolved.

There was another class of young men who were very unlike the serious disciples of James Mill in everything except their interest in politics. They belonged to the distinguished company of the dandies, that had taken the place of the *beaux* who had flourished under the Regency. Carlyle a few years later defined a dandy as " a clothes-wearing Man, a Man whose trade, office, and existence consists in the wearing of clothes." But this was certainly not a fair definition of the dandies of the twenties. There were literary dandies, who, as Lady Palmerston testified, cared more for books than for coats and neckcloths ; and there were dandies who combined literature and politics, and who had brains as active and ambitions as colossal as the shabbiest among the philosophers.

Benjamin Disraeli was the full flower—a little overblown even—of dandyism. He lounged in fashionable drawing-rooms and delighted in being petted and admired by fine ladies. We see him sitting in Lady Blessington's magnificent *salon* " with the last rays of the sunlight reflected from the gorgeous gold flowers of a splendidly embroidered waistcoat," a quantity of gold chains about his neck and pockets, a white stick with a black cord and tassel in his hand, and a thick mass of jet black ringlets falling over his left cheek almost to his collarless stock, and again at Mrs Bulwer's dinner-table, in green velvet trousers, canary-coloured waistcoat, low shoes with silver buckles, lace at his wrists, and his hair in ringlets. Yet when he met Lord Melbourne in Mrs Norton's drawing-room and the Home Secretary said genially, "Well, now tell me what you want to be," this preposterous young man of twenty-four gravely answered, "I want to be Prime Minister." He meant it quite seriously, and it was to the attainment of that end, not to the consideration of his clothes, that his chief energies were devoted.

The dandy politicians had not as many theories as the Utilitarians, and they did not rely for the building-up of their systems of government on the maxims found in books. They went about in society, and watched the people in high places, and formed their own opinions concerning the men who ruled England and the methods of each. Then some of them wrote books in which they put not only a picture of what they had seen, but also a great deal about their own beliefs and hopes and ambitions; and so there came into existence a series of novels which, in a light satiric fashion, and with a good deal of what we now might call 'high-flown nonsense,' did succeed in showing how, in certain circles of society, politics were affecting national life. These novels were read not only by all the dandies and all the aristocratic ladies and gentlemen who were familiar with the life they pictured, but also by the great middle-class reading public who took the volume recommended at the circulating library as that which every one was reading.

Hazlitt wrote an essay, which he called *The Dandy School*, on these novelists, and denounced them for ignoring all ranks of society except the fashionable and the highly placed. According to them, he said, "the great business of life is a sort of masquerade or melodrama, got up for effect by the particular desire of the Great"; and he cited Theodore Hook, the editor of the Tory paper *John Bull*, and Benjamin Disraeli, the author of *Vivian Grey*, as the chief offenders.

The hero of *Vivian Grey* is, in all important points, Disraeli himself. Like Disraeli, he read widely in the library of a scholarly father, and like him he decided that

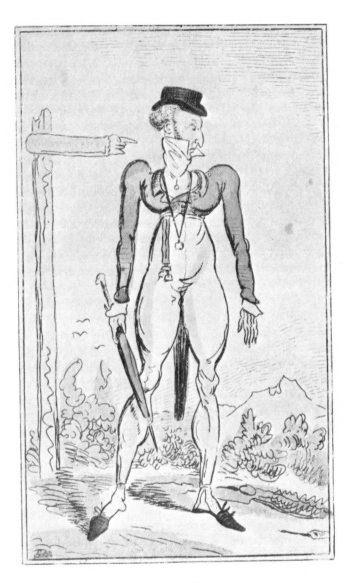

A Genuine Dandy

A satirical sketch by George Cruikshank

it was useless for a youth who wished quickly to make a name and figure in the world to go to a university. For a time he hesitated as to what career he should follow, until there came a moment when

> The inexplicable longings of his soul, which had so often perplexed him, were at length explained. The want, the indefinable want, which he had so constantly experienced was at last supplied ; the grand object on which to bring the powers of his mind to bear and work was at last provided. He paced his chamber in an agitated spirit and panted for the senate.

Nearly all the gentlemen who wrote these books and nearly all their heroes " panted for the senate." Robert Plumer Ward, who had the distinction of beginning the series, was older than most of the band, and had been in Parliament since 1802, so that he had the light of experience to guide him and was able to mark out a way in which his youthful followers could tread with confidence. His hero, Tremaine, is a young Whig Member of Parliament, with an estate in Yorkshire, whose name is " known in the political world for talents and integrity, in the fashionable as an ornament of the higher circles." He finds his political friends treacherous and self-seeking, and in disgust he retires to his Yorkshire estate, resolved to live for himself alone and have nothing to do with public affairs ; but he is brought to a better mind by the influence of a neighbouring clergyman-squire, Mr Evelyn, and his lovely and accomplished daughter, Georgina. Dozens of the pages of the book are taken up with arguments on religion and moral philosophy between Tremaine and Evelyn, and the discussions on " the compatibility of free-will with foreknowledge " and " the indiscerptibility of consciousness " are worthy of the Benthamites themselves. But with all this the appeal of politics to the ordinary man is not forgotten, and farmers and squires discuss practical Parliamentary questions with a fervour almost equal to that of the high-souled theorists. " What can be so interesting," said a fox-hunter to a politician, " as a hard-run chase ? " " What ? " replied the politician. " Why, a hard-run division in the House of Commons."

K 145

THE ENGLISHMAN AND HIS BOOKS

Tremaine was certainly the success of the season. Harriet Martineau said that she read " Mr Ward's novel *Tremaine*, which was making a prodigious noise, and which perfectly enchanted me, except by its bad philosophy." Five years later it was still being read. Mrs Gore makes some of her fine ladies and gentlemen of 1830 call Tremaine a " sentimental driveller " and reject his ideas with scorn.

Vivian Grey, which came anonymously in 1826, made an even greater sensation, and Robert Plumer Ward was one of the foremost in testifying to the interest it excited. " All are talking of *Vivian Grey*," he wrote to Disraeli.

> Its wit, raciness and boldness are admired everywhere. From Sir George and Lady Nugent's accounts it is spreading in London, where it excited curiosity and also resentment. I observed this at Lord Maryborough's dinner on Monday, where were many public men and some fine ladies who all admired but a little felt the satire. Vivian Grey himself is abused as a hypocrite. In short you have set everybody a-guessing.

In another letter Ward tells of a dinner at Lord Gifford's where he met "much of the *beau monde*, as well as graver characters, bishops and judges," and here too the chief topic of conversation was *Vivian Grey*.

By and by it leaked out that the author of the much-talked-of work was an obscure young man of twenty-one, who knew nothing whatever of the political matters and the political personages that he had treated so familiarly, and then there came a reaction. Mortified readers, annoyed at having taken the book with seriousness, now abused it roundly, and for a time young Benjamin Disraeli was crushed to the earth. But he soon rose again, and his book rose with him, and from various quarters came indications that it was still being read. It is on Clarissa Trant's book-list for 1827, and handsome, stately Miss Rosina Wheeler, soon to become Mrs Bulwer, read it in the same year. In 1828 Lady Morgan wrote that she was reading *Vivian Grey* " at night and in bed in the morning." Mrs Norton read it, learned whole pages of it by heart, and admired it excessively, as also did Madame D'Arblay, now seventy-four years old, whom a few years later Disraeli gratefully declared to be " the staunchest admirer I have in London."

Granby, by Thomas Lister, who had married the sister of Lord Auckland and so allied himself with the great Whig family of the Edens, appeared in the same year as *Vivian Grey*, and although it did not make such a sensation it was widely read and soon established itself as a favourite. It gives a finished picture of a dandy, Mr Vincent Trebeck, who is, however, too selfish to concern himself with public affairs. There is Sir Thomas Jermyn, Member for Rotten-town, which was a Government borough, and " therefore his politics were ministerial." There is Lady Crosstown, who is strong-minded and disagreeable and a Radical, and who once, to the horror of her friends, sent a card for one of her parties to the demagogue Hunt. There is Lady Highbury, who is anti-Catholic because she was " disappointed at Rome—ill-used, she says, about a front place at one of the ceremonies in Holy Week."

In 1827 came Robert Plumer Ward's *De Vere, or The Man of Independence*, which its author openly called a political novel. It dealt with the period of Chatham's last administration, more than fifty years before, but there was much in it that could be, and was, applied by its readers to the affairs of their own day.

Edward Bulwer's *Pelham*, which came in 1828, was, like *Vivian Grey*, largely autobiographical. Bulwer had travelled on the Continent since leaving Cambridge and had developed into a dandy of the most elegant type. " He adopted a style of dress and manner different to that of other people," said Miss Cunningham, one of the friends he met in Paris, " and he liked to be noted for it. My mother often laughed at him for his vanity, and his ' beautiful curls ' were a standing joke among his friends." He was not very tall, so he wore a very tall hat to add to his height, and he dressed with the very greatest care—not showily, like Disraeli, but with extreme elegance. He had not yet taken up the Radical opinions for which he became noted a little later, but he was extremely interested in politics, and so was his hero, Pelham, who eventually went into Parliament.

THE ENGLISHMAN AND HIS BOOKS

For two months after *Pelham* was published it attracted little notice ; then suddenly, and without any apparent reason for the change, it became the rage. Everybody began to talk about it and to discover its outstanding merit. One day when Bulwer was paying a visit to Cambridge he was stopped before the door of the Senate House by George Burgess, a well-known tutor of the university. " I had no idea, Bulwer," said this distinguished critic, " that you had it in you to write such a book." " Well," replied the youthful author, " no man knows what he can do till he tries." Bulwer became the lion of the season, and *Pelham* was quoted everywhere. It even had an influence on the fashions. " I did not like that blue coat you wore when I last saw you," the hero's mother, Lady Frances, is represented as having written to her son, " you look best in black ; which is a great compliment, for people must be very distinguished in appearance to do so." Up to that time the coats worn for evening dress had been of different colours—brown, green, or blue according to the fancy of the wearer, but soon after the publication of *Pelham* black became the invariable wear.

Mrs Gore, in her *Manners of the Day* (1830), complains that " Ours is the age of aristocratic literature, and such novels as *Tremaine, Granby*, and *Pelham*," but she herself has a weakness for the nobility, and Thackeray caricatured her in one of his *Novels by Eminent Hands—Lords and Liveries*, by the author of *Dukes and Déjeuners, Hearts and Diamonds, Marchionesses and Milliners*. She is interested in the affairs of the day also, and has almost as many references to politics as the novelists of the dandy school. Politics, indeed, were becoming more and more the absorbing subject of interest for the whole nation. " It is considered a mark of fine young ladies," says another of Mrs Gore's heroines, " to ' doat on the Duke of Wellington ' or to ' adore the present ministry,' the intellectual coteries affecting the latter creed, the exclusive the former." " Society is become a sort of battlefield, for every man (and woman too) is nothing if not political," declared Fanny Kemble in 1831.

148

LITERARY LADIES

Mrs Hall   Mary Russell Mitford   Harriet Martineau   Mrs Norton   Lady Blessington
Letitia Elizabeth Landon (L.E.L.)   Lady Morgan   Jane Porter
(author of *Thaddeus of Warsaw*)

From a drawing by Daniel Maclise, R.A.

BOOKS AND POLITICS

Harriet Martineau, trying perseveringly to obtain a publisher for her *Illustrations of Political Economy*, was met everywhere with the reply that the attention of the public was so taken up with the cholera and the Reform Bill that there was no chance for any new publication to succeed. This seemed to her hard, since her *Illustrations* was intended to instruct the very class into whose hands the Reform Bill would put power, and she believed that it would supply a national need. " I could never even have started the work," she said, " but for my thorough, well-considered, steady conviction that the work was wanted —was even craved by the popular mind." She found a publisher at last, and, in spite of Mr James Mill's prediction that her method of publication could not possibly succeed, five thousand of the first number were sold in a month, and later numbers had an even larger sale. The Duchess of Kent procured a set for her daughter, the Princess Victoria, and Lord Durham was instructed to inform Miss Martineau that the royal pupil was enjoying her readings immensely and was particularly attached to *Ella of Garveloch*. This was very gratifying to the author, since *Ella of Garveloch* had been violently attacked by some of her critics. It was a story of a Highland fishing village, and was intended to illustrate the principles of population, as laid down by Malthus. A certain section of society professed to be shocked by its treatment; it was indelicate, they said, and quite unfit to meet the eyes of young ladies. Harriet Martineau stood stoutly by her guns, and by and by came the royal approval and the approval of many other influential people, and the tumult died away.

At length, in 1832, came the Reform Bill; and after that, as Disraeli says, the New Generation, with a new political literature of its own.

CHAPTER IX

WORKING-MEN READERS

THE last decade of the eighteenth century, which saw the beginnings of so many new things, saw the emergence of a new class of working-men readers. Most of these were handicraftsmen in the big manufacturing towns, though there were small tradesmen, country mechanics, and farm labourers among them. They had little education and a narrow experience, but they had an immense curiosity. The dullness and monotony of their lives they felt to be unbearable, and they had a strong, blind faith that further knowledge would show them the way to better things. The urge that they felt toward learning was of the same kind that in earlier days had driven the young men, and sometimes the middle-aged also, out upon the road toward the medieval university. In this later time it drove them toward books.

Up to the beginning of the century the working men of England had seemed to be content with the ballads and chapbooks, the Bible and the religious works, that were easily within their reach. To these had been added the "Cheap Repository Tracts" and the sixpenny "blue books" in which Southey and Shelley had delighted, and which were reprints of the 'horrid' stories of the Minerva Press. Respectable working-class people, especially country families that had been settled in the same place for several generations, had usually collected a store of solid books bought mainly for the purpose of providing suitable reading for Sunday afternoons—as worthy Mr Tulliver read Jeremy Taylor's *Holy Living* and *Holy Dying* and Mrs Zachariah Coleman, wife of a journeyman printer of Islington, read Boston's *Fourfold State.* Mrs Gaskell says that the small farmers of Cumberland and Westmorland read " no light or ephemeral literature, but the grave, solid books brought round by the pedlar, such as the *Paradise Lost* and *Regained*, Gesner's *Death of Abel*, *The Spiritual Quixote* and *The Pilgrim's Progress*, were to be found in nearly every house." Year after year the pedlar brought round the same selection, and the two books of which he sold the most copies were *The Pilgrim's Progress* and *Robinson Crusoe*. These two books were read by almost everybody who read at all, from the working man to the prince. The pedlar had copies that he would sell for a few pence, and those who bought nothing else bought these. It would be interesting to try to trace the influence which the almost universal reading of these two books had on the people of eighteenth-century England. The tendency of both was certainly democratic, and it may be that they helped to make the working man feel that he had an equal right with his ' betters ' to many things—including knowledge—that had so far been out of his reach.

But the great mass of working men troubled themselves little about books. Many of them could not read, and of those who could the greater number were satisfied with a weekly newspaper. It was not until this new class, hungry for knowledge, arose that there was any real demand for an extension of the means and opportunities for reading.

Their demand was clear and insistent. Books they must have. They bought as many as they could, but books were dear and wages low. They borrowed if, as seldom happened, they were lucky enough to know anyone with books to lend. They seized on chance opportunities, read stray pages used as waste paper, or snatches from books displayed in shops. They would walk miles if there was a book to be had at the end of the journey. No sort of book came amiss to them ; they read history, travels, biography, science, fiction, poetry, but the subject that interested them most was politics. Each of them had decided views on the way the country should be governed. Each had his own vision of a perfect state. It was not in most cases anything very romantic or splendid. It was not the fairy-tale country of beauty and delight, nor was it Wordsworth's happy valley where man lived in close and joyous communion with nature. It was a very definite man-made paradise, to be created by the will of the people, and to exist for the good of the people. High wages, short hours, cheap food, and political power were to be its gifts to the working man. How it was to be brought into being he was not quite clear, but he believed that books would help him to find out.

A typical workman of this class was Francis Place. He was born in 1771, in a sponging-house kept by his father, and he was lucky enough to be sent to school fairly regularly from the time he was four years old until he was fourteen, though the schools were very poor ones and he learned little, except to read, that was of any value to him. At fourteen he was apprenticed to a leather breeches maker, and his education was regarded as finished. There were no books in his father's house, and he had no money to buy any for himself. " But," he says,

> my desire for information was too strong to be turned aside. Often have I been sent away from a bookstall when the owner became offended at my standing reading, which I used to do until I was turned away. I used to borrow books from a man who kept a small shop in Maiden Lane, Covent Garden, leaving a small sum as a deposit, and paying a trifle for reading them, having only one at a time.

Imaginative works made no appeal to him ; he mentions slightingly that he read at this period " *Pilgrim's Progress* and parts of other equally absurd books."

When he was nineteen and earning only fourteen shillings a week as a journeyman tailor he married, and he and his wife went through some very hard times together. They lived in one room in a court off the Strand, and their joint weekly earnings amounted to only seventeen shillings. Sometimes they were near actual starvation. There were several strikes and trade disputes among the tailors in the years that followed, and Francis Place took an active part in all of them. Young as he was, his fellows soon began to look upon him as a leader. He was staunch and brave and resourceful, and he never lost heart even when he had been out of work for months and was hungry and penniless. He struggled hard to keep his self-respect and live decently, and even in the days of their worst poverty he and his wife were known among their neighbours as "the lady and gentleman."

Books were still his passion and delight. During the first year of his married life he lived in the house of an old woman who took charge of chambers in the Temple, and she brought him home books borrowed from the rooms which she cleaned. In the course of a year he worked, he says, through

> the histories of Greece and Rome, and some translated works of Greek and Roman writers, Hume, Smollett, Fielding's novels and Robertson's works ; some of Hume's essays, some translations from French writers, and much on geography ; some books on anatomy and surgery ; some relating to science and the arts and many magazines. He had worked all the problems in the Introduction to Guthrie's Geography and had made some small progress in geometry.

He read also Blackstone, Hale's *Common Law*, Adam Smith, Locke, and Euclid.

In 1791 Thomas Paine—himself a working man who had led a wandering life and followed many trades—published his book *The Rights of Man*, which was intended as an answer to Burke's *Reflections on the French Revolution*. It was a narrow, unenlightened book, influencing chiefly by its vehemence and the easy assurance with which it set to work to remodel the universe. But it had power and sincerity, and it spoke to the uneducated classes in a language they could understand. All over England working men— eager, dissatisfied, questioning, looking for a way out of the conditions that oppressed them and raging blindly because they could not find it—saw in this book their answer and their clue. Francis Place read it and accepted its doctrines with enthusiasm. The Friends of the People, a society formed to spread democratic principles in England, recited with the faith and almost the reverence that men give to inspired words the Declaration of the Rights of Man on which Paine's book was founded.

> Men are born and always continue free, and equal in respect of their rights. . . . Every citizen has a right, either by himself or by his representative, to a free voice in determining the

necessity of public contributions, the appropriation of them, and their amount, mode of assessment, and duration.

Mark Rutherford (the pen-name of William Hale White) tells in his *Revolution in Tanner's Lane* how Jean Caillaud, shoemaker, recited this declaration to Zachariah Coleman, journeyman printer, as they walked down Red Lion Street toward Hatton Garden one April evening. Caillaud was one of the Friends of the People and was urging Coleman to join the society; but Coleman, sober, intelligent, and deeply religious, a deacon of the Pike Street meeting-house, Hackney, and a great reader, hesitated. "My friend," said Caillaud, "study that immortal charter, the Declaration of the Rights of Man. . . . It is the truth, you must come to that, unless you believe in the Divine appointment of dynasties." Zachariah did not—he detested kings and their ministers—and so he too became a disciple of Thomas Paine.

Peaceful, law-abiding people, especially among the middle and upper classes, who had been outraged by the excesses of the French Revolution looked on *The Rights of Man* with horror. It was a wicked and dangerous book, they said, aiming at the destruction of law and order, of loyalty and good citizenship, and glorifying murder and all hateful crimes. Napoleon, it was commonly reported, slept with a copy of it under his pillow, treasuring it for the help it gave him in his plans for the destruction of England. Thomas Poole, of Nether Stowey, the friend of Coleridge, bought a copy in 1791. He was not a revolutionary. His interest in social questions made him desire to read the book which was so strongly stirring the working classes, but his friends and even his own family were horrified at his action and treated him as a kind of political Ishmael. Writing to a friend in 1792, Poole tells how he lent *The Rights of Man* to a cabinet-maker who had expressed a great desire to read it, and how a certain Mr Syme, an attorney, seeing the man reading it, took it from him, tore it, and stamped it underfoot, and then maliciously set all sorts of tales about in the neighbourhood accusing Poole of being a dangerous person who distributed revolutionary literature.

154

So strong was the feeling against it that the book was forbidden, and selling it became an offence, to be punished by fine or imprisonment. Thomas Spence boldly displayed it on his bookstall at the corner of Chancery Lane and Holborn in 1792, for which he served a term in prison. Spence had been brought up in grinding poverty. His father was a net-maker of Newcastle, who had been twice married and had nineteen children. It was impossible for him to pay for any education for them, but he taught them to read, and with Thomas that was enough. Somehow he managed to get hold of books, and the number and variety of the books that he read, so thoroughly that he was able to remember and quote from them, is amazing. We know that before 1796, when he was forty-six years old, he had read the Bible, More's *Utopia*, Swift's *Sermons*, and *Gulliver's Travels*, Voltaire's *Philosophical Dictionary* and *Candide*, Barlow's *Advice to the Privileged Orders*, Murray's *Sermons*, Buchanan's *Travels in the Western Hebrides*, Lord Lyttelton's *Letters from a Persian in England to his Friend at Ispahan*, Ogilvie's *Right of Property in Land*, William Frend's *Peace and Union*, Goldsmith's *Citizen of the World*, Paine's *Rights of Man*, Defoe's *Robinson Crusoe*, and Harrington's *Oceana*; and there were probably many others. His great plan for the regeneration of the world was the nationalization of the land, and he preached this diligently, first in Newcastle, and afterward from his bookstall in London. Everybody knew him—a little, stunted, ragged man, standing by his stall at the corner of Chancery Lane, and giving sharp, irritable answers to tiresome or uncivil customers. Many working men bought the penny weekly paper which he published from 1793 to 1796. He called it *Pigs' Meat, or Lessons for the Swinish Multitude*, in bitter reference to a phrase used by Burke. He was, said Francis Place, " a very simple, very honest, single-minded man, who loved mankind and firmly believed that the time would come when they would be wise, virtuous, and happy."

No efforts of angry and frightened opponents could stop the sale of *The Rights of Man* or lessen its influence. All over the country little groups of men were forming themselves into societies where it was read and discussed. Samuel Bamford the Radical, a Lancashire weaver, tells how his father and a few friends—including a shoemaker, an apothecary, a herb-doctor, and several weavers—used to meet regularly at each other's houses to read Paine's book and discuss Parliamentary reform. Most of them were earnest Methodists of sober and decent life, feeling keenly the hardships of their class. They were derided and abused by their fellows, who called them " Jacobites " or " Painites," but they kept on their way steadily and quietly. When, in 1794, Paine's second book, *The Age of Reason*, was published, they read and discussed that also, in spite of its anti-religious tendency. It aimed at showing that the conception of God as set forth in the Scriptures was incompatible with man's reason and experience, and it argued shrewdly enough, though without any breadth of thought or spiritual insight. To those working men—a considerable number—who were sincerely religious the book came as a shock to the allegiance they had given to the author of *The Rights of Man*. These men were usually attached to an obscure sect of Dissenters, such as "the church assembling in Lantern Yard," of which Silas Marner was a member, and they found some satisfaction for their intellectual needs in endless theological arguments founded on the reading of the Bible and the polemical works of Dissenting divines. But they were as keen reformers as their fellows who cared nothing for religion, or who were professed atheists, proud of what they regarded as emancipation from the bonds of an outworn superstition. These latter welcomed *The Age of Reason* with triumphant satisfaction. Francis Place had never felt any strong attachment to religion, and the works of Hume had undermined what faith he had. *The Age of Reason* completed the work, and he became an agnostic. He was so eager to spread his new views that in 1796 he persuaded one of his friends, Thomas Williams, a small jobbing bookbinder and bookseller, to join with him in producing a new edition of Paine's work, and two thousand copies were sold within the first fortnight.

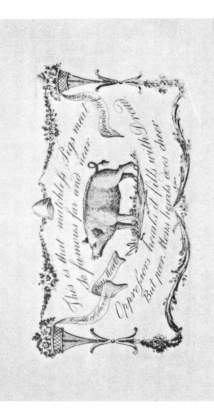

PIGS' MEAT;

OR,

LESSONS

FOR THE

SWINISH MULTITUDE.

PUBLISHED IN WEEKLY PENNY NUMBERS,

Collected by the Poor Man's Advocate (an old Veteran in the Cause of Freedom) in the Course of his Reading for more than Twenty Years.

INTENDED

To promote among the Labouring Part of Mankind proper Ideas of their Situation, of their Importance, and of their Rights.

AND TO CONVINCE THEM

That their forlorn Condition has not been entirely overlooked and forgotten, nor their just Cause unpleaded, neither by their Maker nor by the best and most enlightened of Men in all Ages.

For the oppression of the poor, for the sighing of the needy, now will I arise, saith the Lord, I will set him in safety from him that puffeth at him. PSALM XII. ver. 5.

And the Lord said, I have surely seen the affliction of my people which are in Egypt, and have heard their cry by reason of their task-masters: for I know their sorrows. EXODUS III. ver. 7.

THE SECOND EDITION.

LONDON:

PRINTED FOR T. SPENCE, AT THE HIVE OF LIBERTY, NO. 8, LITTLE-TURNSTILE, HIGH HOLBORN.

OPENING PAGES OF "PIGS' MEAT, OR LESSONS FOR THE SWINISH MULTITUDE"

WORKING-MEN READERS

In 1792 the Corresponding Society, intended to be the working-class wing of the democratic movement, was formed. The two existing societies—the Friends of the People, with its subscription of five guineas, and the Society for Constitutional Information, with one of two and a half guineas—were out of the reach of all except a few of the most prosperous among working men. The germ of the new society can be traced, we are told, to a dinner at the home of Thomas Hardy, "an honest and innocent, religious-minded shoemaker." This informal meeting was followed by others of the same kind.

> In January 1792 nine persons, all acquainted with each other, finished their daily labour and met at the sign of the Bell in Exeter Street. After bread and cheese and porter for supper, they lighted their pipes, discussed the hardness of the times and the dearness of all the necessaries of life, and finally turned to their subject, Parliamentary reform.

One of these nine persons was Thomas Holcroft. He was the son of a poor cobbler, and had been stable-boy, hawker, clerk, schoolmaster, actor, and author. Now, after years of poverty and hard striving, he was at last, at the age of forty-six, making for himself a position and a comfortable income by his novels and his plays. As a boy he had had little education. His father had taught him to read, and he had read everything that had come in his way—chap-books, plays, a great deal of religious literature, and, since money had been more plentiful, a great many works on history and politics. He was an ardent reformer and an enthusiastic member of the Corresponding Society which he had helped to found.

The society, with its entrance fee of a shilling and its subscription of a penny a week, attracted large numbers of working men. Francis Place joined it in 1794. " In this society," he says,

> I met with many clever, inquisitive, upright men, and among them I greatly enlarged my acquaintance. . . . We had book subscriptions—the books for which any one subscribed were read by all the members in rotation who chose to read them before they were finally consigned to the subscriber.

One of the books that Place was able to read through this society was Godwin's *Political Justice*, published in 1793. Its effect among working men was stronger, if not as widespread and immediately felt, as that of *The Rights of Man*. Readers were attracted by its smooth and persuasive style, so different from the violence of denunciation and the crude arguments used by Paine. Its price—three guineas—put it beyond the buying power of even the most prosperous working men, but very soon the many clubs that had lately been formed bought copies for the use of their members. Nearly every circulating library had at least one copy; and in 1797, when a new edition was published at fourteen shillings, many of Godwin's admirers managed to buy it that they might keep it as a precious personal possession. Thomas Spence read it, and quoted it in his periodical *Pigs' Meat*. Francis Place read it at a time when he was hesitating whether he should take the decisive step of giving up his journeyman's work and starting as a master. Failure meant ruin, and his wife was terrified at the thought of the risk that must be run. He himself was doubtful and afraid. " Mr Godwin's book," he says, " extinguished this fear in me."

Henceforward he went steadily on, step by step, until he won a position of independence and comfort. He still lived frugally. " The only things I bought," he says, " were books, and not many of them." In time, however, he got together a collection such as no working tailor had probably ever had before. Most of them were on historical, political, or legal subjects. Francis Place's imagination did not strengthen as the years passed by, nor did his sense of humour develop. He read neither novels nor poetry, and he has not recorded any visits to the play. He kept his books in the parlour behind his shop, carefully concealed from all except the small circle of friends who were like-minded to him. But sometimes a customer would catch a glimpse of them, and would ask questions, and then almost always the work which was to have been given to Place was taken elsewhere, for few people would believe that a man who was interested in books could be at the same time a good tailor.

158

As he grew more prosperous in his business he found himself able to give an increasing amount of time to public affairs. He was very active in the famous Westminster election of 1807, when Sir Francis Burdett was the Radical candidate. Little by little, through reading and observation and intercourse with the leading men of affairs, his grasp of the political situation strengthened, until at length he attained the remarkable position of the man behind the scenes who pulls the strings and manipulates the machinery which controls the movements of the actors on the stage. Times were very bad for the lower classes in England, and there were many working men besides Francis Place who passionately felt that some great change was necessary in the government of the country. The war still went on. Food was so dear that many must go hungry. The introduction of machinery had thrown numbers out of employment ; and there seemed no way in which the suffering classes could make their grievances known and insist upon relief.

More and more eagerly intelligent working men turned to books, some with a fierce desire to meet those whom they looked upon as their oppressors on more equal terms, some earnestly wishing to understand what was wrong, some simply seeking an escape from the hard monotony of their lives. There was Robert Owen, busy evolving those views and projects which gained for him the name of the " founder of Socialism." He was the son of a saddler and ironmonger in Newtown, South Wales. When he was eleven years old he was sent to London to a situation in a draper's shop, and he went on from one situation to another until he became overseer at a cotton mill, first at Manchester, and afterward in South Lanarkshire. His passion for reading began with his childhood. Before he left his father's house he had read *Robinson Crusoe*, *The Pilgrim's Progress*, Hervey's *Meditations among the Tombs*, Young's *Night Thoughts*, Cook's *Voyages*, Richardson's and other standard novels. All through his life he read, devouring books with the eager, untiring energy he brought to all his work. He was a black-haired, strong-featured, sturdy man, brimming over with theories, and of a sanguine temperament that was never discouraged by the rather chilly fashion in which his plans were often received, even by his brother-democrats. In 1813 he brought to London the manuscript of his book *A New View of Society*. " He introduced himself to me," said Francis Place, " and I found him a man of kind manners and good intentions, of an imperturbable temper and an enthusiastic desire to promote the happiness of mankind." Place considered Owen's scheme of little practical value, though its promoter declared that he " possessed the means, and was resolved to produce a great change in the manners and habits of the whole of the people from the most exalted to the most depressed," and that his project was " simple, easy of adoption, and so plainly efficacious that it must be embraced by every thinking man the moment he was made to understand it." Place was inclined to look down upon him as a mere dabbler in the deep waters of politics. " Never having read a metaphysical book or heard a metaphysical conversation, he had no clear conception of his subject, and his views were obscure," said this upholder of Philosophic Radicalism ; and later he added, speaking of this meeting, " Mr Owen then was and is still convinced that he was the first who had ever observed that man was the creature of circumstances." George Eliot met Owen years later, and was not impressed by his eloquence. " I think if his system prosper," she said, " it will be in spite of its founder and not because of his advocacy."

In 1812 appeared *Childe Harold's Pilgrimage*, and there followed a tremendous burst of enthusiasm, which made Byron the best read and the most eagerly discussed writer of his day. Working men were ready and able to feel and judge the merits of the new poet and to make their voices heard even among the clamour that rose on every side. Practical, unimaginative politicians—Owen and Place and their like —were unmoved and scornful. They would probably all have agreed whole-heartedly with George Eliot's Felix Holt, the Loamshire Radical, who some years later, when *The Bride of Abydos*, *The Corsair*, and *Lara* had followed *Childe Harold*, roughly reproved Miss Esther Lyon for reading them. Esther was the adopted daughter of Rufus Lyon, pastor of the church in Malthouse Lane, and inclined, so Felix believed, to the sin of fine-ladyism. " What ! do you stuff your memory with Byron, Miss Lyon ? " he asked scornfully, and when Esther replied with stiffness, " I have a great admiration for Byron," he proceeded to denounce the popular poet roundly.

> A misanthropic debauchee whose notion of a hero was that he should disorder his stomach and despise mankind. His corsairs and renegades, his Alps and Manfreds, are the most paltry puppets that were ever pulled by the strings of lust and pride . . . gentlemen of unspeakable woes, who employ a hair dresser and look seriously at themselves in the glass.

There were working men, however, who held opinions very different from those of this loud-voiced, shaggy-headed, strong-limbed young watchmaker of Treby Magna. Zachariah Coleman, living in a dull lodging in Rosoman Street, Clerkenwell, married to a cold, unsympathetic wife, and conscious that he had missed the best joys of existence, found his heart warm to Byron. He had felt no temptation to read the much-lauded poet until a chance friend had lent him a copy of *The Corsair*. Idly he began to read it, until the words reached his heart, and

> he unconsciously found himself declaiming several of the most glowing and eloquent lines aloud. . . . Zachariah found in *The Corsair* exactly what answered to his own inmost self, down to its very depths. The lofty style, the scorn of what is mean and base, the courage—root of all virtue—that dares and evermore dares in the very last extremity, the love of the illimitable, of freedom, and the cadences like the fall of waves on a seashore were attractive to him beyond measure.

" It is all very well," says Mark Rutherford, the creator of Zachariah, who, though he started life as a Dissenting minister, had spent many years as a working man, leading a toilsome, dreary life among the poorest of his fellows,

> for the happy and well-to-do to talk scornfully of poetic senti-mentality. Those to whom a natural outlet to their affection is denied know better. They instinctively turn to books which are the farthest removed from the commonplace, and are in a sense unreal. Not to the prosperous man, a dweller in beautiful scenery, well-married to an intelligent wife, is Byron precious, but to the poor wretch, say some City clerk, with an

aspiration beyond his desk, who has two rooms in Camberwell, and who before he knew what he was doing made a marriage—well—which was a mistake.

Zachariah, with many another unfortunate toiler, felt all this from his heart ; felt, too, the influence of his reading in his daily life. " The vision of Medora will not intensify the shadow over Rosoman Street, but will soften it."

Up in the north, where the great iron-manufacturing towns were year by year spreading grime and ugliness farther over the fresh, wild countryside, lived Ebenezer Elliott, the son of a clerk in an iron-foundry. He was ten years younger than Owen and Place—who had been born in the same year —and less physically robust. He felt as strongly as they did the unhappy condition of the people, and longed as ardently to set things right ; and he suffered more intensely than their less sensitive natures could ever suffer from the misery he saw around him. He hated and dreaded poverty for himself and for others ; it never really touched him, but it came very near, and he met it constantly among the workers round about his home. Books were for him a means of escape and a means of delight. He was brought up in a strictly religious home, and he knew the Bible almost by heart by the time he was twelve years old. He read all the books which he found in the " little parlour, like the cabin of a ship," above which was the chamber where he was born. There were Thomson's *Seasons*, Barrow's *Sermons*, Ray's *Wisdom of God*, Derham's *Physico-Theology*, Young's *Night Thoughts*, Hervey's *Meditations among the Tombs*, Herepin's *Travels*, Shenstone's *Poems*, and Sowerby's *Botany*. It was the picture of a primrose in this last book which, he says, made him a poet. Later he read much poetry—Wordsworth, though he praised him but grudgingly, Southey, whom he loved, Shelley, Keats, and Byron, whom he almost idolized. He thought *Childe Harold* " the finest masterpiece of melody our noble English tongue can boast," and he prophesied that Byron and his poems would live " when the bones of his blasphemers shall have rotted."

Poetry and the visions that it brought helped John Clare, son of a farm-labourer of Helpstone, near Peterborough,

162

through a youth of hardship and bitter poverty. His father was disabled, and lived on the parish allowance, and John, when he was seven years old, was taken from school and set to watch the sheep and geese on the village green. He had learned to read, and now his passionate desire was to find books, and he devoured every one he could get hold of, from *Robinson Crusoe* to Bonnycastle's *Arithmetic* and Ward's *Algebra*. When he was a little older he worked in the fields, and then at the village inn. One day, soon after his thirteenth birthday, he was sent by his master on an errand to Stamford, and there he saw in a shop window a copy of Thomson's *Seasons*. Its price was eighteenpence, and though he had no money of his own he determined that, some way or other, the book should be his. His mother, moved by his entreaties, managed to scrape together sevenpence toward the price. The rest he borrowed from several friends, and on the next Sunday morning he started before it was light to walk the seven miles to Stamford. The shop was closed, and he returned empty-handed, but next morning he set out again, and this time came back with his treasure.

After that he worked as a gardener, then as a farm-labourer, and in 1812, when he was nineteen years old, he enlisted; but his regiment was soon disbanded, and he came home bringing second-hand copies of two books which he had bought with pence hardly scraped together—*Paradise Lost* and *The Tempest*. He had begun writing poetry himself, and by and by he won some recognition and was able to earn a modest livelihood by contributing to the *London* and other magazines.

By this time the war was over, but peace brought no change for the better in the lot of the working man. Years must pass before the country would recover from the effects of the long struggle ; and the great changes in industrial conditions following the introduction of machinery increased the distress. The Corn Law of 1815 made things still worse, and the poor man was brought very near to starvation. Ebenezer Elliott, his heart wrung by the misery he saw all around, wrote his *Corn Law Rhymes*, which put the workers' case so poignantly that thinking men and women all over England were roused to sympathy.

> Child, is thy father dead ?
>> Father is gone !
> Why did they tax his bread ?
>> God's will be done !
> Mother has sold her bed :
> Better to die than wed !
> Where shall she lay her head ?
> Home we have none !

The cry for Parliamentary reform grew louder. It seemed to the sufferers that through that alone could they hope for any relief. More and more eagerly the working man sought for the knowledge that he believed would be a weapon in his hand to help him in the fight he must wage. William Cobbett, the son of an innkeeper, had started in 1802 a weekly newspaper, which he called *The Weekly Political Register*, specially designed to meet the needs of the farmer and the small trader. At first it was Tory in its principles, but as time went on it veered round until it became strongly Radical. Its price—tenpence—prevented its being very widely read among working men, but in 1817 the price was reduced to twopence, and then the circulation rapidly increased, until between forty and fifty thousand copies were sold each week. Cobbett became the political oracle of a large part of the nation, and thousands of working men waited eagerly for each issue of the *Register*. It advocated Parliamentary reform, and went so far as to demand universal suffrage and annual Parliaments ; it denounced rioting, but it denounced much more strongly the repressive measures of the Government. It did its best to rouse the people of the country to united action, and gibed at those who hoped that good things would come to them without any effort on their own part.

> Open your mouth and shut your eyes,
> And God will love you, and send you a prize.

All through the agitations and riotings of the eighteen-twenties the intelligent working man's desire to read and to learn went on increasing. Francis Place had removed

164

to a shop at Charing Cross, and had set up there his now large and comprehensive library ; and he took care that from this library political literature setting forward the reformers' point of view could be obtained by all who cared to ask for it. In 1817 he retired from business and left the shop to his son, and from that time onward he occupied himself entirely with books and politics. Four years before he had been introduced to James Mill, and the two, finding they had much in common, worked together for the en-franchisement of the people. Mill came often to the Charing Cross Library, which had become " a sort of gossip shop for such persons as were in any way engaged in public matters having the good of the people for their object." It came to be called the " Civic Palace," and " was frequented very much in the manner of a common coffee-room." " There is an old gentleman still alive and active," says Professor Graham Wallas, in his *Life of Francis Place*, written in 1898, " who can remember being taken as a boy, about 1820, up into a big room at the back of Place's shop, and being told in a reverential tone that this was the headquarters of English Radicalism." Besides books, the library contained Parlia-mentary papers, pamphlets, and newspaper cuttings, all bound and lettered and in scrupulous order. Here Place sat nearly all day on a high stool before his desk, talking to the many visitors who came into his room ; helping and directing them if they came for information ; talking, planning, discussing ; spinning like a diligent spider the threads that were to connect this central web with the political world around.

The ideas of the reformers began to spread from the big manufacturing towns into the remoter parts of the country, and towns like Treby Magna,

> which had lived quietly through the great earthquakes of the French Revolution and the Napoleonic wars, which had remained unmoved by *The Rights of Man* and saw little in Mr Cobbett's *Weekly Political Register*, except that he held eccentric views about potatoes, began at last to know the higher pains of a dim political consciousness.

It was in some cases very dim, and led to a political faith

which was almost grotesque. The ignorant working man, like the ignorant members of the classes above him, expected the Reform Bill to bring him, immediately and permanently, into a blissful state of ease and plenty. Mrs Edward Bulwer said that in 1831 she heard a ragged fellow crying the King's Speech in the streets.

> Good news for the poor ! Great and glorious speech of His Most Gracious Majesty William IV ! The Reform Bill will pass ! Then you'll have your beef and mutton for a penny a pound. And then you'll be as fine as peacocks for a mere trifle. To say nothing of ale at a penny a quart in which you may drink His Majesty's health and His Majesty's ministers' health and the glorious Reform Bill without a-ruining of yourselves.

The sober, intelligent working man had no such illusions. His books had helped him to form clearer and juster views. He had learned to value intellectual as well as material blessings, and he was ready for the fuller opportunities that the coming years were to bring him.

CHAPTER X

A PERFORMANCE OF "THE ROAD TO RUIN," OCTOBER 1802

SEVEN o'clock on an evening of late October, a chill wind and a drizzle of rain. Outside Covent Garden Theatre a crowd is gathering waiting for the opening of the doors. The play to-night is a favourite one, Holcroft's *Road to Ruin*; and as it has not been acted for more than a year the audience is likely to be large, and late-comers will have little chance of a place. Streams of noisy, swaggering boys and flaunting, loud-voiced girls are pouring in from the side streets round about the market. Sober, prosperous-looking tradesmen and decent working men, their wives on their arms, are stepping carefully through the greasy ooze of black mud that covers the roadway. Family parties, with anxious though smiling mammas trying to restrain the excited, happy children, splash valiantly along, caring for nothing but the chance of getting a good place. Weedy young shopmen walk proudly with their pretty seamstress sweethearts. Half-drunken men and women advance uncertainly, singing snatches of coarse songs.

Here are Mr and Mrs Jones, come from their flourishing haberdasher's shop in Holborn, with Mrs Jones's sister, Miss Julia Dawkins, and her mother's lodger, Miss Laura Montreville. Julia is short, round, rosy, and sentimental; Miss Laura is tall and surpassingly lovely.

" Fancy ! " says good-natured Mrs Jones, " here's Miss never seed a play in her life. Howsoever, she'll see a good one to-night, an' it'll be something she can talk of when she gets back to Scotland."

" I wish it was a tragedy," sighs Miss Julia, in a deep, low voice. Last week she borrowed from the circulating library *The Hut and the Castle*, and she is at present imagining herself the heroine, " the pensive Alethea."

167

Miss Laura is interested and amused by the lively scene, though the loud voices frighten her a little, and she refuses to press in among the throng, even at the risk of having to put up with a seat at the back when she gets inside the theatre.

" We must have some oranges," says kindly little Mr Jones, intent on making his theatre party a success ; and he beckons one of the ragged, clamorous girls who are shrilling out " Chase an orange, chase a nonpareil " and buys a generous supply. " Buy a bill of the play," resounds on the other side, and his hand goes into his pocket once more, and the flimsy playbills are passed round. The girl makes a coarse, good-natured jest on his luck in having so many ladies under his charge, and beaming Mr Jones is ready with his reply. Miss Julia titters, then, remembering " the pensive Alethea," frames her rosy mouth to what she hopes is " a wan smile."

When it is nearly time for the doors to open the coaches begin to drive up, and the shouting link-boys hurry with their flaring lights to guide the quality toward the dark doorways. The coach steps are let down, and gay parties hurry into the theatre. There are young ladies with hair dressed high in front and falling in ringlets behind, in long, short-waisted frocks, with bright sashes and little puffed sleeves ; young gentlemen in knee-breeches, silk stockings, cut-away coats, lace cravats, and powdered heads ; mammas rustling in rich silks ; papas with gorgeously embroidered waistcoats and elaborate wigs. There are fine ladies of the Court and fine ladies of the town ; there are haughty gentlemen, faultlessly attired, just come from my lord's dinner-table, and gentlemen whose clothes were once even more splendid, but are now a trifle tarnished and dingy, who have evidently been dining in less exalted company.

The doors are opened, and now comes a great rush. There is shrieking and pushing and rough language as the crowd struggles up the narrow staircases to the one-shilling and two-shilling galleries. Decent men shield their female companions with their arms and with their bodies, though there is in most cases a sort of rough politeness shown to women who are obviously gentle-mannered and shrink from making their own way. But many women neither ask for nor desire any forbearance. They are as able as the men to force their way forward, and they do it, laughing, shouting, jesting, using their elbows and their feet to push and tread their neighbours out of their way. But, though rough, the struggle is for the most part good-tempered, and when at last the gallery is reached and the rush for places is over there are no injuries to be recorded save a few torn gowns, crushed hats, bruised sides, and aching toes.

" Thank God we are safe ! " breathes a pleasant-faced, middle-aged lady, as she settles down in her seat, puts her bonnet straight, and tries to find the fastening of her twisted, disordered shawl. " The crowding up these inconvenient staircases gets worse each time we come. There is a rent in the back of my gown, and my arms I am sure are black and blue."

" I ought not to have b-b-rought you among all this gallery rabble," says her companion penitently. He is a slender youth with a dark, beautiful, wistful face and a whimsical smile. " But never m-m-ind, M-Mary. When we are rich we will go into the p-pit."

" Nonsense," replies the lady briskly. " You know you always say that the gallery is the best place of all for enjoying a play socially. And when should we see among the respectable citizens in the pit such a face as that of the man in front of us?—no, not there, to the left." She lowers her voice, and the brother and sister proceed with much enjoyment to make their comments on the motley company around them.

Meanwhile the good people in the pit have taken their places and have disposed of their extra wrappings, their umbrellas, and their oranges as conveniently as circumstances allow. They are thrifty folk, resolved to get the fullest possible measure of entertainment for the three and sixpence they have paid at the door, and they begin by studying the bill of the play to see what is in store for them.

" Munden ! " exclaims Miss Julia Dawkins ecstatically,

" and old Dornton is one of his best parts ! Do you not *adore* Munden ? " she demands of Miss Laura, who is sitting next to her ; but the young lady shakes her head.

" I know nothing of him," she replies, " his fame has not reached Scotland. But I have read and greatly admired some novels written by Thomas Holcroft, the author of the play. Did he not write *Anna St Ives* and *Hugh Trevor* ? "

A small man with a massive head and a gentle, almost nervous, manner who is sitting in the row in front of them turns round and looks at Miss Laura with interest. He is the famous William Godwin, author of *Political Justice*, and the buxom, good-looking lady sitting beside him is his lately married second wife. Holcroft is one of his greatest friends, and he has a good mind to tell the young lady so, but his wife claims his attention, and the impulse passes. Holcroft is probably in the house somewhere with his daughter—the pair, so alike in their strong, ugly features and determined expression, sitting in some remote corner, waiting for the applause which will send them, thrilled and happy, back to their lodgings in Beaumont Street.

The three rows of handsome boxes, with their green and gold paint and their fawn-coloured hangings, are filling rapidly. One blank front after another lights up with a glow of colour and a brightness of jewels as, fans fluttering, silks rustling, the ladies take their places. The gentlemen, scarcely less resplendent, follow, and the pit makes its not inaudible comments on the manners and appearance of ' the quality.'

There is one box which draws every one's attention, it is filled with such a happy, laughing group of young people, with a comely mamma and a beaming papa as guardians of the flock. The centre of all the merriment seems to be a handsome, dark-eyed youth, whose face is alight with fun and high spirits. This is Master Henry Leigh Hunt, aged sixteen, fresh from the Sixth Form of Christ's Hospital. He knows all about the actors and the play and goes on from one anecdote to another, all drawn from his own experiences as a playgoer, for he has a passion for the theatre and goes as often as he can. Some day he hopes to be more

AT A COMEDY

Richard Dighton

than a spectator ; he has already written a play, which his
friends believe to be a work of genius.

In another box are seated a handsome, portly, exceedingly
well-dressed gentleman, a dignified lady of middle age, and
a plump, plain-faced, beaming girl of fifteen. The gentleman
is the fascinating, graceless Mr Mitford of Bertram House,
Hampshire. He has already spent one fortune, and is
now engaged in squandering the remains of a second—
his daughter Mary's. The money he is spending to-night
in bringing Mary and her governess, Miss Rowden, from the
boarding-school in Hans Place for an evening at the play
ought to have gone to pay long-standing bills at the butcher's
and the baker's. Mary, who adores her father, is especially
grateful for the treat ; Miss Rowden appreciates it as the
act of a truly courteous gentleman ; even Mrs Mitford, left
at home in Hampshire, has no fault to find with her husband.

As the music strikes up a gentleman, young, sturdily
built, and with a fine, keen face, comes to the front of one
of the boxes and looks round the great theatre with an air
of troubled distaste. " Whenever I come to a London
theatre," he says, addressing the other occupants of the
box in general, but more especially a distinguished-looking
gentleman of foreign appearance who is standing at the
back,

> I am thankful that I have never been attacked by an ambition
> to write stage plays. I do not think the character of the audi-
> ence in London is such that one could have the least pleasure
> in pleasing them. One half come to prosecute their debaucheries,
> another set to snooze off their beefsteaks and port wine ; a
> third are critics of the fourth column of a newspaper. Fashion,
> wit, or literature there is not, and on the whole I would far
> rather write verses for mine honest friend Punch and his
> audience.

He looks round at his companions and sees that their mirth
is checked and that they are looking a little perplexed and
uneasy at this very sweeping denunciation. " Come," he
says, with a genial, sunny smile that makes everybody feel
happy again, " what am I about ? A wild man from
Scotland coming here to hold forth on the manners and
morals of polished Londoners ! and when I ought to be

171

thinking of nothing except what is behind that green curtain. After all, the play's the thing " ; and the gentleman, whose name is Walter Scott, sits down, just as an actor comes before the curtain and the whole audience turns toward the stage. The catcalling, whistling, and stamping up in the gallery ceases, the pit leaves off sucking oranges and making remarks on its neighbours. The music stops, and the actor begins to speak his Prologue.

The Prologue has little to do with the play. It touches on contemporary events, and refers in high-flown terms to the new ideas which Holcroft and Godwin are trying very hard to spread throughout the country, and it ends with the lines :

> Freedom, at length, said he, like a torrent is spreading and swelling
> To sweep away pride and reach the most miserable dwelling,
> To ease, happiness, art, science, wit, and genius give birth,
> Ay, to fertilize a world, and renovate old earth.

The galleries applaud loudly, especially those that are in most need of renovation ; the pit is more decorous, but righteously emphatic ; the boxes are divided, but scornful for the most part. The actor bows and retires, the green curtain goes up, and the play begins.

The scene shows a room, plainly furnished, and, sitting before his desk, an elderly man dressed in a grey coat with black buttons, black silk waistcoat, knee-breeches, and white cravat. There is an enthusiastic outburst of applause, and whispers of " Munden," " old Dornton," go round. It is indeed Munden—Charles Lamb's Munden—" the king of broad comedy," " the mover of tears." To-night he is a solid, sober City merchant, making angry inquiries of his clerk and of his manager, Mr Sulky, concerning his graceless son. He is determined to be stern and angry, yet every now and then his love for the boy and even a little pride in the high spirits that lead him into his worst escapades will break through. But these gleams of tenderness are violently quenched in the storm of rage that comes when he hears that the young scapegrace has that day gone rapidly forward on the road to ruin and has lost ten thousand pounds by

172

backing horses at the races. To pay this sum will, old Dornton knows, endanger the credit of the firm and may bring ruin ; and his pride in his firm is, he persuades himself, stronger than his love for his boy. All these succeeding emotions appear plainly on his face—this wonderful Munden who, as the young man sitting up in the gallery with his sister is to write years after, " literally *makes faces*."

> When you think he has exhausted his battery of looks, in unaccountable warfare with your gravity, suddenly he sprouts out an entirely new set of features, like Hydra. He is not one, but legion. Not so much a comedian as a company. If his name could be multiplied like his countenance, it might fill a play-bill.

But on the greater part of the audience this wonderful power of Munden's is lost. They are too far away to distinguish subtle changes of countenance. In an Elizabethan theatre there would have been delight and appreciation down to the last ragamuffin in the pit. In this huge building only broad spectacular effects can reach to every part. The dramatist must write for the galleries, and must make his plays spectacles, even if he ruin them as works of art.

By and by young Dornton comes in, and then there is another storm, the boy's easy, careless, affectionate ways by turns infuriating and softening his father. Harry does not believe that his debts will bring the firm to ruin. He has been brought up to think its resources inexhaustible, and he has heard this cry of " Ruin ! " so many times before. He really loves his father, and is at the bottom a gallant lad, honest and generous, but he has no conception of the value of money.

At the end of the scene comes one of the touches that have made the play famous. Harry entreats his father to bid him good-night.

> *Harry.* Reproach me with my follies, strike out my name, disinherit me, I deserve it all, and more,—but say, " Good-night, Harry ! "
> *Dornton.* I won't—I won't—I won't.
> *Harry.* Poverty is a trifle ; we can whistle it off ;—but enmity——
> *Dornton.* I will not.

Harry. Sleep in enmity! And who can say how soundly? Come, good-night.

Dornton. I won't, I won't.   [*Hurries off.*

Harry. Say you so? Why, then, my noble-hearted dad, I am indeed a scoundrel.   [*Re-enter Mr Dornton.*

Dornton. Good-night!

Harry. Good-night! and heaven eternally bless you, my father.

Played as Munden and Holman play it, this little incident melts the whole house to tears. The curtain goes down to the sound of sobs and weeping, for in those days no one was ashamed of crying at the play. It was, indeed, considered graceful and becoming in a female to show such emotion; it proved that she possessed that fashionable and genteel quality, sensibility. Some men also are weeping, others have put on a woebegone countenance, and are murmuring their sympathy with the general feeling. Miss Julia Dawkins is shedding tears in floods, or, in her own more chaste language, is "paying a watery tribute to the sorrows of the gallant hero"; her sister sniffs and chokes, Miss Laura dries her eyes with the finest of lawn pocket-handkerchiefs, and Mr Jones follows with his bandanna. Plump little Miss Mitford is sobbing piteously, Miss Rowden drops a ladylike tear, while Papa looks on approvingly.

The next scene introduces Sophia and Mrs Warren. Sophia is very young, very pretty, and is meant to be very charming, though to the critical she may appear simply silly. She is the daughter of Mrs Warren's first husband, and has been brought up at "Grandmamma's in Gloucestershire." She is in love with Harry Dornton and he with her, but Mrs Warren also is in love with Harry and determined to win him. The difference in age does not deter her; she dresses as youthfully as Sophia and flatters herself she looks no older. Sophia is penniless, but Mrs Warren has fifty thousand pounds; her second husband has lately died abroad, and, no will being forthcoming, she has inherited his entire fortune. There is a will, however, in which the late Mr Warren expresses his distrust of his wife's professions of affection and leaves her only six hundred pounds a year. The rest is to be divided equally between his illegitimate

SCENE FROM "THE ROAD TO RUIN"
Gabrielle Enthoven Collection, Victoria and Albert Museum

174

son Milford, who is Harry Dornton's greatest friend, and Sophia. The will has been sent by a messenger to Mr Sulky, who is named in it as trustee, but the messenger, misled by the similarity in names, has taken it to Mr Silky, a smooth-tongued, rascally lawyer. Silky, seeing how the mistake can be turned to his own advantage, conceals the will, intending to make terms with Mrs Warren for its destruction.

All this the audience learns little by little as the play goes on. There are love scenes between Harry and Sophia, and pathetic scenes between Harry and old Dornton. Sagacious Mr Sulky begins to have his doubts of plausible Mr Silky. In the second act the famous Goldfinch makes his appearance. He is a suitor of Mrs Warren's, attracted by the fame of her fifty thousand pounds. It is easy to see from the moment he comes on the stage that Goldfinch is a ' horsy ' man—one of the ' young bloods ' that the society of the day holds to be at the top of the fashion. He is dressed in a scarlet frock-coat, buff waistcoat, white breeches, and top-boots. He carries a whip, which he continually cracks by way of adding point to his remarks.

Now comes the turn of the galleries. Goldfinch is a dashing fellow, and he woos the widow in noisy fashion, with a great deal of movement and gesticulation and an overpowering flow of words. There is no subtlety here, no need to watch the play of countenance or listen to the fine modulations of the voice. The shilling gallery is wild with delight ; this is the sort of acting it can appreciate. Goldfinch says nothing that is really witty or humorous, little that is even smart. It is just a rattle of nonsense, with a few catch phrases—" That's your sort ! " " I'm the lad ! "—coming over and over again. Yet all the time he is on the stage there is a gurgle of laughter, which breaks into a roar at the recurrence of the familiar tags or at any specially exuberant flowers of speech. There is one sentence, " Curse all dancing-masters and their umbrellas," with which he concludes an account of an accident he has met with while driving, which tickles the audience so greatly that it rocks in a helpless paroxysm of laughter. " Gentleman Lewis," which is the

175

name by which the actor of Goldfinch is known to all regular playgoers, is famous for parts of this kind. He is never vulgar, and his high spirits and natural lively air of enjoyment make him irresistible.

The play goes on, pathos alternating with humour. Harry Dornton, when at last he realizes that his recklessness has in truth ruined his father, is overcome with remorse. Heartbroken, he resolves to marry Mrs Warren, that her money may repair the mischief he has done. He proposes and is gladly accepted. But Goldfinch is not the man to be set aside in this manner. He plots with Silky to force the widow into marriage with himself. Meanwhile Sulky's suspicions of foul play with regard to the missing will are strengthened. He and Milford call upon the widow to try to obtain some information from her, and while waiting for her to be told of their presence hear her coming up the stairs accompanied by Goldfinch and Silky. They hide in two cupboards in the room and overhear the conversation that follows. Silky is bargaining with Mrs Warren to induce her to sign a paper and to pay him a large sum of money for his silence with regard to the existence of the will. At the critical moment Milford and Sulky burst from their hiding-places and the whole plot is disclosed. Harry wins his Sophia and her fortune, and is completely reconciled to his father, whose heart has been melted at hearing of the boy's intended sacrifice of himself to the widow. The firm is saved and all ends happily. Harry and Milford have been arrested on the Road to Ruin, and their feet are now set upon the highway of morality, which leads to happiness, riches, and, finally, perfection.

The theatre begins to empty itself. Going down from the gallery is almost as perilous an adventure as coming up, and the quieter folk wait until the rush is over. A noisy crowd pours into the street, shouting its crude comments on the play. " That's your sort ! " is heard on every side. Some are reeling drunkenly; some are quarrelling; groups are making off to public-houses and even more disreputable places, to finish the evening with low dissipation. The decent part of the audience makes its way as quickly as possible through the crowd in front of the theatre to the quiet streets beyond. The rain is over now, and the moonlight makes the help of the link-boys almost unnecessary, though they run officiously to and fro, lighting the ladies and gentlemen to their coaches. Master Leigh Hunt and his party drive off merrily. Lordly Mr Mitford calls a coach and takes his grateful and admiring daughter and her governess back to Hans Place ; then, pleasantly conscious that he is a model father, repairs to his luxurious hotel.

Charles Lamb and his sister, coming comfortably down from the deserted gallery, meet Mr and Mrs Godwin, and stop to exchange greetings. John Hazlitt the painter and his younger brother William, who have also been in the gallery, come up, and they all go off together. They have a good deal to say about the play and the actors, and if we could follow them we should find it well worth listening to ; as we cannot we have to be content with what two of them wrote about it in later years for the reading of the public at large.

Miss Julia Dawkins trips skittishly along between her short, rotund brother-in-law and the tall, gracious Miss Montreville. She is Sophia now, all smiles and pouts and titters, *naïve* questions, and arch glances.

" I think nothing is so delightful as a play ! " she cries. " I should like to go to one every night. That charming Harry ! how I love him ! "

" Goldfinch was all to nothing the best of the lot," declares Mr Jones. " What do you think, miss ? "

" Here, come along," says his wife good-naturedly, " never mind bothering Miss about it just now. There's a nice bit of hot supper waiting at home, which is better than any play to my thinking." And, still to the sound of Miss Julia's raptures, they make their way to Holborn.

CHAPTER XI

PERIODICALS AND THEIR READERS

PERIODICAL literature in England began with *The Tatler* and *The Spectator* of Steele and Addison. During the years 1711 and 1712 *The Spectator* appeared as regularly as the coffee-pot at every polite breakfast-table, and it had an immense influence on the opinions and manners of the day. But the taste for such literature did not flourish. As the years went on the demand for it grew less, and consequently the supply dwindled. The newspaper took the place of the more literary periodical, and for reading of other kinds the public turned to books, which were becoming rapidly cheaper as well as more plentiful. During the years that brought the eighteenth century to a close there was no periodical which formed an important part of the country's reading. There was *The Gentleman's Magazine*, founded in 1731, which appeared monthly, and was read for its articles in the form of letters on a variety of topics, as well as for its news. It had long obituary accounts of all the notable people who had died during the month, one or two pages of original verse, and notices of new publications—these being for the most part volumes of sermons and very learned but now absolutely forgotten works. It had a large and steady circulation, especially among country families and the professional classes, and scholarly gentlemen and bookish young ladies all over the country were in the habit, like the Reverend Dr Brown, the delightful vicar of Praed's poem, of amusing their leisure by writing " nothings for Sylvanus Urban," which was the name under which the editor of *The Gentleman's Magazine* was known to his readers. For the younger generation, nourished upon the ideas and the ideals of the revolutionary period in Europe, it had no interest, and even their elders, who read it diligently,

178

could not claim that its contents were in any sense real literature.

There were also several reviews, of which the chief were *The Monthly Review* and *The Critical Review*, but these were little more than the organs by means of which particular publishing firms puffed their wares. Most of the critical articles they contained were written by undistinguished writers who were very poorly paid and were allowed no freedom of judgment, but, poor as these articles were, they had many readers, for there was now a large section of the public that was keenly interested in books, and anxious to know what was best to buy and to read.

In the midst of all this dullness a bright light flashed when, in November 1797, there appeared the first number of a new weekly paper, *The Anti-Jacobin*. It was started by George Canning, then a young man of twenty-seven, for the purpose of supporting the anti-revolutionary policy of the younger Pitt. William Gifford, well known for his satirical verse, was its editor, and George Ellis, the friend of Walter Scott, and John Hookham Frere, another satiric poet, were, with Canning, its chief contributors. They were all devoted to Pitt, and thoroughly enjoyed hurling their keen shafts of ridicule at his opponents. The articles that appeared in the paper were written in a spirit of lofty patriotism, and called upon their readers to be true to the ancient morals and ancient manners " that have preserv'd this proud isle for many a rugged age." But the series of parodies that appeared in the " Poet's Corner " of *The Anti-Jacobin* gave to it its especial brilliance and its claim to be considered as a really literary periodical. Even now their wit and their high spirits make them excellent reading, and it is difficult to refrain from quoting at length. They ridiculed the new sentimentalism—borrowed from the Germans—and the new sympathy with lawlessness—due to the example of France—and they attacked also particular individuals in the ranks of the Whigs and the Radicals. The poet Southey, who, although he had by this time left most of his youthful revolutionary follies behind him, was still regarded as a fair butt, was one of *The Anti-*

Jacobin's favourite victims. He had written a poem which began :

> Cold was the night wind ; drifting fast the snows fell ;
> Wide were the downs and shelterless and naked,
> When a poor wanderer struggled on her journey,
>   Weary and way-sore.

Gleefully the young men of *The Anti-Jacobin* fell upon this, and wrote a parody which they called *The Friend of Humanity and the Knife-grinder*. "The Friend of Humanity" was the nickname that had been given to a certain Mr Tierney, a Whig Member of Parliament, who was very eloquent concerning the wrongs of the lower classes. The parody began :

> Needy knife-grinder ! whither are you going ?
> Rough is your road, your wheel is out of order ;
> Bleak blows the blast—your hat has got a hole in't,
>   So have your breeches.

It went on to enumerate all the probable wrongs that this victim of tyranny had suffered, and to urge him to revolt.

> Have you not read *The Rights of Man*, by Tom Paine ?
> Drops of compassion tremble on my eyelids,
> Ready to fall as soon as you have told your
>   Pitiful story.

But the knife-grinder most disappointingly replied :

> Story ! God bless you ! I have none to tell, sir,
> Only last night a-drinking at the Chequers,
> This poor old hat and breeches as you see were
>   Torn in a scuffle.

In another issue appeared an *Epitaph on Mrs Brownrigg* (the woman who had been hanged for ill-treating and killing her two girl apprentices), which was a parody on Southey's epitaph on Henry Marten, the Regicide.

> Harsh laws ! but time shall come
> When France shall reign, and laws be all repeal'd.

Then came a play called *The Rovers*, in the German senti-mental style, with a hero drawn from Sir Robert Adair, another Whig Member. It contained a ballad called *Sweet Matilda Pottingen* :

180

"THE FRIEND OF HUMANITY AND THE KNIFE-GRINDER"
James Gillray

180·

PERIODICALS AND THEIR READERS

> There, there for thee my passion grew
> Sweet, sweet Matilda Pottingen !
> Thou wast the daughter of my Tu-
> tor, Law Professor at the U-
>   -niversity of Göttingen,
>   -niversity of Göttingen.

Week after week hundreds of readers turned eagerly to the Poet's Corner of *The Anti-Jacobin* and read these parodies with shouts of laughter. Lines and couplets were quoted and discussed until they became common sayings all over the country. Some of them have survived until to-day; for example :

> A steady Patriot of the World alone,
> The Friend of every Country—but his own;

and

> Give me th' avow'd, the erect, the manly foe,
> Bold I can meet—perhaps may turn his blow ;
> But of all plagues, good heav'n, thy wrath can send,
> Save, save, oh, save me from a candid friend !

In July 1798 Canning and his friends decided that *The Anti-Jacobin* had done its work, and that it would be wiser to stop before the jest had lost its savour—as such jests are apt to do if long continued. So the temporary illumination vanished, and dullness reigned as before.

Many people complained of this dullness, but apparently it did not occur to anyone to try to dissipate it until one evening, early in 1802, three young men—Francis Jeffrey, Sydney Smith, and Henry Brougham—met at Jeffrey's lodgings in a house in Edinburgh. There, half in jest, they planned to start a quarterly review which was to be entirely different from any of the reviews then in existence. It was to take upon itself to be the judge and arbiter with regard to all new books. It was to be witty, satirical, cutting—readier to blame than to praise—and above all it was to provide the general reader with something that would both impress and entertain him. In politics it was to be mildly Whiggish.

The project was looked upon as something in the nature of a frolic, and its originators scarcely expected it to have any permanent success. The first number appeared in October 1802, under the title of *The Edinburgh Review*. At once it leaped into popularity. The public imagination was captured by its lordly assumption of omniscience in matters literary; the public taste was delighted with the brilliance and audacity of its critical articles. When the second number came out there was an eager crowd waiting to buy it. With each number its circulation increased; without a struggle *The Edinburgh Review* had established itself as the supreme literary authority of Scotland and England.

By November 1808 it had attained to such a position that Walter Scott wrote: "No genteel family *can* pretend to be without it, because, independent of its politics, it gives the only valuable literary criticism that can be met with." He used the word 'genteel' not with the suspicion of a sneer as a writer of to-day might use it, but with the meaning ascribed to it by Crabb in his *English Synonyms*—"suited to the station of a gentleman"—and in this sense his readers understood it. Scott's acquaintance among genteel families was large, though perhaps scarcely larger than his acquaintance among ungenteel ones. He knew all the people best worth knowing in Edinburgh, and at this time Edinburgh was a recognized centre of learning and culture. It rivalled London, if not in the rank and fashion, in the distinction of its society. Now that the Continent was closed to Englishmen by the war, and the Grand Tour no longer possible, many of the great families of the south sent their sons to Edinburgh as to a foreign capital. At the time when the *Edinburgh* was established, Henry Temple, son of Viscount Palmerston, was living at the house of Dugald Stewart, the most eminent among the many eminent professors of the Edinburgh University; and in this year 1808, when Scott wrote, Michael Hicks Beach was there, with Sydney Smith as his tutor.

Next in social importance to the professors came the advocates, whom Scott met daily at the Parliament House, among them some of the most famous lawyers in Scotland, such as William Erskine, afterward Lord Kinneder. We have Scott's word for it that *The Edinburgh Review* was to be found in the sober, handsome houses of all these learned and legal gentlemen, and that it was read by them and by their wives, by their sons and by their daughters, so that at their dignified evening parties, where conversation was the chief diversion, they might be ready to discuss the judgments pronounced by the great tribunal upon such authors as had had the temerity to publish books during the three months lately passed. Most of the seven hundred and eighty-four copies of the first number that were sold in 1802 went to these genteel families of Edinburgh.

There were also many genteel families in the southern part of the kingdom concerning whose literary habits Scott could speak with authority. He had friends and acquaintances at many places up and down the country. At Lichfield, which he visited in 1807, his friendship with Miss Seward made him free of the houses of the famous group that gathered round Dr Darwin. At Oxford he knew Richard Heber, Member of Parliament for the university, and his famous half-brother, afterward Bishop of Calcutta. In Hampshire he had stayed for a time with his scholarly friend Mr William Stewart Rose. In Yorkshire he spent many happy holidays at Rokeby Park, the beautiful home of Mr John Morritt. He had a large acquaintance in London, including Mr George Ellis, antiquarian and contributor to *The Anti-Jacobin*, through whom he had become intimate with Mr Canning, Joanna Baillie and her circle at Hampstead, Dr Hughes, Canon Prebendary of St Paul's, and his wife, and Mr Charles Dumergue, surgeon-dentist to the royal family and a relative of Mrs Scott's. It was to these genteel English families and others like them that the greatly increased circulation of the *Edinburgh*—of which in November 1808 nine thousand copies were sold—was largely due.

Thomas De Quincey, who in 1809 came to live in the cottage at Grasmere from which Wordsworth had just removed, throws a little more light on this honourable company of *Edinburgh* readers. He is describing the society of the Lake District, and trying to show why Wordsworth is entirely without honour as a poet among his neighbours, gentle as well as simple. "Almost all the world," he says, "had surrendered their opinions and their literary consciences into the keeping of *The Edinburgh Review*." De Quincey speaks with his usual largeness of phrase, but the truth is within it. The *Edinburgh* had become the fashion. Therefore the large class of people who had a mild enjoyment of literature, but no very decided tastes, and the still larger class that cared scarcely at all about literature, but cared a great deal about being in the fashion, were delighted to be saved the trouble of making up their own minds about the merits of a book and were only too glad to allow the *Edinburgh* to make their minds up for them ; and from both these classes came a substantial number of subscribers.

Then, as Henry Brougham said at a later date, the *Review* had two legs to stand on—literature and politics—and the right leg was politics. It was this right leg that took it into the great Whig families of the day—the Edens, the Lambs, and the Temples. Its blue and buff cover—taken from the blue coat and buff waistcoat of Charles James Fox —was the outward and visible sign of the Whiggish doctrine within. The Tories at first took it for its literature and put up with its politics ; but as the years went on, and the *Edinburgh* opposed the war against Napoleon with more and more bitterness, and denounced with increasing contumely the great British leader, General Wellesley, the indignant Tories began to feel that they were buying their wit and their criticism at too high a price. Scott, in its early days, had contributed occasional articles to the review, but in 1808 he wrote to George Ellis :

> Consider, of the numbers who read this work, how many are there likely to separate the literature from the politics—how many youths are there upon whose minds the flashy and bold character of the work is likely to make an indelible impression ; and think what the consequence is likely to be.

It was clear to these staunch Tories that something must be done. First of all Scott renounced the *Edinburgh*. He wrote to Constable, the editor, requesting that his name might be removed from the list of subscribers. " *The*

Edinburgh Review," he said, " *had become* such as to render it impossible for me to continue a contributor to it. *Now* it is such as I can no longer continue to receive or read it." The loss of so eminent a subscriber was a blow, even to the *Edinburgh.* " The list of the then subscribers," said Mr Cadell, a partner in the firm, " exhibits in an indignant dash of Constable's pen opposite Mr Scott's name the word, ' Stopt.' "

Next a small band of Tories—Scott, Ellis, Canning, Heber, Stewart Rose, William Gifford (who had been the editor of *The Anti-Jacobin*), Robert Dundas, the Lord Advocate, and John Murray, a young publisher of Fleet Street—put their heads together to consider how they could establish a rival review. It was to be as witty, as dashing, and as authoritative as the *Edinburgh*, but its politics were to be those of its founders. As a result *The Quarterly Review* came into being, and the first number was issued in February 1809. The Tories welcomed it with joy. Four thousand copies were printed, and all these were quickly sold, and more demanded ; and its originators congratulated themselves on having struck a shrewd blow at the pestilent *Edinburgh*.

But it appeared as time went on that though the new review flourished the sale of the older one was scarcely affected. The people who felt a strong interest in literature took both. Writers and men of letters were almost obliged to do so if they would keep up with the movements of the day. At the Macaulays' house at Clapham " the *Edinburgh* and the *Quarterly* were a standing dish." Mr and Miss Edgeworth read both, and so did Mrs Barbauld and Samuel Rogers, the poet. Even those who abused the periodicals read them. Mrs Gore wrote indignantly that " the reptile battery of flippant periodical criticism had opened its battery on all that was superior or rebellious to the routine of established customs," but it is clear that she read both the *Edinburgh* and the *Quarterly*. By 1817 the circulation of both reviews had reached the highest point to which either ever attained—about fourteen thousand in each case.

THE ENGLISHMAN AND HIS BOOKS

The *Quarterly*, run as it was by men who had left the daring recklessness of youth behind them, never managed to attain to the dash and vigour of its rival. Its authority over its readers was as great; its pronouncements were dreaded, and when they came were accepted as final. " I have not read the *Quarterly*," wrote Lady Wharncliffe to her mother, in a letter concerning a certain cousin, Lady Emmeline Stuart Wortley, who had published a book of poems, "and am almost afraid of it, as I shall find Emmeline and *it* at Wortley when I get back, and I fear she will be much annoyed, and I shall feel conscious and sorry for her, poor thing, tho' I wish it may do her good." A sentence in the review was enough to destroy a writer's reputation. When Southey wrote in an article on *The Essays of Elia* " It wants only sounder religious feeling to be as delightful as it is original," the hint of unorthodoxy stopped the sale of the book at once. But though the *Quarterly* could thus impress its readers, it could not entertain them; it shone, but it did not sparkle. Its youthful readers found it just a trifle heavy. That interesting young lady, the heroine of Mrs Jameson's *The Diary of an Ennuyée*, who at the age of twenty-five was crossed in love and retired heart-broken to Naples, received there copies of the two reviews, and moralized thus concerning them:

> Methinks these two reviews stalk through the literary world like the two giants in Pulci's *Morgante Maggiore*; the one pounding, slaying, mangling, despoiling with blunt fury, like the hearty, orthodox, club-armed Morgante; the other like sneering, witty, half-pagan, half-baptised Margutte, slashing and cutting and piercing through thick and thin.

It became clear to a keen-eyed, able, and ambitious book-seller named William Blackwood, who was John Murray's agent in Edinburgh, that there was a large body of readers—made up for the most part of the young and the ardent—who would eagerly welcome a periodical lighter and more entertaining in character than either of the two reviews. In this faith he set to work. He determined to found a publication which should be a magazine, not a review, and he looked about him for some young, clever, audacious young

186

men who would help him in his enterprise. He wanted to make his appearance with something that would startle the reading public ; if it shocked them a little too, so much the better.

The two men that at last he fixed upon were not as brilliant as he had hoped his editors might be. They were both Scottish, and one of them had been the editor of *The Farmer's Magazine*. They did their best, but it was not in them to appreciate or even to understand William Blackwood's ideals, and they only succeeded in producing " a meek and mild miscellany," which was very far from the thing he wanted. Six numbers of it were published under the title of *The Edinburgh Magazine*, but it drew little attention, and the irritated publisher felt that a new start must be made.

He had made his business premises in Princes Street a recognized meeting-place for Edinburgh men of letters. Writers and advocates and university students dropped in there to look over new publications and discuss literary events, and among this little society he found, when he was almost in despair, just the two young men he was looking for. One was John Gibson Lockhart, aged twenty-three, late of Oxford and now studying for the Scottish Bar, the other John Wilson, aged thirty-two, also from Oxford, but with ten years of authorship between him and the university. Later on these two were joined by James Hogg, the shepherd poet of Ettrick. The three entered with zest into William Blackwood's plans. He managed to get rid of his two earlier editors ; and with the seventh number of the magazine his design of startling the world was magnificently and almost too successfully accomplished.

The number contained two articles—one on " the Cockney Poets," under which name were included Hunt, Keats, Lamb, Shelley, and Hazlitt, and one on the *Biographia Literaria* of Coleridge—which were as scathing as anything that had appeared in the *Edinburgh* or the *Quarterly* and even more violent and abusive. But these were at first scarcely noticed in the tumult that arose concerning a third article, which was called *A Chaldee MS*. This was gravely announced as a translation of an old manuscript discovered in the " great library of Paris." It told, in Biblical language and with Biblical imagery, the history of *The Edinburgh Magazine*. " I looked and behold a man clothed in plain apparel stood in the door of his house ; and I saw his name and the number of his house, and his name was as it had been the colour of ebony." This, of course, was Blackwood, and there followed a description of the two editors of the first six numbers of the magazine. Both these men happened to be lame and walk with sticks, and of these it was said that they made a great noise in their going, as it were the noise of thunder, but they quickly disappeared and made way for the new band. Then came Wilson, " the beautiful leopard from the valley of the palm-trees," Lockhart, " the scorpion which delighted to sting the faces of men," and Hogg, " the great wild boar from the forest of Lebanon, and he roused up his spirit, and I saw him whetting his dreadful tusks for battle." There follows an account of the uneasiness with which another Edinburgh publisher, Archibald Constable, nicknamed " the Crafty," looked upon Blackwood's activities and of a visit that he made to Walter Scott, to try to induce that great writer to join with him in a literary project which would bring great glory to his own publishing house. " And in those days and at that time," said the *Chaldee MS.*,

> there lived also a man that was crafty in counsel and cunning in all manner of working, an upright and a just man, comely and well-favoured. . . . He said unto himself, I will arise and go unto a magician which is of my friends ; of a surety he will devise some remedy, and free me out of all my distresses. So he arose and came in to that great magician which hath his dwelling in the old fastness, hard by the River Jordan, which is by the Border.

But Scott would not promise to help him, and " the man which is Crafty saw tnat the magician loved him not."

So far it seems to us harmless enough, though many of the good folk of Edinburgh were horrified at what they considered a blasphemous use of the language of Scripture. But there followed an account of some of the notabilities of

Edinburgh, and here some of the thrusts were deadly. There was a certain advocate, Mr John Graham Dalyell, whom the writers had in mind when they wrote of

> a beast that he loved not, a beast that he had in his courts to hew wood and to draw water and to do all manner of unclean things. His face was like the face of an ape, and he chattered continually, and his nether parts were uncomely, nevertheless his thighs were hairy, and he skipped with a branch of a tree in his hand.

Mr Dalyell, most injudiciously, as it would seem, openly recognized this portrait and was furious. So were a good many others who were similarly attacked, and such a storm arose as Edinburgh had never seen before. There were threats of lawsuits and threats of violence, shoals of indignant letters, and challenges to duels. William Blackwood and his lieutenants rubbed their hands gleefully; here was the great send-off for which they had hoped. Everybody was reading the magazine, and those who were not smarting under its attacks were laughing uproariously. Scott, though his kindly nature and his common sense told him that such personalities were both malicious and unwise, could not help chuckling over them. Mrs Oliphant says that her mother, who was a staunch Whig, nevertheless enjoyed the *Chaldee MS.* immensely, and was never tired of talking about the ferment the innocent-looking, brown-covered magazine had caused throughout Edinburgh.

By and by William Blackwood began to wonder if the jest had not gone a little too far. Some of the threatened lawsuits were taking unpleasantly definite form. Mr John Dalyell, who seems to have been a gentleman astonishingly deficient in humour, made an application to the court stating that while he was "reposing in the bosom of his family, following his lawful avocations and at peace and unity with all mankind," William Blackwood, of Princes Street,

> actuated by deliberate malignity and without any provocation whatever on the part of the said John Graham Dalyell did insert and publish a wicked, false, and scandalous libel, grossly calumniating the person of the said John Graham Dalyell in an indecent, irreverent, and blasphemous application of Scripture

189

language, and in false, malevolent or wanton mockery of personal infirmities and holding them up as a subject of public scorn and derision.

The publisher saw that something must be done. The *Chaldee MS.* was withdrawn, and further issues of the magazine were published without it. Some judicious apologies were made and irate readers propitiated. Scott was induced to lend his powerful influence in stilling the storm. Gradually it all blew over, and the ruffled plumage of the Edinburgh notabilities allowed itself to be smoothed down. Mr Dalyell's lawsuit went on, but that served usefully as the means of keeping the name of the magazine in men's mouths. It was called *Blackwood's Magazine* now, by which name its fame had spread to England, and a large circle of very much intrigued readers waited expectantly for its next issue.

It remained for the publisher to deal with those who had been outraged by the violent article on the Cockney Poets. Leigh Hunt and Hazlitt both threatened legal proceedings. Hazlitt, who had been treated with actual scurrility and contemptuously alluded to as "pimpled Hazlitt," began an action ; and William Blackwood found it advisable to escape further trouble by paying the costs of the proceedings and an additional sum as compensation.

He did not, however, insist on the tone of the reviews being altered, and his three editors went on their intrepid, turbulent way. The violence of their attacks cost them a good many subscribers. Henry Mackenzie, author of *The Man of Feeling*, declared that the magazine contained things so offensive that he would not wish it to be found lying on his table. Mr Fraser Tytler, the historian, requested that the publisher would have the goodness to direct his clerk not to send him any more copies, as he was disgusted with its personal attacks on inoffensive people. But there were others who delighted in its pungent criticisms. Isaac d'Israeli, father of the still more famous Benjamin, was one of these, and that stern old Tory, the Reverend Patrick Brontë, was another. "Mr Driver lends us *Blackwood's Magazine*, the most able periodical there is," wrote Mr

190

Brontë's thirteen-year-old daughter Charlotte in 1829; and, she added, " The Editor is Mr Christopher North, an old man seventy-four years of age." " Christopher North " was the pen-name of John Wilson, but he was forty-four, not seventy-four, when this was written, and as rollicking and turbulent as he had been when he helped to shock Edinburgh with the *Chaldee MS.*

Two years after the founding of *Blackwood's* came *The London Magazine*; once again the example of the North was followed by the South. There had been a *London Magazine* since 1732, but it had been of small distinction. In 1820 it started with a new editor, as a publication of an entirely different character. It was fortunate in attracting a splendid group of contributors—Lamb and Hazlitt, De Quincey, Horace Smith, Bryan Procter. This was the group of writers specially obnoxious to *Blackwood's*, and for a good many years war raged between them. The *London* was not a whit behind its rival in the offensiveness of its personalities, and the pen of Hazlitt was as sharp-pointed as the pen of Lockhart. It had a distinguished but not a very fortunate career, and it lasted only until 1829.

Wilson, writing in *Blackwood's* in 1820, boasted that the circulation of his magazine was " somewhere below 17,000," that of the *Edinburgh* upward of 7000, the *Quarterly* about 14,000, *The Gentleman's Magazine* about 4000, but his figures cannot be taken as very reliable.

These four publications—the *Edinburgh*, the *Quarterly*, *Blackwood's*, and the *London*—supplied the wants of the general body of readers who cared for periodicals. Various sects and classes had also their own particular magazine. The Evangelicals had *The Christian Observer*, edited by Zachary Macaulay, which was diligently read by all the members of the Clapham Sect. Jonathan Gray wrote for it, and George Eliot in her youthful days contributed a poem. Its readers looked to it to give them the pure and undefiled Evangelical teaching on doctrine, morals, and manners, and very seldom did it fail them. But on one occasion there came a deplorable lapse. The unsuspicious subscribers one morning opened their paper and read, with fast-growing horror, a letter which defended works of fiction and eulogized Fielding and Smollett. Scandalized, they took up their pens and wrote to the editor, condemning in violent terms this outrage on Evangelical principles. One gentleman announced that he had committed the obnoxious number to the flames and should thenceforward cease to take the magazine. Mr Macaulay in the next issue stoutly defended his action, though in the meantime it had been revealed to him that his anonymous contributor was his own fifteen-year-old son.

The Unitarians also had their magazine, called *The Monthly Repository*, edited by W. J. Fox, a noted man in his day, and a staunch Radical and Benthamite. He preached on Sundays at the chapel in South Place, Finsbury, and his rousing discourses, half politics and half religion, were called by the admiring though irreverent younger members of his congregation " Sunday ticklers." Harriet Martineau, when she was nineteen years old, sent the first article she ever wrote to the *Repository*, and it was published anonymously. It was called *Women Writers on Practical Divinity*, and was considered by her brother and by other readers to be quite above the average in style and reasoning power. Thomas Noon Talfourd, in his early days, also wrote for the *Repository*. Miss Martineau remembered his first attempt, *On the System of Malthus*, which, she said, resolved itself into " a sentimental vindication of long engagements." " It was prodigiously admired by very young people," she went on, " but was too luscious for my taste, though some of my family lived on it for a while."

For more frivolous people there was *The Lady's Magazine, or Entertaining Companion for the Fair Sex, appropriated solely to their Use and Amusement*. It was read also, however, by members of what its editor would probably have called the " sterner sex." Clarissa Trant wrote to her brother: " I know you are fond of reading, but I also remember that you used sometimes to peruse the *larmoyante* love-tales contained in *The Lady's Magazine* in preference to the more solid stuff of our good authors "; and Mr Harbottle, of Theodore Hook's *The Parson's Daughter*, enjoyed looking

The Genius of the Lady's Magazine weeping over
the Tomb of her Royal Highnefs the Princefs Amelia

ILLUSTRATION FROM "THE LADY'S MAGAZINE," 1810

over old numbers of this entertaining periodical while he sipped his wine after dinner. Miss Branwell brought a pile of *Lady's Magazines* with her from Penzance in 1822, when she came to Haworth to take charge of her sister's motherless children, and Charlotte Brontë remembered reading them by stealth " with the most exquisite pleasure." It is probable that she owed some of this pleasure to the graceful sketches called *Our Village*, by Miss Mitford, which appeared regularly in *The Lady's Magazine* from 1819 to 1824 and made the fortune of that lucky periodical.

The time had not yet come when the tastes of children were to be carefully considered in the issue of periodicals. There was a *Child's Companion, or Sunday Scholar's Reward*, and a *Children's Magazine, or Monthly Repository of Instruction and Delight*, but in both the provision for " instruction " greatly outweighed that for " delight." We hear also of *The Monthly Preceptor*, a periodical which claimed to give " A Complete Course of Instruction on every useful subject, particularly Natural and Experimental Philosophy, Moral Philosophy, Natural History, Botany, Ancient and Modern History, Biography and the Manners and Customs of Nations Ancient and Modern, Languages, English Law, Penmanship, Mathematics and the *Belles Lettres*." Prizes to the value of fifteen shillings and upward were given each month for the best answers to questions set, and in the first number of the paper, issued in 1800, it was announced that Master James Henry Leigh Hunt and Master Thomas Love Peacock, both aged fourteen, had won prizes for poetical answers to the question, " Is history or biography the more improving study ? " Master Peacock's prize was *Elegant Extracts in Verse* epitomized. Later on in the same year Master Henry Kirke White, the son of a Nottingham butcher, and afterward sizar of St John's College, Cambridge, won a silver medal for a translation from Horace, and in the year following he won a pair of twelve-inch globes for an imaginary tour from London to Edinburgh. It would seem that there were persons of judgment on the editorial staff of *The Monthly Preceptor* who were able to recognize merit when they found it.

THE ENGLISHMAN AND HIS BOOKS

As the years went on the number of periodicals multiplied, and their form and contents changed to meet the changing demands of their readers. But each year that passed made it more unlikely that there would ever arise another conqueror who would mount with one stride to the throne of the supreme dictator, or another Prospero who, by means of spells written on the page of a magazine, would raise a storm that should rage through a whole city.

CHAPTER XII

LECTURERS AND THEIR AUDIENCES

IN the early years of the nineteenth century the higher classes of London society had given up going regularly to the play. The people had taken possession of the theatre ; the robust tastes and ideals of the middle class ruled it ; and ladies and gentlemen who cultivated delicacy and refinement found little to please them in the full-blooded dramas that delighted shopkeepers and manufacturers. So they went only occasionally, just to sample a new play, or to see the performance of some famous actor or actress—Kean or Kemble or Mrs Siddons or the boy tragedian, William Betty, who in 1804 took the town by storm.

This falling-off in play-going caused other recreations to come into fashion, and among these was the public lecture. Various learned societies had instituted courses of lectures, and they had been well attended ; Sir James Mackintosh had lectured at Lincoln's Inn, John Flaxman at the Royal Academy, and Sir Humphry Davy at the Royal Institution. Then, in the autumn of 1804, it was announced that a course of lectures on moral philosophy would be given by the Reverend Sydney Smith ; and at once there was a great rush for tickets. Everybody knew or had heard of Sydney Smith, who preached so eloquently, wrote such brilliant articles for the *Edinburgh,* and as a diner-out had no equal. His jokes and witty sayings were remembered and repeated until they were well known all over the town. It is not certain that all the people who bought tickets for the lectures desired earnestly to be instructed in moral philosophy, but they all felt sure that an hour passed in the company of Sydney Smith would be full of interest and entertainment and well worth the money to be paid.

On November 10, when the course of lectures was to

begin, fashionable ladies and gentlemen ordered their carriages to be at their doors in good time, that they might reach the hall early and secure a front seat. But only those who took care to be very early indeed had any chance of getting near the front. An hour before the time announced for the beginning of the lecture Albemarle Street and Grafton Street were blocked with carriages, the great hall was full to the very last seat, and latecomers had to be thankful if room could be made for them in the lobbies and passages, where, with the doors of the hall left open, they might hope to hear something of what was going on inside. Fine ladies in big feathered hats and long, high-waisted gowns complained peevishly of draughts and discomfort; dandies the most exquisite saw with anguish their lace cravats disordered and their polished toes trodden upon; damsels of the Blue-stocking type edged their way persistently toward the open door; dignified elderly gentlemen strove to remain dignified, though pressed before and behind. Yet nobody attempted to go away; and when, by and by, a portly, rubicund clergyman appeared, smiling genially, behind the lecture-table the people who could not see him joined in the applause with those who could.

The first lecture was an introductory one, defining the subject, and it was as witty and delightful as everybody had expected it to be, so that there was an even greater crowd at those which succeeded it. Some people, like Francis Horner, the great authority on political economy, and Mrs Marcet, of " Nat. Phil." fame, were drawn by interest in the subject. " I was a perfect enthusiast during the delivery of those lectures," said Mrs Marcet. " He who at one moment inspired his hearers with such awe and reverence by the solemn piety of his manner that his discourse seemed converted into a sermon, at others, by the brilliancy of his wit, made us die of laughing."

Another lady, less severely learned than Mrs Marcet, represents the class that looked upon the lectures rather as a social function than as a means of instruction. This is Miss Berry, the elder of the two beautiful sisters famous as the friends of Horace Walpole. In 1804 Miss Mary and

"Fine ladies in big feathered hats and long,
high-waisted gowns"

Miss Agnes Berry were living in Curzon Street, where all the wits and beauties and notable people of the day gathered at their evening parties. Sydney Smith knew their drawing-room well and had often seen Miss Mary queening it there, so that if he read, as most likely he did, the poem that she wrote, *On buying a New Bonnet to go to one of Sydney Smith's Lectures*, he must have been extremely flattered to find that she regarded it as an event of such social importance as to require a careful toilet.

> Lo where the gaily vestured throng,
> Fair Learning's train are seen,
> Wedged in close ranks her walls along,
> And up her benches green.

Thus Miss Berry began ; and she went on to demonstrate how, in spite of the arguments of the moralist, a new bonnet was absolutely necessary ; then finished with the sobering reflection that

> The simplest bonnet in Pall Mall
> Is sold for one pound eight.

The twelfth lecture of the course was on "Taste," and as the lecturer was coming into the hall—he had no carriage, so he walked from his home in Doughty Street, trudging sturdily along and often arriving with muddy shoes—he met a lady at the entrance. She had a bright, charming face and waving brown hair, and she was dressed in blue, with white feathers in her blue bonnet.

" Oh, Mrs Opie," said Sydney Smith, holding out his hand, " I am going to quote from one of your poems this evening, so don't fall asleep, or you may miss it," and he went on, smiling his quizzical smile.

Mrs Opie, who looked just as pretty as when she was the beautiful Miss Alderson of Norwich, and scarcely any older, was pleasantly fluttered. What should she do ? She felt she could hardly sit on her chair while her verses were quoted from the platform, and yet she would love to hear them. She appealed to her husband.

" Come in, or we shall get no seat," said John Opie, R.A., who was sometimes not quite as polite to his wife as he might have been ; and they went in.

THE ENGLISHMAN AND HIS BOOKS

There was the usual large audience, and everybody seemed to be talking eagerly, for this was March 1805, and all England was wondering if Napoleon's fleet would really cross the Channel, and what Mr Pitt would do in the matter of Lord Melville. But the sight of the lecturer standing by his table, so sturdy, so unperturbed, and so thoroughly English, gave them a pleasant feeling of confidence, and they settled down to listen to him, forgetting Napoleon and Lord Melville and all other troublers of the peace of the country.

At the back of the hall stood a group of undergraduates just down from Oxford, and among them a yellow-headed youth with blue eyes and a fresh boyish face. He listened to the lecture as attentively as did Mrs Opie, and remembered it so well that forty years later, when he was Sir Robert Peel, Prime Minister of England, he could quote passages from it.

The lecturer began by pointing out that " taste " was a metaphorical expression borrowed from a physical sensation, and went on to discourse upon the different ways in which it could be applied; and in due time came Mrs Opie's poem.

> We do not speak of taste in connection with the discernment of some quality which is undeniable and obvious. If a man were to discover that vinegar were sour we should give him no great credit for natural taste. If he were to discover the true language of feeling in this little poem of Mrs Opie's he would deserve no credit, for the fact is too striking for hesitation.

> Go, youth beloved ! in distant glades
>   New friends, new hopes, new joys to find !
> Yet sometimes deign, midst fairer maids,
>   To think on her thou leav'st behind.
> Thy love, thy fate, dear youth, to share,
>   Must never be my happy lot ;
> But thou may'st grant this humble prayer,
>   Forget me not, forget me not !

He read two verses so charmingly that they sounded like the very highest poetry, and everybody was enraptured. The poetess blushed deeply and hung her head, feeling that every eye was upon her. But only a few of the audience knew her, and though these whispered to their neighbours the little stir was soon over, and the lecturer went on.

> In considering the lighter virtues we may perhaps talk of taste, but for the graver virtues and vices certainly not. The Scythians always ate their grandfathers ; they behaved very respectfully to them for a long time ; but as soon as the grandfathers became old and troublesome, and began to tell long stories, they immediately ate them. Nothing could be more improper and even disrespectful than dining off such near and venerable relatives; yet we could not with any propriety accuse them of bad taste in morals.

He went on to talk of how natural taste was affected by association and convention, and of the difficulties in the way of setting up a standard of taste ; and he finished by assuring his hearers of his own conviction that the progress of good taste, though slow, was certain and irresistible.

The lecture had not been very learned or original, and the jokes had not been up to Mr Smith's highest efforts ; but the charm of his manner, the happy geniality that he managed to spread throughout the hall, the intonations of his pleasant voice, that gave everything he said a fuller and more piquant meaning, the glances and gestures that gave point and savour to a very ordinary witticism—these, taken together, carried his audience completely away. They applauded enthusiastically, and when he had made his bow and retired the ladies and gentlemen said to one another that dear Mr Smith had been better than ever this evening, and what a delightful man he was, and how should they get through the crowd—really, it was a shame to issue so many tickets. In fact, the whole course was such a brilliant triumph for the lecturer that the Royal Institution invited Mr Smith to deliver another course in the autumn of 1806 ; which he did, and drew still greater crowds, so that galleries had to be put up in the hall to accommodate them. It was, Mr Smith jestingly declared, " the most successful swindle of the season."

Other lecturers came and went at the Royal Institution, and season after season the hall was filled by eager audiences who wanted to hear what Dalton, or Humphry Davy, or Faraday had to tell them about the latest discoveries in science. But none of these lectures made such a social sensation as those given by Sydney Smith had done. They were serious scientific expositions, not fashionable functions. In 1808 Coleridge lectured on "Poetry and the Fine Arts," and at first attracted crowded audiences. De Quincey says that he has seen all Albemarle Street closed by a lock of carriages of women of distinction, until the servants of the Institute, or their own footmen, advanced to the carriage doors with the intelligence that Mr Coleridge had been suddenly taken ill. De Quincey speaks as if this happened many times, but Charles Lamb mentions two occasions only; it is certain, however, that Coleridge was often late, that his lectures were ill-prepared and unsatisfactory, and that his popularity rapidly declined and his audiences dwindled.

The vogue of the lecture spread, and in various parts of London attempts were made to obtain audiences for courses on literature or art or some other subject of general interest. In the autumn of 1811 Coleridge began a course of lectures on "Shakespeare and Milton, in Illustration of the Principles of Poetry," at the Philosophical Society's rooms in Fleet Street. They were, at least at first, almost as popular as those of Sydney Smith. "We are going in a party to hear the new Art of Poetry by the reformed schismatic," wrote Lord Byron in his diary, and again, a little later: "To-morrow I dine with Rogers and am to hear Coleridge, who is a sort of rage at present." Crabb Robinson saw Byron and Rogers at this lecture, which was given on January 20, 1812. The poet, he says, "was well wrapped up, but I recognized his club foot, and indeed his countenance and general appearance." Robinson estimates that there were usually about a hundred and fifty people present at the lectures, and he confirms Byron's statement that Coleridge had become the rage. He reports that the lectures varied greatly in quality. There were four on *Romeo and Juliet*, and one of these was "incomparably the best of the course, spirited, methodical, and for the most part intelligible, though profound"; but the next, also on *Romeo and Juliet*, was the worst he had heard. The course ended, we are told, with *éclat*. In the last lecture, which was given in

LONDON FASHIONABLE WALKING DRESSES, 1812

June, Coleridge surpassed himself; several passages were "more than brilliant," and the applause from a large audience was enthusiastic.

Meantime Hazlitt had been lecturing at the Russell Institute, Great Coram Street, on "The History of Human Philosophy." In October 1811 he wrote to Crabb Robinson telling him of the proposed course and saying that he had already thirty subscribers and wanted ten or a dozen more. Robinson induced John Payne Collier and James Buck, brother of Mrs Clarkson, to take tickets, at two guineas each. He did not look forward to the course having any great success. "No subject is in itself less adapted to a lecture than metaphysical philosophy," he wrote in his diary, "no manner less adapted to recommend abstract matter than Hazlitt's."

Robinson's misgivings were well founded. Hazlitt had none of Sydney Smith's charm of manner and none of his power of setting up friendly relations with his audience. He had no humour or lightness of touch, no tact, and no regard for the susceptibilities of his hearers. That which he had to give was of high and rare value, but he could not offer it with the winning grace shown by the popular Mr Smith in dispensing his trifles. Nor had he Coleridge's moments of inspired brilliance and compelling eloquence. He was neither a society favourite nor a "reformed schismatic." Such reputation as he had was that of a severe critic, apt to bear hardly on other people's opinions and prejudices.

To the first lecture of the course Robinson escorted Mrs Charles Aikin, whom he had known when she was Miss Wakefield—"a charming girl" he had noted in his diary. She had married a nephew of Mrs Barbauld, and had introduced Robinson to the Barbauld circle. The lecture, we hear, was excellent in substance, but the lecturer read it in a low, monotonous voice, very rapidly, with his eyes fixed on his book. Not once did he look at his audience. "As he seems to have no conception of the difference between a lecture and a book," said Robinson, "his lectures cannot possibly be popular, hardly tolerable."

There was another member of the audience who was

disposed to sit in judgment upon Hazlitt for his faults of manner and delivery, and this was Dr John Stoddart, the lecturer's brother-in-law, whom Charles Lamb called " a cold-hearted, well-bred, conceited disciple of Godwin." Dr Stoddart took upon himself to write to Hazlitt pointing out his defects and advising him how to cure them. Hazlitt, already depressed by the sense of failure, felt the hard criticisms keenly, and was disposed to give up the lectures in despair ; but his friends did what they could to hearten him, and next time he succeeded better. " He delivered himself well," said Robinson, " that is loud, and with a tone of confidence which, being forced, had sometimes the air of arrogance ; this, however, did not offend (except perhaps a few) and he was interrupted by applause several times. His lecture was on Locke."

There were two more lectures on Locke, and at the second of these Robinson noted that Hazlitt's manner was " now very respectable." Then came a lecture on "Disinterestedness," but apparently interest was waning, for " the attendance was thin." To the next lecture, which was on "Self-love," he escorted Mrs Flaxman, and to the one which followed, on the philosophy of Hartley, he took Miss Benger, who was quite a famous authoress in her day, and intimate with all the celebrities. Both these lectures, he complained, were dull. The next, on Helvetius and the doctrine of selfishness, was " interesting and animated." The last lecture of the course was on April 27, and Robinson described it as " very well delivered and full of shrewd observation," but we do not hear how many of the audience had survived to the end, or what general opinion said with regard to the lecturer.

For six years Hazlitt lectured no more ; then on the second Tuesday of the year 1818 we hear of him beginning a course on the English poets at the Surrey Institution.

The Surrey Institution had been established in 1807, and was planned on similar lines to those of the Royal Institution in Albemarle Street. It stood in Blackfriars Road, near the Surrey end of the bridge, and it contained a fine library, reading-rooms, scientific laboratories, and a lecture-room.

It was hoped to make it a centre of education and culture for London south of the river, and much was expected from the English literature lectures that were to be given by Hazlitt.

The audience that gathered to hear him was very different from the select and fashionable assembly that had hung upon the words of Sydney Smith. Fine ladies and gentlemen would not deign to cross the river, and Mr Hazlitt must be content with the people who lived in the neighbourhood of the institution. Most of these were small manufacturers and tradesmen, with a few professional men and a sprinkling of a lower class. Close by stood the chapel where for more than thirty years the famous Rowland Hill had preached and ministered to a devoted following, and many of these pious, narrow, conventionally minded Dissenters were among Hazlitt's hearers. For them the lecture was no light and pleasing substitute for a play, for they regarded the theatre as the home of Satan. They came for edification and for such solid instruction as it befitted respectable citizens to receive. Talfourd, who attended the lectures regularly, described the audience as being one with which Hazlitt had " an imperfect sympathy." It was made up chiefly, he said, of

> Dissenters, who agreed with him in his hatred of Lord Castle-maine [whom they regarded as responsible for the oppressive measures of the Government, which had aroused great discontent] but who " loved no play " ; of Quakers, who approved him as the opponent of slavery and capital punishment, but who " heard no music " ; of citizens devoted to the main chance who had a hankering after the improvement of the mind but to whom his favourite doctrine of its natural disinterestedness was a riddle ; of a few enemies who came to sneer, and a few friends who were eager to learn and admire.

These friends made a band large enough to provide some leaven to the heaviness of the audience. John Keats, who came regularly, says that he usually met many people whom he knew. John Hunt, brother of Leigh Hunt, came with his son Henry, now seventeen years old, and helping his father with *The Examiner*. Thomas Bewick, the painter, an enthusiastic admirer of Hazlitt's, was there, and John Landseer, the engraver, with his two sons, Thomas and

Edwin, who were both of them at this time pupils of Benjamin Haydon. Crabb Robinson came to most of the lectures, though he often left them in a state of high indignation at the lecturer's unflattering remarks concerning the poetry of Wordsworth. Talfourd, now a spruce young law-student of twenty-three, Bryan Procter, also a lawyer, but beginning to be known for his plays and his lyrics, Charles Wells, a young solicitor's clerk and devoted to Hazlitt, and George Patmore, the secretary of the Surrey Institution, were always in their places, so that when the lecturer looked round at his audience he could see here and there a sympathetic face, and take heart.

He was much less nervous now than he had been when he had given his first not very successful course. He stood up calmly at the lecture-table, and spoke clearly and earnestly. His looks would have been in his favour with an audience of real discrimination, but as he was neither of the Byronic type, which was still the popular ideal of beauty, nor big and sleek and fair like that model of manly perfection the Prince Regent, his hearers saw in him nothing to admire. His dark, piercing eyes and shock of brown, wavy hair made him look very unlike the conventional lecturer, and careful mothers of families among the audience doubtless noticed that his clothes were shabby and ill-brushed and his neck-cloth carelessly tied.

Week after week he took his place and looked round the hall, which, though it was not crowded, was always fairly well filled. Here and there the responsive faces of one or other of his friends lit up the scene, but the general effect was of row after row of stolid countenances, indifferent or faintly disapproving. Hazlitt did his best to move them. He brought them the finest thoughts of the greatest poets, with his own stirring and illuminating comments; but there was only the slightest show of interest. When he had tried again and again and his highest efforts had failed to rouse them, his irritable temper mastered him, and deliberately he flung out some startling paradox or some unorthodox comment which he knew would shock his hearers into liveliness. In his lecture on the writers of Queen Anne's day he drew a

204

parallel between Swift and Voltaire, and the audience listened with growing horror while he dared in calm and even speech to praise the intellectual powers of an infidel—and an infidel of that abandoned country France. Hazlitt proceeded to quote Cowper's lines on the pious cottager :

> Just knows, and knows no more, her Bible true—
> A truth the brilliant Frenchman never knew.

A storm of applause (of the sentiment, not of the lecturer) broke out. The audience put themselves in the place of the cottager, and received the lines as a tribute to their own superiority. At another time the name of Hannah More was mentioned. " She is a lady," said Hazlitt, " who has written a good deal that I have never read." " More pity for you ! " cried a stern voice from the body of the hall ; and Hazlitt smiled his slightly sardonic smile and went on unmoved. Sometimes one or two outraged hearers would give vent to their feelings in hisses. Hazlitt would look steadily toward them for a moment, then turn to his manuscript, and read again, slowly and impressively, the sentence which had called forth the demonstration. Once Crabb Robinson so far forgot himself as to offend in this unseemly fashion. " He was so contemptuous in speaking of Wordsworth's letter to Burns that I lost my temper and hissed," said Robinson, " but I was on the outside of the room and I hurried away almost immediately afterwards."

Reports of Hazlitt's sins against Wordsworth were carried to Charles Lamb, but he did not regard them as seriously as did that devoted admirer of the poet Henry Crabb Robinson. Charles Lamb often allowed himself a few jests at Wordsworth's expense, and he had some sympathy with Hazlitt's scorn of the great man's vanity and egotism. " W. H. goes on lecturing against W. W.," wrote Lamb, " and making copious use of quotations from said W. W. to give a zest to said lectures." But in the last lecture of his course Hazlitt made fine and ample amends for the slighting references that had gone before. " As Mr Wordsworth's poems have been little known to the public," he said,

> or chiefly through garbled extracts from them, I will here
> give an entire poem (one that has always been a favourite

205

with me) that the reader may know what it is that the admirers of this author find to be delighted with in his poetry. Those who do not feel the beauty and force of it may save themselves the trouble of enquiring further.

Then he read to them the whole of *Hart-leap Well*, with its clear declaration of Wordsworth's poetic aim and method,

> The moving accident is not my trade ;
> To freeze the blood I have no ready arts :
> 'Tis my delight, alone in summer shade,
> To pipe a simple song to thinking hearts,

and its characteristic final stanza :

> " One lesson, Shepherd, let us two divide,
> Taught both by what she [Nature] shows, and
> what conceals ;
> Never to blend our pleasure or our pride
> With sorrow of the meanest thing that feels."

On the whole the lectures had been a success. Hazlitt had fought sturdily against the apathy and hostility of the audience, and had gained their respect almost in spite of themselves. Bewick says that he had obtained complete command over them and had become quite a favourite.

The lectures were published, and at first sold very well ; then the *Quarterly* stepped in with its authoritative and damaging criticism. " Mr Hazlitt's knowledge of Shakespeare and of the English language are on a par with the purity of his morals and the depth of his understanding," declared this " savage and tartarly " review. " Sometimes he breaks forth into a poetical strain, but more frequently he descends to that simple style of eloquence which is in use among washer-women, the class of females with whom, as we learn from *The Round Table*, he and his friend Mr Hunt particularly delight to associate." *The Round Table* was the name given to the literary pages of *The Examiner*, to which Hazlitt and Hunt contributed. Nearly every one who had heard the lectures was furiously indignant at the *Quarterly's* criticism ; but there was no appeal against it, and, Hazlitt says, not another copy of the book was sold.

Coleridge, during this winter season of 1818, was giving a course of lectures at Fleur-de-Lys Court, Fetter Lane. His lectures were on the same day of the week as those of Hazlitt, but at a later hour, so that Crabb Robinson was able to hurry off from the Surrey Institution, cross Blackfriars Bridge, and reach Fetter Lane only a little late for the lecture. " Rushed off to hear Coleridge's opening lecture on Shakespeare," he wrote in his diary on January 27. " I was gratified unexpectedly by finding a large and respectable audience, generally of very superior persons—in physiognomy rather than in dress. But the lecture was heavy."

Thomas Allsop, the devoted and admiring friend of Charles Lamb, gave a similar account of the gathering at Fetter Lane. The lectures, he said, " were constantly thronged by the most attentive and intelligent auditory I have ever seen." The difference between this audience and that which attended Coleridge's earlier lectures is significant. He was no longer " the rage." The fashionable world had grown tired of him, and now neglected his lectures for some newer diversion. But the value and originality of his Shakespearean criticism had been recognized by those men and women who really cared about literature and were eager for new light and leading. Hence he was drawing an audience of a character very different from the fashionable crowd that had come to be entertained by Sydney Smith or the respectable company, moved by a conscientious but unenlightened desire for self-improvement, that had ' sat under ' Hazlitt. His vexatious carelessness and unpunctuality, his irritating lapses into wordy dullness, were overlooked by those who saw the true worth of what he had to give ; and so it came to pass that Crabb Robinson's " superior persons " gathered at Fleur-de-Lys Court.

Charles Lamb was not among them.

> Lectures are not to my taste, whatever the lecturer may be. If *read* they are dismal flat, and you can't think why you are brought together to hear a man read his works which you could read so much better at leisure yourself. If delivered extempore I am always in pain lest the gift of utterance should suddenly fail the orator in the middle, as it did me at a dinner given in honour of me at the London Tavern. " Gentlemen," I said, and there I stopped.

Charles Lamb thus puts the case against the lecture, but

there is a good deal to be said on the other side. There were many Englishmen and Englishwomen in his day who felt that a lecture was equal to a book *plus* the personality of the lecturer *plus* the stimulus that comes from the meeting together of a number of people for a common purpose, and there have been many since who have felt the same. The value of the last two elements varies immensely according to circumstances, but it is probable that it will always prove too great for the vogue of the lecture to die out.

CHAPTER XIII

LONDON READERS IN THE DAYS OF THE REGENCY

*Being Extracts from the Letters of an American Youth
to his Mother*

BRUNSWICK SQUARE
January 1812

MY DEAR MOTHER,

I am now settled quite happily here, and am beginning to understand something about the work in my uncle's house of business. At the end of my projected sojourn of five years I shall, I hope, have mastered it thoroughly, and shall return home fitted to be a real help to my father in all that concerns his trade with England. Meantime I intend to profit in other ways also by my stay and to enjoy to the full the life of this great capital. All my surroundings are strange and interesting to me, the men and women no less than the actual scenes and buildings. I will tell you in the journal-letters I send you as much about my experiences as is possible, but there will be a great deal that I cannot record and which must wait until the happy day when I see and talk with you once more. I will not forget the special request that you made to me before I left. I will try, as you wish, to give you a full and detailed account of what the people of London are reading, and what are the opinions of the public about the books of the day ; and I will send you from time to time, as my purse will permit, copies of the books which are here regarded as the greatest works of contemporary genius. I will not fail to insert a paragraph on this subject in each letter I write to you, and will take pains that my account shall be both accurate and circumstantial. You will doubtless find that many changes have taken place in the public taste since you lived in London more than twenty years ago, and I shall feel amply repaid for any trouble this record may cost me if it can please or interest my dearest mother.

THE ENGLISHMAN AND HIS BOOKS

February 2. I will begin by telling you what books are read in my uncle's house. Since I wrote to you last I have begun a campaign of investigation which may have many difficulties, and even, I can assure you, some dangers. First, I penetrated into my uncle's sanctum, where, as I suspected, he kept a store of books for his private reading. This room is not actually forbidden ground to the family, but it is seldom that anyone enters it without special occasion, and I felt some little trepidation as I opened the door last Tuesday evening and crossed the room to the small set of bookshelves fastened against the opposite wall. I had learned to think very highly of my uncle's good sense in business matters and of his kindness, especially to me, who must be in some respects a trial to his good-nature, but I knew nothing of his literary tastes. On the top shelf of the bookcase was a row of well-worn volumes, and I was proceeding to enter the titles of these in my notebook when I heard a step, and my uncle stood behind me. There was nothing to be done but to tell him why I had come there, begging his pardon for what might seem a lack of respect towards him in entering his private room unbidden.

As you know, he is something of a humorist, and the situation appeared to amuse him.

" Ho ! ho ! " he said, " so you are conducting an inquiry into my reading ! Let me see if I can help you."

He turned to the bookcase and looked at the volumes with an air of keen appreciation.

" Those shabby fellows up there," he said, " were my beloved companions when I was not much older than you are now. How I remember reading Godwin's *Political Justice*—it opened a new world to me—and Tom Paine's *Rights of Man* and Arthur Young's *Travels in France* and Southey's *Wat Tyler*! They made a red-hot revolutionist of me for a year or two, as they did of many another. That fat little volume is Cowper's poems, and these thin ones are Crabbe's—*The Village* and *The Library* and *The Borough*— that one came out only last year. Good tales all of them, not mawkish rubbish such as that maudlin Lake fellow, Wordsworth, writes. I bought his *Lyrical Ballads* when it first came out, thinking it would be after the fashion of Southey "—here he took down a thin volume in paper boards—" but I couldn't read the stuff.

> "'Oh! what's the matter? What's the matter?
> What is't that ails young Harry Gill?'"

He read the lines in a mocking tone, then shut the book impatiently and put it back in its place.

"But here's the poet for my money—Walter Scott. Here's *The Lay of the Last Minstrel* and *Marmion* and *The Lady of the Lake*. I forget while I am reading them that I am a staid London merchant, and long for a sword in my hand, and a good horse under me."

I took one of the volumes and turned over its pages curiously, for I had heard the poems spoken of with enthusiasm by many people since my arrival in London.

"You haven't read them?" asked my uncle. "Here, take them, boy, and read them at once."

I took them very joyfully.

"Novels too," he went on, "I read plenty of them once, and do still, though not the sort your aunt gets from the circulating library. Here's *Clarissa Harlowe* and *Tom Jones* and *Amelia* and *Tristram Shandy* and *Humphry Clinker* and *Peregrine Pickle* and *John Buncle* and *Caleb Williams* and *Hugh Trevor* and *Hermsprong*. I've read them all over and over again. There's nothing like them now. Some of Miss Edgeworth's I can read—there's *Castle Rackrent*, I enjoyed that. And here's a new book I've just bought that's very good reading too in its way—*Sense and Sensibility*, by a Miss Jane Austen. And here on the lower shelves are the more sober books—Rollin's *Ancient History*, Gibbon's *Decline and Fall*, Smith's *Wealth of Nations*, Bentham's *Principles of Morals and Legislation*, Boswell's *Johnson*— a rare book, that. I knew them all once, and I read them now sometimes, but I'm getting lazy in my reading. I can't keep up with all the new publications. If you want to know about them you must go to your cousin Robert. He calls himself a Wordsworthian, and the last time he came home he was raving about some new poet—a boy who had been expelled from the university."

THE ENGLISHMAN AND HIS BOOKS

Robert is twenty, and at Oxford. I have seen him only once.

"Now get along and leave me to my work," said my uncle, "and take these—they will tell you more about the new books than I can." He thrust the *Edinburgh* and the *Quarterly* into my hands, and I went out.

February 12. It is with great regret that I find myself obliged to confess that I have at present made no progress in my investigations into the reading of this household, having given all my leisure moments to the poems of Mr Scott, lent me by my uncle. Words cannot describe the effect they have had upon my mind. They are, indeed, marvellous works. I have read them over and over until I can now repeat long passages from them by heart. It is now seven years since the *Lay* was published, and four since the appearance of *Marmion*. Yet the whole town is still reading them, and large new editions are sent out each year. Of the three I think that *Marmion* is my favourite, though it is difficult to choose where all are so exquisite. I sat up the whole of one night reading this wonderful poem, for I could not tear myself from its entrancing pages, and now stirring passages from it ring in my ears as I go about my daily work.

February 18. Yesterday I resumed my investigations, and endeavoured to discover something concerning the reading of my aunt and my cousin Julia. Julia, as you know, is eighteen, and just out of the schoolroom. She is, I believe, considered a beauty, and she has many admirers.

I am always a little shy of going into my aunt's drawing-room unless I am specially invited to do so. It is an extremely handsome apartment, and there are many elegant ornaments tastefully disposed about it. But, having dressed myself with more than my usual care, I went courageously up last evening. I examined first the fine bookcase, which contains several rows of beautifully bound books. I saw Shakespeare and Milton and *The Pilgrim's Progress*, the works of Dr Johnson and of Edmund Burke, and Oliver Goldsmith's *Vicar of Wakefield*, with *Evelina*, *Cecilia*, *Camilla*, and one or two of Miss Edgeworth's novels—all the books that I know so well in the old bookcase at home.

" Which of these books do you like best ? " I asked my cousin.

" Those old things! " she replied. " I never look at them."

" They are quite out of the fashion," said my aunt languidly. She was sitting in a comfortable chair by the fire, and had a book on her lap. I must tell you that nothing that is out of the fashion has any value for my aunt. She admires only the latest mode in dress, furniture, and manners, and, as it appears, in books also. She held up the volume she was reading.

" This was published only last week," she said. " It is called *The Monastery of St Columba*. It is in five volumes, and I am told that everybody is reading it, and the book-sellers cannot get enough copies to supply their customers. It is a delightful story." And she returned to it with an air of great enjoyment.

" We had a parcel of charming novels sent from Mr Lane's library yesterday," said my cousin, going to a side table that was covered with books. " I dote upon them. This one is so horrid you can't think. It is called *The Fatal Revenge, or The Family of Montorio*. Is not that a sweet title ? I sat up all night reading it."

I spent nearly an hour turning over the books and trying to fix some of the titles in my memory. There was *The Scottish Chiefs, Self-control, The Houses of Osma and Almeria, or The Convent of Ildefonso, Woman, or Ida of Athens*, and several others. On another table lay magazines such as *The Lady's Magazine, or Entertaining Companion for the Fair Sex*, but these I need not describe, as you know them.

February 21. My next adventure promised to be more dangerous than those that had gone before. I had to find out what was being read in the schoolroom. The school-room in this house is sacred territory. It is presided over by a severe but depressed-looking lady, named Miss Mordaunt, whom I sometimes meet on the stairs or in the drawing-room when I venture there after dinner. She never speaks to me, except for a formal greeting, and I am afraid to speak to her. But I am on very good terms with her pupils Harriet and Eliza, aged fifteen and thirteen, and John, aged ten. I meet them sometimes when they are sent out to walk round the square before breakfast, and sometimes, on holidays, I am allowed to play at ball with them in the garden. One such occasion, fortunately for me, came yesterday, and I asked them to tell me what books they read when they had finished their lessons. They were very ready to give me a great deal of information, and invited me to visit their schoolroom, encouraging me by saying that Miss Mordaunt was out, and their mother retired to her own apartment. I quaked, but I would not seem to fail in courage, so I followed them.

They have *Sandford and Merton* and Miss Edgeworth's *Parent's Assistant* and *Moral Tales*, with several volumes of Mrs Barbauld's *Evenings at Home*. They own a good many of Newbery's publications, and John went very proudly to fetch a copy of *Industry and Idleness: a Pleasing and Instructive Tale*, which he had received as a present on his birthday, a few days before. They have Lamb's *Tales from Shakespeare* and Jane and Ann Taylor's *Original Poems*. They spoke with great affection of an old illustrated copy of *The Pilgrim's Progress* that had served the whole family in turn. Harriet told me proudly that she had lately been allowed to read *Thaddeus of Warsaw*, and that she had cried over it for several days. She seemed to regard this as a proof that she was fit to leave Miss Mordaunt's territory and take her place with her sister in the drawing-room.

February 26. There remained only the kitchen to be explored, and I prepared the way for my investigations there by a talk with Parker, the butler. He is a sober, middle-aged man, and my uncle looks upon him as the mainstay of the establishment. His wife is the cook, and his niece Fanny is the housemaid.

Parker's reading appeared to be limited to the newspaper. He read my uncle's *Morning Chronicle* and my aunt's *Morning Post*, and when my cousin was at home there was *The Examiner*, but Parker did not think very much of that. He had no time for any other kind of reading, he said ; but his wife and the girls were for ever at some book or other, though he had never taken the trouble to find out what they were all about. So I descended to the kitchen. I am well known to the female servants, and, I may say, rather a favourite with them. I found Mrs Parker, very clean and respectable-looking, reading a tract. The tract was called *The Road to Hell, or Are you a Drunkard ?* and she seemed to be enjoying it mightily. She was quite pleased when I asked her about it, and showed me a pile of similar publications which she kept in the dresser drawer. It appears that she is one of the Evangelicals, or, as they are called here, the Clapham Sect. She presented me with a tract called *The Converted Cobbler, or A Word to the Blasphemer*, which I received, I hope, with becoming gratitude. As soon as I could get away from Mrs Parker's lengthy exposition of her faith I went to see what Fanny and Emma were giggling over at the other side of the table. Fanny was reading aloud—since Emma, alack ! is " no scholar "—from a blue paper-covered volume—a sort of debased edition of a Minerva novel—entitled *The True History of Jane Shore*. They both said they were enjoying it very much, though Fanny confessed to preferring a story " with more love in it, like," and Emma wanted " fighting, an' crimes, an' 'orrible murders, if you please, sir." She confessed that she sometimes borrowed *The Halfpenny Annals of Crime* and *The History of the Most Celebrated Murderers of All Countries* from red-headed Joseph, the boot-boy.

And now I have tried to tell you something of the books that are read in the house, almost from the garret to the cellar. I will proceed next to some account of the reading of the London world in general.

March 20. Only two words are required to tell you what the town is reading at present, and those two are—*Childe Harold*. Nobody reads, talks, or thinks of anything else. It is, I believe, a sort of epic poem, written by Lord Byron, a young peer twenty-four years old, who is well known in London for his dissipations, his handsome face, and his club foot. He wrote some verses five years ago which were very harshly treated by the reviewers, but these are almost forgotten, though they made some stir at the time. His latest poem has set the whole town raving. Wherever I go I am

asked : " Are you not *charmed* with Lord Byron's poem ? "
" Do you not *adore Childe Harold* ? " When I reply that
I have not read it, I am looked upon with compassion and
disgust, as one who has voluntarily surrendered his privileges
as a reasonable being. But I am determined I will not read
it. I am sickened by the commotion that is being made
about it, the rantings and sighings, the raptures and tears
that are being spent upon what I judge, from all I have heard,
to be a piece of bombastic and sentimental extravagance.

A few days ago I came back from my uncle's office and
found my cousin Julia with a young lady visitor in the morning-room. They were both reading out of one book, which
lay open on the table before them. Both were in a state of
high excitement, and from time to time one read aloud in
rapturous tones some line or passage from the book, and
the other uttered ecstatic ejaculations. I heard something
about " blood-red tresses deepening in the sun," " milk-
white crests," " gold spurs," " And must they fall, the young,
the proud, the brave ? " and, what disgusted me most of all,
and so fixed itself in my memory, " For he through Sin's
long labyrinth had run." My cousin's pretty eyes were wet,
and so were those of her companion. My aunt sat in her
comfortable chair listening, and occasionally repeating a
line after one or other of the girls as if to commit it to
memory—I knew she was preparing to repeat it at her next
dinner-party in order to impress her visitors.

As soon as I entered they called to me. " Oh, cousin,
listen to Lord Byron's new poem ! Such a splendid hero !—
dark and stern and terrible !—and such a lovely heroine !
such descriptions of divine scenery ! "—and so on. But
I would not listen.

" A Minerva novel in verse," I said. " Pretty reading for
sentimental young ladies."

" Oh, but, cousin, it is written by Lord Byron ! He is *so*
handsome and *so* interesting and only twenty-four."

I took up the book, turned over the pages, and read a few
lines here and there.

> Oh ! many a time and oft had Harold loved,
> Or dreamed he loved, since rapture is a dream ; . . .

"Childe Harold's Pilgrimage"

J. M. W. Turner

IN THE DAYS OF THE REGENCY

Pleasure's pall'd victim! life-abhorring gloom
Wrote on his faded brow curst Cain's unresting doom.

" A very foolish young man, to my mind," I said scornfully. " I like Mrs Radcliffe's heroes better " ; and I went quickly out of the room to escape their clatter.

I was a little surprised the next evening to see my uncle sit and read the book steadily, scarcely looking off its pages for more than an hour, and answering quite at random anyone who addressed him. But even this did not prepare me for the state of things which, in the course of a few days, has come to pass in my uncle's house of business. The clerks with whom I work have each a copy of the poem, and they spout lines from it at every opportunity, and rave about its beauties in a way that is almost intolerable. They have begun to imitate its noble author, who affects a scornful and melancholy demeanour and a peculiar style of dress. He wears his hair longer than is usual, has discarded his neckcloth, and has adopted a peculiar style of collar, open in front to display the beauties of his throat. To see Thompson, who is short and fair and fat, striding about the counting-house with a Byronic collar above his shabby jacket and a Byronic frown upon his chubby and usually beaming face, his flaxen hair grown wispy for want of cutting, is enough to warn any sane person against reading *Childe Harold*. Macilray, dark and long and bony, carries it off better, but he wears spectacles, and in his efforts to flash dark fire from his eyes he makes some most extraordinary grimaces. My uncle's head clerk complains that he is constantly finding the beginnings of *Odes to Despair* and *Lines on a Fatal Passion* in the desks of these young men, and that, in consequence, the work is neglected. The only good thing about the whole matter is that Lord Byron is said to be sardonic and reserved, and therefore his followers maintain, when they remember to do so, a dark and haughty silence.

August 14. The Byron fever still rages. The bookshops are filled with copies of his poems, and no drawing-room table is without one. He has become the idol of fashionable society. His admirers are never tired of telling how he was the guest of honour at a certain duchess's ball, and how another duchess was quite ill with chagrin because she could not secure him for her dinner-party. The fairest and most nobly born ladies, it is said, learn his poems by heart, hang upon his words, court him, flatter him, boast of his smiles, and exult when a rival is treated with coldness. His demeanour towards his fair admirers is reported to be very haughty and disdainful, sometimes verging on rudeness, and this but inflames them the more. Lady Caroline Lamb, wife of a son of Lord Melbourne's, is mentioned as one of his most ardent admirers.

May 1813. There is another poem by Lord Byron just out. It is called *The Giaour* and is, I gather, of the same character as *Childe Harold*. It has raised its noble author to the giddiest heights of popularity. He is regarded almost as a demi-god, and the tales of his wild escapades that fly about the town only add to his charm in the eyes of his worshippers. Everywhere I go the talk is still of him. In my aunt's drawing-room questions as to whether his name is to be pronounced *By*ron or By*ron*, and whether the G in 'Giaour' is hard or soft, are discussed gravely, as matters of the highest importance. Whenever one passes the Albany one is sure to see a small crowd gathered waiting to catch a glimpse of his lordship as he emerges from his lodgings or returns after some festivity. He is at once recognized by his lameness, and this is said to give him great annoyance, for he cannot bear to be reminded of what he feels to be his one defect. The Prince Regent himself commanded that Lord Byron should be presented to him at a ball, and paid him many compliments on his work. It is reported, though I do not know with how much truth, that the conversation turned on the poems of Walter Scott. The Prince expressed his admiration of *The Lay of the Last Minstrel, Marmion,* and *The Lady of the Lake,* and Byron replied with the warmest and most enthusiastic praises of these works. If this is true, it was handsomely done. But why, if he can thus admire true poetry, does he not see how different and inferior is his own?

October 21. Last night my uncle gave a dinner-party. There were twelve guests present—business friends of my uncle's, with their wives, their sons, and their daughters. The talk was almost entirely of Lord Byron. One speaker especially engaged my attention. He was a gentleman of mature years, with a countenance that was both shrewd and kindly. He said that *Childe Harold* had opened a new world to him. He had read no poetry since his boyhood until, induced by curiosity, he had taken up the book about which every one was talking. He said, too, that he had discovered that many of the men whom he employed were fervent admirers of Byron—not the young men only, but the sober, middle-aged fathers of families also. Much had been said, he added, against Lord Byron's character, but for his part he considered that the man who had brought this marvellous brightness into hundreds of dull lives must be regarded as a public benefactor.

Another guest told of a girl of fifteen who, hearing by chance two lines from *The Giaour*, was haunted by them and could not rest until she had obtained the entire work. Yet another related how the little daughter of one of his friends, Mr Barrett, a child of ten years, dreamed day and night of dressing up as a boy and running away to become the page of the poet she idolized. They agreed that a good many people—Mr Scott, for example, Mr Wordsworth, Mr Southey, and Mrs Barbauld—were shocked by the morality of the poems and repelled by their gloom and pessimism, but even these owned that they had had great pleasure in reading them and praised them for many of their qualities. One gentleman spoke of a Miss Mary Russell Mitford, a clever young lady of twenty-five, who dislikes *Childe Harold* heartily; and another said that Mr Samuel Rogers, the poet, had told him that he had sent the book to his friend, Mr Thomas Grenville, who had altogether condemned it, saying, " It is written in a deadly spirit of scorn and hate, which curdles the blood, and chills every kindly feeling instead of stirring and promoting them."

I felt much vexation at not being able to join myself with these latter critics and denounce the poems of which the world has become so unaccountably enraptured ; but as I had read neither *Childe Harold* nor *The Giaour* I could not do so. I resolved, however much I might dislike the task, to read them at once, that I might be able to expose their worthlessness. Meantime I called upon the company, and my uncle especially, not to forget their old allegiance to Mr Scott, whose new poem, *Rokeby*, I praised with great warmth. " And," I said, " to prove that there are many who still value him highly, I must tell you that I have seen a letter from an undergraduate at Oxford who says that the booksellers' shops were besieged for early copies, and that he who had been so fortunate as to secure one was followed to his chambers by a tribe of friends all as eager to hear it read as ever were jockeys to hear the result of a match at Newmarket, that bets were made as to whether the older or the younger poet would win in the race for popularity, and that Scott had many backers."

" That may be," replied one of the guests, " but what do you say to the falling off of the sales ?   Twenty thousand copies of *The Lady of the Lake* were sold in four months, and it is credibly reported that the sales of *Rokeby* amount to little more than half that number."   To this I could not reply, as I had reason to believe the statement to be true ; and soon afterwards the party broke up.   I had noticed that Parker, my uncle's butler, had appeared greatly interested in the discussion, and as I was passing from the room I said to him : " Are you too a reader of Lord Byron ? "   He looked somewhat embarrassed.

" Not to say a reader, sir," he replied, " but Fanny, she reads his lordship's works out in the kitchen, sir, and I listen at odd times when my duties do not call me away. All the women in the kitchen, sir, my wife and all, they rave about his lordship and his poems."

" And what do you think of them ? " I asked.

" They are the only reading I ever took to," he answered, " but they do seem to liven a man up, and make him see things he never saw before."

I could say nothing, so I went on my way upstairs. Stolid Parker and his pious wife, flighty Fanny and clumsy Emma, all gloating over Lord Byron like their betters !   It was too much.

IN THE DAYS OF THE REGENCY

April 6, 1814. It is a long time since I inserted in my journal-letter the literary paragraph that I promised you, and I must begin this one with a confession. I am now a devoted admirer of Lord Byron, but I flatter myself that mine is not the foolish, unreasoning rapture of the multitude, but the calm, considered judgment of an intelligent reader who has studied the poems and weighed their merits. I read, as I told you I should do, *Childe Harold* and *The Giaour*, and also *The Bride of Abydos* and *The Corsair*, which have since appeared, and I found in them beauties which I could not but approve and admire. The descriptions are superb, and as I read strange and beautiful lands unfold themselves before my eyes. I no longer desire to accept my uncle's offer and remain with him with a view to a partnership in his business, and must beg of you to represent to my father that I feel myself unfitted for such a life. I wish to travel, at least for a few years, and if my father does not think fit to supply me with the necessary funds I will take ship as a sailor, or in any humble capacity, that I may have a chance of those adventures which never come to dull clogs chained to a desk in a counting-house. Like Childe Harold, I will visit the " renown'd, romantic land " of Spain ; like Conrad, I will sail where the waves of the Ægean spread " their long array of sapphire and of gold." How noble are all Lord Byron's heroes ! I picture them with the princely, almost godlike poise of the head that distinguishes their creator, for I have seen Lord Byron now several times as he has emerged from some festivity of which he has been the dazzling and admired centre.

August 21. I have received your letter, and will, as you wish, remain here until the term originally fixed for my stay is ended, but I think it right to assure you that there is no chance that I shall change my mind and give up the dazzling possibilities that Lord Byron's poems have placed before me. I wish to be a dutiful son, and am not unmindful of the affection and care that you and my father have lavished upon me ; but I feel within me longings for a fuller and a larger life. Until the time comes when I may cast off my fetters I will try to accomplish the dull and irksome tasks set me in such a manner as will gain your approbation.

March 1815. You ask me if anyone reads anything at all except the works of Lord Byron, so I will endeavour to give you some account of the other books which engage some of the public attention. Last July there appeared a new novel called *Waverley, or 'Tis Sixty Years Since*, which took the town by storm. It was published anonymously, and there have been all sorts of guesses as to its authorship. I have read it, and agree that it is a work of genius, though its hero is a commonplace creature enough beside the glorious figures that live in the pages of Byron. There are also two works from the pen of a young lady named Miss Jane Austen, of which my uncle thinks very highly. I think I mentioned in a previous letter that he had praised her *Sense and Sensibility*. She has now published *Pride and Prejudice* and *Mansfield Park*, and from these my uncle professes to have obtained a higher degree of enjoyment than he has done from any novel since *John Buncle*. I do not myself care for them. They seem to me tame and commonplace, with nothing to excite the fancy or fire the spirit. They are, however, attracting a considerable number of readers, especially among people of a somewhat fastidious literary taste.

Southey's *Don Roderick*, an epic poem, I find pleasant enough reading, though it does not compare with Byron. Wordsworth has published a long poem called *The Excursion*, which has excited even more ridicule than the *Lyrical Ballads*.

This, I think, is all that I can tell you of London's reading, and these works the public only glances at in its intervals between reading and rereading Byron. For, indeed, everything else in comparison seems pale and insipid. Lord Byron is now married to a Miss Milbanke, and lives in Piccadilly Terrace. He has published no poems since his marriage, and all London is eagerly awaiting a work from him under his altered circumstances.

February 1816. London is in a ferment. Lord Byron and his wife have separated, and he is being charged with sins of the most dark and terrible description. All the charges are vague, and no one seems to know what it really is that he is supposed to have done. The rank and fashion of the town, however, are resolved to put all the blame upon him, and to regard his wife as an injured saint. It is said that he went last night to a rout and that the fine ladies who up to this time have flattered and caressed him literally turned their backs upon him. He is cut by every one. Among people of less exalted rank, however, he still has faithful admirers. I for one shall never believe that the author of those divine poems can be base ; and Macilray, Thompson, and I have resolved to stand up for him against the world.

April 1816. Lord Byron has left the country. The glory of England has departed. None can blame him, for the treatment he has received has been vile beyond description. My blood boils in my veins when I think of it.

I am willing, since you wish it, to return home and consult with you and my father as to my future career. But my mind is made up. Nothing can take from me the vision which Lord Byron's poems have opened up before me, and to those visions I will be true.

CHAPTER XIV

THE WAVERLEY NOVELS AND THEIR READERS

THE summer of 1814 came in with pleasant stirrings of relief and hopefulness all over the British Islands. The war, it was joyfully proclaimed, was over. For the first time for eleven years the country was at peace. Napoleon was safely disposed of in Elba, and would, so the hopeful believed, trouble Europe no more. There remained only the settlement of a continent that had suffered a disintegrating upheaval at his hands, and in this England naturally took the liveliest interest. All through the bright, crowded weeks of that memorable summer the newspapers made enthralling reading, and there were many people who read little else. Books were put aside, and new publications had but a poor chance of receiving proper attention. Byron still kept his place, and his two latest works, *Lara* and *The Corsair*, were declared to be even more entrancing than those that had gone before. All the new Minerva novels were furnished with heroes handsome, dark, unhappy, and wicked, whose curling lips and bare-throated negligence of attire were of the true Byronic type, so that the popularity of the novel increased with that of the poet, and love-lorn maidens and moon-struck youths conspired to build up the fortunes of the astute William Lane. But the sale of Scott's *Rokeby* showed a sad falling-off compared with that of *Marmion*; Southey's *Don Roderick* attracted little attention; *Mansfield Park* had a small though appreciative circle of admirers; and Wordsworth's *Poems* lay unsold on the shelves of the booksellers.

On July 7, in the midst of all the excitement and rejoicing, there came from an Edinburgh firm of publishers a new novel called *Waverley, or 'Tis Sixty Years Since*. It was in three small volumes, poorly printed on poor paper, and its price was one guinea. There was no author's name on its title-

224

page, and nothing to mark it out from the other novels that were appearing by hundreds. Yet very soon people began to talk about it, and before the summer was over all the Edinburgh worthies who loved a good book, and knew one when they saw it, had grown quite excited over *Waverley* and its unknown author. Some vowed that it was the work of Jeffrey, editor of *The Edinburgh Review*, and argued stoutly with those who were equally certain that it was the work of Professor Dugald Stewart ; there was a party in favour of William Erskine, and a stronger party which maintained that there were passages in the book which could have been written by no one but Walter Scott ; while others admitted that there was a flavour of Scott about it, but were inclined to believe that the author was the poet's brother Thomas.

The fame of the book spread southward from Edinburgh and reached London. The first edition of a thousand copies was sold out in five weeks, and the delighted publishers bestirred themselves to get out another and a larger edition with as much speed as possible. Through the long, hot days of August, when London was in a flutter of excitement at the presence of foreign royalties, and the Prince Regent with his illustrious guests showed himself to cheering crowds at innumerable reviews and theatrical performances and dinners and balls, people yet found time to read *Waverley*. The Prince Regent read it, and so did Lord Byron, and, following these great examples, all fashionable and literary society read it too.

John Murray, the enterprising publisher of the *Quarterly*, managed to get hold of an early copy, and, reading it, had no doubt at all as to the author. He wrote on the title-page " By Walter Scott," and sent the book on to Canning. Canning found the opening chapters dull, and decided that the bookseller's keen judgment was for once at fault. " You are quite mistaken," he said when he saw John Murray next day, " it cannot be by Walter Scott." Murray held to his opinion, and Canning returned to the book and finished it. " Yes, it is so, you are right," he said. " Walter Scott and no one else." The copy was next sent on to Mrs Murray, who

P

was away on a visit. "Pray read *Waverley*," wrote her husband, "it is excellent. No dark passages; no secret chambers; no wind howling in long galleries." His trained perception showed him that here was an entirely new type of novel, strong and full of adventure, and not relying for its interest on the worn-out tricks of the school of Mrs Radcliffe.

Another person who was fortunate enough to receive one of the first edition copies was Miss Maria Edgeworth, of Edgeworthstown, County Longford, Ireland. It was eighteen years now since Madame D'Arblay's *Camilla* had reached the big, teeming mansion, and though there had been many changes, life was going on in much the same way as it had done in those earlier days. The fourth Mrs Edgeworth was now reigning, and the eighteenth child had been born. Mr Edgeworth was as active, as autocratic, and as full of ideas as ever; on the day the copy of *Waverley* arrived he was, his daughter records, experimenting in the dairy with a wonderful rat-trap of his own design, which the recent disappearance of two pounds of butter had made necessary. Miss Edgeworth was forty-seven years old now, a brisk, lively little lady who had won a high reputation as a writer, and had been the lion of a London season. The rule concerning poems and novels had been somewhat relaxed at Edgeworthstown, and when the three small volumes of *Waverley*, with the inscription, "From the Author," arrived they were received with rapture. Not a doubt had Maria as to who was the author, and she headed the letter of thanks that she wrote to John Ballantyne, who had forwarded the volumes, "*Aut Scotus, aut diabolus.*" "We have this moment finished *Waverley*," she went on. "It was read aloud to this large family, and I wish the author could have seen the impression it made." "We went to Coolure, and had a pleasant day," she wrote to her aunt.

Waverley was in everybody's hands. The Admiral does not like it. The hero, he says, is such a shuffling fellow. While he was saying this I had in my pocket a letter from Miss Fanshawe, received this morning, saying it was delightful. Mr and Mrs Pollard have spent a day here, and brought with them Miss Napier. We talked over *Waverley* with her. I am

ILLUSTRATION TO "WAVERLEY," BY GEORGE CRUIKSHANK

226

more delighted with it than I can tell you; it is a work of first-rate genius.

By October *Waverley* had made its way into the English circulating libraries. Miss Mary Russell Mitford found it in the weekly parcel she received from Reading, along with *The Miraculous Nuptials, The Invisible Hand,* and other works of the same kind, in which she delighted. Miss Mitford was twenty-seven years old now, and prided herself on her fine literary taste ; and, indeed, it was surprisingly good considering that it had been nourished largely on Minerva novels, of which she had read four or five a week ever since she had left school in 1806. She was still plain and plump, and still lived in the fine house at Grasely, and read her novels in the comfortable morning-room, with its crimson carpet and curtains. Like Miss Edgeworth, she quickly made up her mind as to the authorship of *Waverley*. " Have you read Walter Scott's *Waverley* ? " she wrote to Sir William Elford, who was one of several people with whom she kept up a literary correspondence. " I have ventured to say Walter Scott's, though I hear he denies it, just as a young girl denies the imputation of a lover ; but if there be any belief in internal evidence it must be his." Sir William, it appears, was not so certain, and wrote giving some of the arguments on the other side. Miss Mitford's faith was only slightly shaken. " I am still firmly of opinion that Walter Scott had some hand in *Waverley*," she wrote two months later, " and I know not the evidence that should induce me to believe that Dugald Stewart had anything to do with it."

When *Guy Mannering* appeared in February 1815 Miss Mitford became an advocate on the other side. " I do not think that Scott wrote *Guy Mannering*," she declared, " it is not nearly so like him as *Waverley*." But most people held staunchly to the belief that the two novels were by the same hand, and that that hand was Walter Scott's. The three unpretentious-looking volumes of *Guy Mannering* took their places beside the three *Waverleys* on every drawing-room table. At afternoon kettledrums and evening parties fine ladies in short-waisted satin gowns, and with tall feathers waving gracefully above their piled-up hair, vowed that they should never rest until they found out who really had written those delightful stories, and fine gentlemen in knee-breeches and lace cravats offered long odds on the favourite and found nobody willing to take them.

Crabb Robinson, who sometimes found himself in fashionable drawing-rooms, heard a good deal about the new work ; but he had been following the fate of Wordsworth's *Excursion*, which had been published at nearly the same time as *Waverley*, and had concerned himself little about other writers. But one day in March 1815 he dined with John Payne Collier, and at the table the subject of conversation was, of course, *Waverley*. When Mrs Collier found that Crabb Robinson had not read the book of which everybody was talking she offered to lend it to him, and he took it back with him to his chambers, resolving to read it very carefully, and form his own opinion on the much lauded work. He ordered his tea to be brought in, then locked his door, and sat down to read steadily through the first volume ; and he recorded in his diary that the book had " more than the usual portion of good sense " " and might enjoy though not immortality, at least a long life." It was, on the whole, a generous verdict, seeing that *Waverley* was selling by thousands, and that scarcely anyone spoke of *The Excursion* except to mock at it. He might have been pardoned if he had felt some of the jealousy which Jane Austen affected when she wrote in 1815 to Cassandra : " Walter Scott has no business to write novels, especially good ones. It is not fair. I do not mean to like *Waverley* if I can help it, but I fear I must."

During the twelve years that followed the appearance of *Guy Mannering* the Waverley Novels came regularly, one or sometimes two in a year. All the novel-readers in the country, and many who would have spurned that title, and who hated William Lane and denounced his library, waited impatiently for each new issue. Rumours as to the subject of the next novel and the date of its appearance flew about the town ; and fashionable ladies, like the three Misses Clifton in *Granby*, who wished to be thought a little ' blue ' took care always to know something about the new Scotch novel before anyone else did.

THE WAVERLEY NOVELS

On December 1, 1816, came the first of the series of *Tales of my Landlord*, the publisher in this case being John Murray. A fortnight later this happy man wrote to Scott :

> I believe I might, under any oath that might be proposed, swear that I never experienced such unmixed pleasure as the reading of this exquisite work has afforded me ; and if you could see me as the author's literary chamberlain receiving the unanimous and vehement praises of every one who has read it, and the curses of those whose needs my scanty supply could not satisfy, you might judge of the sincerity with which I now entreat you to assure him of the most complete success. Lord Holland said, when I asked his opinion,—" Opinion ! We did not one of us go to bed last night—nothing slept but my gout." Frere, Hallam, Boswell, Lord Glenbervie, William Lamb, all agree that it surpasses all the other novels. Gifford's estimate is increased at every reperusal. Heber says there are only two men in the world—Walter Scott and Lord Byron. Between you, you have given existence to a THIRD.
>
> Ever your faithful servant,
JOHN MURRAY

" The whole world," said that industrious contributor to the Minerva Press, Mrs Kitty Cuthbertson, in her Introduction to *The Hut and the Castle*,

> from the learned heads of universities to the ragged pupils of our national schools, consume their leisure hours in reading the works of one prolific novelist ; he who supersedes the pursuit of old black letter literature ; he from whose heroines our fair ones form their manners ; he whose muse supplies the patriot with strains for melodies to whet their courage and their sword. And who can dare to enter the lists, even to seek for food, where such a mighty warrior rides triumphant ? nay, now rides, like Phœbus, in his daily race alone.

This, as Bottom says, was lofty ; and there is more in the same strain. Jane Austen's playful complaint, " It is not fair," becomes when translated into the diction of this other lady novelist (so beloved of young Thomas Macaulay) :

> The eagle has forsaken his own track and descended from the lofty soar of epic poetry to pipe in the hedgerows, where all the finches used to chirp their humble lays that drew for them the boon of bread from many a patronizing damsel's hand.

In spite of all complaints, playful or pathetic, Walter Scott continued to write good novels ; the eagle remained upon the hedgerow, though it is by no means certain that he supplanted the finches in the favour of the patronizing damsels. Hazlitt says most decidedly that he did not. " If put to the vote of all the milliner's girls in London," declares this uncompromising critic, " *Old Mortality* or even *The Heart of Midlothian* would not carry the day (or at least not very triumphantly) over a common Minerva Press novel." He tells how he once asked for the Scotch novels at the circulating library of a country watering-place. The young lady who kept the library in conjunction with a milliner's shop had a poor opinion of these works. They were so dry she could hardly get through them, she said, and she advised him to try *Agnes*. She did not know that this shabby, slouching, loud-voiced stranger was a man whose opinion concerning books would be listened to respectfully by almost every one in England, and she did not know that he dearly loved the Waverley Novels. No one praised Scott more finely than Hazlitt did. " His works (taken together) are almost like a new edition of human nature," he wrote. " This is indeed to be an author."

Francis Place would have been in agreement with the young lady of the circulating library as to the difficulty of getting through the Waverley Novels ; he had tried several at different times, he said, and had never been able to finish one of them. But he would not have read a page of one of her favourite Minerva Press productions, and she would have found his books drier even than the Waverleys. In the two classes represented by these so widely different types of readers were to be found most of those who in that generation refused allegiance to Walter Scott. The young lady had a crowd of empty-headed, ill-educated girls behind her ; the Radical workman stood for a smaller company—including probably Bentham, the two Mills, and the rest of the Utilitarians—whose intellect had developed at the expense of their imagination and their humour.

These two classes, however, formed but a small proportion of the reading public, and the enthusiasm of the rest gave them small chance of making themselves felt. Macaulay, then a student at Cambridge, used to walk out for miles along the London road to meet the coach that was bringing a new Waverley. Lord Glenbervie, formerly Chief Secretary for Ireland, told John Murray, with tears in his eyes, that the first series of *Tales of my Landlord* had been a cordial that had saved Lady Glenbervie's life. Sydney Smith in his country parish declared that when a new Waverley appeared " turnips, sermons, and justice business were all forgotten," and an American lady wrote to a friend of Scott's saying that she had called her farm in Massachusetts "Charlie's Hope" after the farm in *Rob Roy* and declaring that she could never be happy until she knew who really had written all those wonderful novels.

Most people in England had by this time made up their minds that "the Great Unknown" was Scott, though as late as January 1817 Lord Glenbervie wrote in his diary:

> Who is the author of *Waverley*, *Guy Mannering*, *The Antiquary*, and *The Tales of My Landlord*? All the world seems agreed that the same author (or perhaps co-authors) wrote the *Tales* and the three other most successful novels, so successful that they will probably occupy a distinguished and permanent place among English classics, and form a sort of epoch in that species of writing.

Scott still persisted in his silence, and outside the small circle of friends who were in his confidence he never by word or sign gave any support to the general belief in his authorship. Novel followed novel, each without a name on its title-page ; the sales mounted higher and higher ; readers grew used to welcoming a new Waverley at least once a year, and could scarcely think of the time when the supply should fail them.

In December 1819 came *Ivanhoe*. It had an immediate sale of twelve thousand copies, although the price of the three volumes—which were larger and more finely printed on better paper than the others had been—was raised to thirty shillings. Readers in England declared that it was better than any that had gone before, and though all loyal Scots maintained that the new novel lost vastly by the scene being changed from Scotland to England, they agreed that it was a wonderful story. John Allen wrote off to Constable, the publisher: "Pray make the author go on. I am sure he has five or six more novels in him, therefore five or six more holidays for the whole kingdom." " I was sure you would like *Ivanhoe*," said Miss Mitford to her friend Mrs Hofland. " Rebecca is divine." Every one fell in love with the beautiful, unhappy Jewish heroine. Mary Hays, writing from her shabby lodging in a dingy London street to her friend, the stout-hearted Mrs Fenwick, described Rebecca as a " holy creature," whose " excellences are perfect specimens of the Moral-Sublime." Mrs Fenwick was in Barbados at this time, with her daughter Eliza, struggling hopefully to establish a school for young ladies, by which she expected to make the family fortunes. She replied that she had read eight of Scott's novels with delight, and that she " found in *Ivanhoe* a chivalric, lofty tone that inspires enthusiasm." She thought Rebecca " the most saintly creature I ever met in print," and her father " a masterly portrait of the characteristic features, both good and bad, of that extraordinary people." William Thackeray, then a fair-haired, chubby boy at a preparatory school, loved Rebecca too, but with a less exalted and more personal affection than that felt by these excellent ladies. He dreamed of her at night, and drew portraits of her in his school-books by day. " Rebecca, daughter of Isaac of York," he wrote long afterward,

> I have loved thee faithfully for forty years ! Thou wert twenty years old (say) and I but twelve when I knew thee. At sixty odd, love, most of the ladies of thy Orient race have lost the bloom of youth, and bulged beyond the line of beauty, but to me thou art ever young and fair, and I will do battle with any felon Templar who assails thy fair name.

In 1820 came *The Monastery* and *The Abbot*, which were neither of them nearly as much liked as *Ivanhoe*. Countess Cowper called them both " strange hodge-podges " that bore the marks of having been " written hastily and without much thought." Miss Mitford thought *The Monastery* showed a falling-off, and Mrs Fenwick declared that the book pained her. " I did not like," she said, " that this genius should adopt a supernatural agency, and that of no dignified kind. It has, however, fine portraits and beautiful passages."

Kenilworth, which appeared in the next year, won back all

the old popularity, and the triumphant series went on with *The Pirate, The Fortunes of Nigel, Peveril of the Peak,* and *Quentin Durward.* Byron, who had read all the Waverley Novels and took them with him in his restless wanderings all over Europe, wrote impatiently from Pisa to say that he had not received *The Pirate,* published a year before. Caroline Stuart-Wortley, daughter of Lady Wharncliffe, was staying at Welbeck with the Duchess of Portland when *Peveril* was published. " It is the most ridiculous thing here," she wrote to her grandmother, Lady Erne, " there are five or six copies in this house, and everybody comes into the room with a volume under their arm."

None of the later novels had quite the marvellous success of the earlier ones, though *The Talisman,* published in 1825, came very near to doing so. But there were frequent reprints of the older favourites, and these were read and reread with interest that never failed. Sir James Mackintosh said he had read *Old Mortality* four times in English and once in French. Mark Rutherford in *The Revolution in Tanner's Lane* shows us a country ironmonger and his wife to whom Walter Scott had been

> what he can only be to people leading a dull life far from the world. He had broken up its monotony and created a new universe. He had introduced them into a royal society of noble friends. . . . *Kenilworth* or *Redgauntlet* was taken down, and the reader was at once in another country and in another age, transported as if by some Arabian charm away from Cowfold cares.

There were many families like these Allens of Cowfold, and many men and women who would have agreed with all their hearts with Mark Rutherford when he went on to say: " If anywhere in another world the blessings which men have conferred here are taken into account in distributing reward, surely the choicest in the store of the Most High will be reserved for his servant Scott ! "

The new generation that was growing up was being nurtured on the Waverley Novels. Fathers read them aloud in the evenings to entranced families, and boys and girls watched for opportunities to seize upon the copies belonging to their elders and snatch a few breathless, golden moments of pure delight. Boys at school held *Ivanhoe* inside their open Latin grammar, and forgot declensions while they fought for Rebecca in the lists, until a heavy blow, not from a knightly lance, but from a schoolmaster's lexicon, brought the contest to an unseemly end. William Makepeace Thackeray remembered, distinctly and unrepentantly, several such incidents in the course of his own school career. Edward FitzGerald never forgot how, being then aged sixteen, he prowled round the booksellers' shops at Ipswich, and, happening on a copy of *The Talisman*, read some pages and saw glimmerings of a new world ; and to Walter Bagehot there came something of the same experience when he was a small boy of eight and his mother read *Quentin Durward* to his step-brother while he was ' doing sums ' in the same room.

The walls of narrow nurseries, cramped schoolrooms, and stuffy parlours suddenly opened out before these lucky young people for whom " the Great Unknown " had worked his magic. They saw strange lands and far-off seas, dark, craggy mountains, and wide spaces where the wind of adventure blew with joyous roughness. Knights in full armour rode down country lanes and through the crowded streets of towns. At any moment one might meet a blue-gowned Edie Ochiltree, a Locksley in his green mantle, Dominie Sampson, learned and uncouth, or poor demented Madge Wildfire. Beside these people, so living and so individual, the children's story-book characters—the Fairchild family, Rosamund deceived by the purple jar, Mr Barlowe and his pupils—sank into mere pale figures of edification. Even Robinson Crusoe and his man Friday and the fascinating company of *The Pilgrim's Progress* seemed a little dim and stiff when the vivid, gallant band from the Waverley Novels poured in to take their places beside them.

Very soon the young people grew joyously familiar with these new companions. Pretty, fair-haired John Ruskin, living the secluded life of a cherished only son in the stately house on Denmark Hill, knew them well by the time he was six years old ; from Saladin to Steenie Micklebaite they bore him company in the solitary nursery and the quiet garden

A Scene from "Peveril of the Peak"

W. Q. Orchardson

Photo T. and R. Annan

234

where most of his leisure time was spent. Eight-year-old Mary Ann Evans knew only a few of them, for she had read none of the novels except part of *Waverley* in a copy that had been lent to her elder sister, and returned before she could finish it. Yet when she looked up from her work of laboriously writing out what she could remember of the story in the pleasant dining-room of Griff House she saw, not her father resting in his big leather chair on one side of the fire and her pale mother busily knitting on the other, but the court of Tully Veolan, the tall figure of the Baron of Bradwardine and the sturdy one of Evan Dhu, and Fergus MacIvor Vich Ian Vohr in his Highland dress, with the eagle's feather in his bonnet.

The little Brontës in their bleak Northern home were free of all Sir Walter's magical realms. Staid Charlotte knew what it was to pass enchanted hours in stately Kenilworth, in the company of my lord of Leicester, poor Amy Robsart, the Great Queen, and the villain Varney. She spoke her pleasure, primly enough, according to her custom. " In my opinion," she wrote to her friend Ellen Nussey, "*Kenilworth* is one of the most interesting works that ever emanated from the great Sir Walter's pen " ; but she felt it, as she felt all pleasures and all pains, with quiet intensity. She was, in almost every respect, unlike high-spirited, tempestuous Fanny Kemble, but in their love of Scott they were at one. " One great intellectual good fortune befell me at this time," wrote Fanny, concerning her fourteenth year, " and that was reading *Guy Mannering*, the first of Walter Scott's novels I ever read—the dearest, therefore."

It was well for these young people that the works of Scott were not classed with ordinary novels, but were held, even by many of the Evangelicals, to have none of the pernicious influence of that banned form of literature. Jonathan Gray read them, and allowed his daughter Margaret to read them. When Margaret was nearly fourteen years old she was taken for a tour in the Isle of Man. " Yesterday it rained all day," she wrote in her diary. " However, we got some of *The Tales of my Landlord*, which we read all day." When they left Douglas to return home she found in the cabin of the ship a copy of *The Fortunes of Nigel*. She took it up, and forgot everything else—forgot to watch the shores of the island as they faded from sight, forgot that she was hungry or thirsty, forgot her companions. She went on reading it all day, and finished it before the evening. Clarissa Trant too read *The Fortunes of Nigel*, and told her brother that though it was not as generally liked as Sir Walter's former books, she thought the character of the times was admirably preserved. Her book-lists show that she read also *St Ronan's Well*, *Redgauntlet*, and *Woodstock*.

But all those Evangelicals who read the Waverley Novels did so at their peril ; they sinned wilfully, not in ignorance, for in a book called *The Student's Guide*, which was well known and highly regarded among them, the evil character of these productions was very fully set out. The book was written by the Reverend John Todd, an American divine, and the English edition was edited by the Reverend Thomas Dale, who was the headmaster of the private school to which John Ruskin went for a time when he was sixteen years old. " Beware of Bad Books," said the pious Mr Todd, and went on to caution his readers especially against Byron, Bulwer, and Scott. He himself had, he admitted, read the pernicious works of these authors ; he had done so because it was his duty to sound " the rocks and quicksands in the sea of literature " that he might warn others against them ; but he solemnly declared that

> the only good he is conscious of ever having received from them is a deep impression that men who possess gifts of such compass and power and so perverted in their application must meet the day of judgment under a responsibility which would be cheaply removed by the price of a world.

The Reverend Mr Dale strongly urged his pupils to accept this book as an infallible guide for their reading. John Ruskin read it, and was infuriated. He considered himself quite as good an Evangelical as Mr Dale, and he considered his mother a far better one ; yet he had been brought up on the Waverley Novels and had been allowed to read both Byron and Bulwer. So when one day Mr Dale set as a theme for an essay " Does the Perusal of Works of Fiction

act favourably or unfavourably on the Moral Character?"
young Ruskin joyously prepared himself for battle. He
wrote a long essay (which is still to be seen in the British
Museum) defending the three authors so piously damned
by the Reverend John Todd against the attacks of " old
maids of jaundiced eye and acidulated lip " who pose as
philosophers and " assert that whatever is amusing must
be criminal." Scott, he declared, was a great moral teacher,
Bulwer a novelist who showed life as it really was, Byron
a genius whose fame had been for a time smirched by the
" crawling things " that had attacked it.

An interesting ' imaginary conversation ' would be that
which might have taken place had Mrs Ruskin ever met
Mrs Warren, wife of a barrister of Norwich, and the two
ladies had conversed on the education of their sons, especially
with regard to this subject of novel-reading. In 1820,
when John Ruskin was a year old and his mother had
already formed her plan for bringing him up to a perfect
manhood, Mrs Warren's eldest son had lately gone to Kingswood boarding-school. From there he wrote to his mother
a terrible confession : " I am afraid that I have injured my
mind by that pernicious kind of amusement, the reading of
novels." He did not say what books he had read nor where
he had obtained them, but he acknowledged that they had
made it difficult for him to give his attention to " Moral
and Religious Subjects." His distracted mother answered
in the highest state of agitation :

> Were I not to check myself I should be hurried away into
> immoderate grief, to the injury of my health, by entertaining
> the melancholy thought that my child has left the *ennobling
> subject* on which Angels delight to dwell and is now about to
> crawl serpentlike among the potsherds of the earth ! Yes,
> my Boy ! could you flourish in romance like the celebrated
> Sir W. Scott with his fictions I should despise your insect-like
> works, and think them fit only for the butterflies of the day.

If she had known, she said, that works of fiction would be
placed within his reach at Kingswood school she would have
taken measures to prevent the terrible consequences that
had followed from his being exposed to this temptation.

237

She had hoped that his previous training would have been sufficient to keep him in the right way. He had never been allowed to read a work of fiction except *The History of the Earl of Moreland*, which was a pious work tending wholly to edification, and *Robinson Crusoe*, which he "had with sufficient admonitions that we did not consider it a proper book for you because, although originally founded on fact, yet it carries with it too much of the character of Novels and Romances." Mrs Warren adjures her son to read, as a corrective to the soul-destroying works of fiction which have done him so much harm, *Macarius on Christian Perfection* and other Evangelical publications.

The Reverend Mr Davies, father of Emily Davies, the founder of Girton College, would have been in entire agreement with Mrs Warren. At his house at Ashling, near Chichester, the novels of Sir Walter Scott were forbidden, and the evenings were spent in reading aloud such improving works as Rollin's *Ancient History* and *Paradise Lost*.

Charles Greville, commenting in his *Memoirs* in 1829 on the prodigious sale of cheap editions of the Waverley Novels, says that it is due to a new class of readers having been produced by the Bell and Lancaster schools. It is certain that a great many among the less educated classes in England and Scotland knew Sir Walter and his works. Mrs Hughes, wife of Canon Hughes, of St Paul's, tells how, in 1824, she and her husband paid a short visit to Edinburgh, and, walking one evening on the Calton, met two old burghers. The visitors made some inquiry about St Leonard's Craigs, and one of the old men pointed them out. " Ye'll hae read they tales ? " he asked. " Oh, yes," said the lady. " Ye'll see that house ower by the red-tiled roof, that is Dumbies' house, and up beyont is the auld Covenanter's—I canna mind the name." " Douce Davie," supplied the lady. " Ay, ay, just sae—weel, and there's a window whar the puir misguided lassie got out after she had the mischance." To these old men Dumbiedikes and Davie Deans and pretty Effie were as real and familiar as their next-door neighbours.

Samuel Rogers told Macaulay that when Sir Walter dined at the house of a certain gentleman in London all the servant-maids asked leave to stand in the passage and see him pass ; and it is recorded that a London fishmonger, having refused to send some Yarmouth bloaters so far as Sussex Place, relented at once when he was told they were for Sir Walter. " Sir Walter Scott ! God bless my soul ! They shall be with him to-night—no, not to-night, for to-morrow morning at seven o'clock a fresh cargo comes in, and he shall have them for his breakfast if I carry them myself. Sir Walter Scott ! "

Two years later, when the author of the Waverley Novels was lying half unconscious and very near to death in St James's Hotel, Jermyn Street, a little group of working men gathered at the corner of the street, and one of them anxiously asked Allan Cunningham as he passed, " Do you know, sir, if this is the street where he is lying ? "—as if, says Mr Lockhart, there were but one deathbed in London.

It is possible that these men who held Sir Walter in such familiar yet reverent affection had not read all, perhaps not any, of his works. But the Waverley Novels, like the Bible and Shakespeare, had even then become part of the Englishman's inheritance. " His thoughts and beauties are so spread abroad that one touches them everywhere ; one is intimate with him by instinct," said one of Miss Austen's characters of Shakespeare. A hundred years ago —fifty years ago—this was true of Scott. It is perhaps not quite true now, though there are still a goodly number ready to claim their heritage and to show themselves the true descendants of those who, in the early days of the nineteenth century, were the first readers of the Waverley Novels.

CHAPTER XV

A SUPPER AT CHARLES LAMB'S AND A DINNER
AT HOLLAND HOUSE

SIR THOMAS NOON TALFOURD, in his *Final Memorials of Charles Lamb*, makes a comparison between the dinners given by Lord and Lady Holland at their Kensington mansion and the Wednesday evening suppers at the lodgings of Charles and Mary Lamb. " These two rare circles of social enjoyment," he says, " may without offence be placed side by side in grateful recollection by those who were fortunate enough to take part in both of them." Sir Thomas was one of these fortunate people, and he has set down something of what he saw and heard at both houses for the benefit of those who have not been so highly favoured. Various writers, notably Hazlitt and Macaulay, have described one or other of the meetings, so that, putting the several accounts together, we are able to see these great men of the past as they gathered to talk and eat and enjoy one another's company in all the ease of pleasant and familiar surroundings. They were readers, every one of them ; they loved books and had a fine taste in selecting their favourites. Books and reading were the things chiefly talked about at Charles Lamb's ; and at Holland House, though politics, perhaps, came first, the second place was given to literature. Nowhere can the Englishman and his books be better studied than in Lamb's homely parlour and Lord Holland's stately dining-room.

The Lambs' famous Wednesday evenings began soon after they came to live at Mitre Court Buildings in the Temple in 1801, and went on, at their various lodgings, until they left London for Enfield in 1827. The brother and sister both disliked visiting. They were shy and uncomfortable in strange houses, and the older they grew the more unwilling they were to leave their own home. But

240

they had many friends, and Charles delighted in company and conversation ; and since he would not visit them, these friends came to visit him. Two or three would drop in almost every evening in the week, and stop, talking and drinking, until the small hours of the morning, so that Charles had no time to himself, could get no work done, and grew harassed and wretched. So it came about that one particular evening in the week was fixed for these visits, and this brought some improvement. " All great men have public days," said Lamb ; and in this way the Wednesday evenings were established.

All who loved good talk and good company were welcome. " Wit and good-fellowship was the motto inscribed over the door," says Hazlitt. " When a stranger came in it was not asked, ' Has he written anything ? ' We were above that pedantry. If he could take a hand at picquet he was welcome to sit down. We abhorred insipidity, affectation, and fine gentlemanliness."

In March 1809 the Lambs removed to No. 4 Inner Temple Lane, and it was during the eight years that they lived in these chambers that the Wednesday evenings were in their greatest glory. Talfourd says that these years were the happiest the brother and sister ever spent. They were in better health and spirits than at most periods of their lives, and there was a little more money coming in to lessen the wearing anxiety as to ways and means. Most of their friends were near enough to come with fair regularity to what Lamb called his ' levee.' " We play at whist," he said, " eat cold meat and hot potatoes, and any gentleman that chooses smokes."

Charles came home from his day's work at the India House about five o'clock, usually very tired and a little out of temper. Mary had a meal ready for him—a savoury steak, or the fried tripe that he loved—and she listened with calm cheerfulness to his peevish laments over the hours wasted in distasteful office work ; and very soon his good humour came back, and he began to laugh at his own complainings, and was his whimsical, delightful self once more. Then he and Mary sat comfortably by the fire for a time—

Charles a small, frail figure dressed in sober black, with a nobly shaped head covered with crisply curling black hair and a face beautiful, humorous, and sad, Mary homely and substantial, her face kindly and intellectual, her garments quaint and old-fashioned. The brother smoked his pipe and read one of his favourite Elizabethans; the sister darned socks and listened appreciatively to passages which Charles now and then read out to her.

Soon after nine o'clock Mary and Becky, the old servant, began to bestir themselves. They pulled the large table over to the side of the room and made it ready for supper to be served upon it later on. They set out two smaller tables with packs of cards and the cribbage board. They tidied the room, putting away the books and papers with which Charles had already contrived to strew it. They swept the hearth, and made the fire burn brightly. The room, with its low, smoke-stained ceiling, its heavy, old-fashioned furniture, and the treasured Hogarth prints in narrow black frames adorning its walls, looked homely and hospitable, and Mary Lamb, surveying it with satisfaction, looked as homely and hospitable as her room.

About ten o'clock footsteps would be heard coming up the three long flights of stairs that led to this high-perched chamber— soft, slow footsteps if, as often happened, the first-comer was William Godwin. He was a small, spare man, with a big head and a small voice, and a manner smooth, gentle, and almost cringing. It was difficult to think of him as the author of the revolutionary *Political Justice* and much easier to associate him with the shop in Skinner Street where he now sold books for children. He still read widely, and considered himself an authority on literary matters; and in argument he was apt to expect his pronouncements to be accepted as final.

Crabb Robinson would perhaps be the next, coming up quickly, eager to discuss Wordsworth's latest poem. He was practising as a lawyer now, and living at Hatton Garden, where he had an excellent collection of books, from which Lamb often borrowed. Then there was Captain Burney, brother of the famous Fanny, who in his younger days had

ONE OF CHARLES LAMB'S HAUNTS IN THE TEMPLE
Looking from Mitre Court to King's Bench Walk.
Photo Herbert Felton

A SUPPER AT CHARLES LAMB'S

been a sailor and adventured into unknown seas with Captain Cook. He was old now—" a humourous old man, . . . with a rough exterior," says Crabb Robinson. Books were his chief companions and his greatest joy, and, like Lamb, he delighted in old dusty tomes that few people read. After him came a gaunt, awkward man in a very shabby coat, and trousers shrunk so that they showed his bony ankles. This was George Dyer, the classical scholar, who was so absorbed in his books that he forgot to buy himself new clothes or even to have his meals. He knew little of Lamb's beloved Elizabethans. " I found," said Charles,

> that he *had* read Shakespeare (whom he called an original but irregular genius) : but it was a good while ago ; and he has dipped into Rowe and Otway, I suppose having found their names in *Johnson's Lives* at full length. He never seemed even to have heard of Fletcher, Ford, Marlowe, Massinger, and the worthies of Dodsley's collection.

Dyer had introduced Lamb to a certain John Rickman, who had forthwith become one of the most regular attendants at the Wednesday evenings during the time that he was in town. " He is a most pleasant hand," wrote Charles to Thomas Manning,

> a fine rattling fellow, has gone through life laughing at solemn apes—himself hugely literate, oppressively full of information in all stuff of conversation, from matter of fact to Xenophon and Plato—can talk Greek with Porson, politics with Thelwall, conjecture with George Dyer, nonsense with me, and anything with anybody, a great farmer, somewhat concerned in an agri- cultural magazine ; reads no poetry but Shakespeare.

One after another the guests came dropping in. There was Jem White, " who carried away half the fun of the world when he died—of my world at least," said Lamb. There was Bryan Procter the poet, and pale-faced Charles Lloyd. There was Basil Montagu, full of his philan- thropic schemes of every sort, and impecunious Ned Phillips. To the later meetings came Thomas Talfourd, who in 1813 had left Dr Valpy's famous school at Reading, where he had been head boy, and come to live as a young law student in chambers in the Inner Temple.

He was a devoted disciple of Charles Lamb, and used to send him fruit from Covent Garden and other offerings; and Lamb introduced him to Wordsworth as "my one admirer."

Then came bustling in John Lamb—"a plump, good-looking man of seven and forty," as Charles described him in 1810. He brought with him one or two of the younger clerks of the South Sea House; they were always begging to be introduced to his famous brother, and John, puzzled and a little scornful that poor Charles had become famous, was yet pleased to take them. All these and many more found their way at one time or another to the hospitable room in the Inner Temple; they were of the Wednesday brotherhood and free of all its privileges.

Godwin and Ned Phillips, who loved their rubber, got the company settled down to cards as soon as possible, and the play and talking began. At first it was light and fragmentary, with puns and nonsense, and some baiting of the credulous George Dyer, whose head was always so deeply buried in his Greek books that he knew nothing at all of what was going on in the world round about him. The others delighted in asking him absurd questions and listening to his grave, considered answers. "What sort of man do you suppose the murderer Williams must have been?" Lamb once asked him; and he replied, "Why, I should think, Mr Lamb, he must have been rather an eccentric character." When the question as to who wrote the Waverley Novels was being discussed he contentedly accepted the assertion of the rest of the company that it must have been Lord Castlereagh.

Soon supper-time came, and Becky brought in the cold roast lamb, the boiled beef, or veal and ham pie, with a smoking dish of roasted potatoes and a frothing can of porter. She put them on the big table, and each man helped himself, while the talk went on briskly. The door opened several times while supper was going on, and late-comers, just out from the theatre, entered noisily, hungry and full of news. Hazlitt and Leigh Hunt, both of them dramatic critics on a newspaper, came regularly; so did

A SUPPER AT CHARLES LAMB'S

Ayrton, who was Director of Music at the Italian Opera; and often some of the famous actors of the time—Kemble and Liston and Lamb's beloved Miss Kelly—dropped in on their way home from the play.

The talk grew faster and louder. Discussions were begun and carried on with quips and personalities that brought shouts of delighted laughter. Hazlitt, for at least the twentieth time, tried to convince Charles Lamb that Fielding was a better writer than Smollett; and Lamb, carrying on the argument vigorously, yet contrived to have something to say in all the conversations that were going on round about him, to stammer out his puns, and shout his friendly, provocative insults. Leigh Hunt's dark, handsome face was full of fire as he discussed the doctrines of Rousseau with serious Charles Lloyd. Godwin expounded his revolutionary philosophy in a mild, pleasant voice, quoting from Locke and Berkeley and Hume. "He is quite a tame creature," Lamb assured Manning, "a middle-sized man both in stature and understanding; whereas from his noisy fame you would expect to find a Briareus Centimanus, or a Tityus tall enough to pull Jupiter from his heavens."

Somebody mentioned *John Buncle*, and Crabb Robinson remarked that he had just finished the first volume, and though it contained little that was readable that little was excellent. At once Lamb and Hazlitt and Leigh Hunt were upon him. "A healthy book," cried Lamb. "John Buncle is a famous fine man formed in Nature's most eccentric hour."

"It is famous reading, indeed," declared Leigh Hunt.

"But only in parts," maintained Crabb Robinson, "you must skip the preachments——"

"Skip nothing," roared Hazlitt. "Skip if you will whole pages of your dull *Excursion*, but read every word of our great John. It is of the rarest flavour," and he smacked his lips, recalling it.

"It is written in the highest spirits of any book I ever read," declared Lamb. "I would not give one page of it for all your *Childe Harolds* or *Ladies of the Lake*."

Crabb Robinson, receiving such a determined attack from these superior authorities, said no more.

Modern novels were scarcely esteemed as literature by these Wednesday evening assemblies. Lamb declared that he could not read them—even the better sort. Narrative teased him, he said; he could not bear *Gil Blas*, and he had no great opinion even of *Waverley*. Mary, listening quietly, smiled. It was an old point of disagreement between them, for she read every novel she could get hold of, and defended her taste stoutly upon occasion. Leigh Hunt was on her side, for he too enjoyed anything in the shape of a story. Hazlitt had nothing to say in favour of the ordinary novels, though he read a good many of them, but the Waverleys were in a different class, and no one praised them more wholeheartedly than he.

As the evening went on the talk mounted. Voices grew eager and tongues were inspired. " It was Lamb," says Hazlitt,

> who always made the best pun and the best remark in the course of the evening. His serious conversation, like his serious writings, is his best. No one ever stammered out such fine, piquant, eloquent things in half a dozen sentences as he does. His jests scald like tears, and he probes a question with a play upon words.

They talked of Shakespeare and Milton, Pope and Dryden, Steele and Addison, Swift and Gray, Smollett, Sterne, and Richardson, Hogarth's prints and Claude's landscapes. They did not care for Dr Johnson, though they admired Boswell's *Life*, and scarcely anyone had a word to say for the *Letters of Junius*. But Lamb was happiest when the talk turned on his beloved Elizabethans. " With what gusto would he describe his favourite authors—Donne or Sir Philip Sidney, and call their most crabbed passages delicious."

One evening they talked of " Persons one would wish to have seen," and Hazlitt has left us a full account of the discussion, which forms one of his most delightful essays.

Sometimes the talk turned on the play, and then each was loud in his praise of his favourite actor or actress and his best-loved playwright. Lamb defended the dramatists of the Restoration period with more than his usual whimsical brilliance. He talked of Munden and John Kemble, of Bensley and Dodd and Jack Bannister, of Mrs Jordan and Miss O'Neill. Hazlitt's favourites were Kean and Kemble and Mrs Siddons. He did not think much of the acting of Munden, and he argued hotly on Kean's claim to be placed above any other English actor.

The din grew greater, and each man raised his voice that he might be heard above it ; and through it all the card-playing went on.

> While the most critical question was pending, while the most difficult problem in philosophy was solving, Phillips cried out, " That's game," and Martin Burney muttered a quotation over the last remains of a veal pie at a side table. An utterly misinformed person might have supposed this a scene of vulgar confusion and uproar.

Sometimes, but at long intervals, Coleridge or Wordsworth came in ; and then the noisy, broken discussions changed to an inspired monologue, with an enthralled though not altogether silent audience. Coleridge would discourse eloquently in his low, beautiful voice on Shakespeare, or Kant, or some abstract question in philosophy ; and the strange music of his language and the flashing visions of pure loveliness that he brought before his hearers' eyes made even the coolest heads among them quite oblivious of the want of connexion and sequence in the rhapsody. It was Hazlitt who once said that Coleridge was an excellent talker if he were allowed to start from no premises and come to no conclusion. Samuel Rogers used to tell a story of how he and Wordsworth once listened while Coleridge spoke uninterruptedly for two hours. Wordsworth showed profound attention, and every now and then nodded his head, as if to signify agreement. When they came away Rogers said, " Well, for my part I could not make head or tail of Coleridge's oration ; pray, did you understand it ? " " Not one syllable of it," was Wordsworth's reply.

When Wordsworth talked it was usually about his own poems or some question arising out of them, and he was apt to be a little querulous if the company did not agree whole-heartedly with him. Lamb reverenced Wordsworth, but he could never resist the temptation to make fun of what seemed to him the poet's egotisms and pomposities. Hazlitt too was, on the whole, an ardent Wordsworthian, but his irritable temper led him sometimes to gibes with more sting in them than Lamb's pleasantries. So it happened once or twice that the poet went away early and a little ruffled; then those who were left took up their ordinary talk until morning came and dawn broke over the tall Temple build-ings and the trees in the court. Wednesday evening was over, and sober, workaday Thursday was upon them.

Turn we now to Talfourd's other ' social circle.' The meetings at Holland House began in the early years of the nineteenth century, when Lord Holland, nephew of Charles James Fox, came back from a long Continental tour, married, and settled down in his magnificent Kensington mansion, and they went on with few breaks until his death in 1840. The master of Holland House was almost as charming and sweet-natured, as wise and as witty, as Charles Lamb. Its mistress was very unlike the kindly, ill-starred Mary. Macaulay described her to his sisters as " a large, bold-looking woman, with the remains of a fine person and the air of Queen Elizabeth." She had also much of that great sovereign's arrogance and brusque outspokenness. Every guest who came to Holland House must submit to be under her orders, and prompt obedience was expected. " Lay down that screen, Lord Russell; you will spoil it," " Mr Allen, take a candle and show Mr Cradock the picture of Buonaparte "—such were the commands that came sharply from time to time. Occasionally there were signs of insub-ordination, as when, in answer to her order, " Ring the bell, Mr Smith," Sydney Smith is said to have replied, " Yes, certainly, and shall I sweep the floor ? " It is to her credit that she took such retorts with good temper, but the occasions when her forbearance was called for were rare. As a rule the guests obeyed, or managed tactfully to disguise their disobedience under some pretext. Lady Holland was a woman of great strength of mind, intelligent, well read,

248

fluent in speech, and, when she chose, pleasing in manner. Yet when the guests at those famous assemblies recalled the scenes over which she had ruled it was not her majestic figure that came most clearly before their eyes, but that of her gentle-mannered and courteous lord, whose cordial kindness made the youngest and rawest member of the group feel at home, and whose conversation, rich in anecdote drawn from a remarkable and crowded experience, gave the greatest charm to the evening no matter how many other brilliant talkers might be present.

Lord Holland was a Whig in the tradition of his uncle, Charles James Fox, and Holland House was, first and foremost, a Whig house, where members of the host's party met and talked over the political affairs of the day. Staunch Tories like Mrs Boscawen could not bear to hear it named. " It is the school of political corruption," declared the old lady, who was now well over eighty years of age, to Lady Morgan, " and spoils all the young men " ; and Sir Robert Lilfield, in Mrs Gore's *Manners of the Day*, denounced it as the " Hall of Eblis." It was, however, very much more than a great political house, and very many things were talked of at its famous banquets besides politics. There were few eminent men in England who had not at one time or another dined at Holland House, and distinguished foreigners considered an invitation to its hospitalities as the crowning honour and opportunity of their stay in England. " It is *the* house in all Europe," declared Charles Greville.

Thomas Noon Talfourd did not attain to the honour of a welcome there until more than fifteen years after the great day that had made him free of the shabby, hospitable apartment in Inner Temple Lane. The enthusiastic, " injudiciously loquacious " (as Crabb Robinson had called him) young law student had become a celebrated lawyer, with some reputation as a poet, and his joy and pride were great when, about 1830, he was invited to join the far-famed company of Lord Holland's guests. A year or two later another young lawyer, Thomas Babington Macaulay, the recently elected Member of Parliament for Calne, made his first appearance at the great house. These two, with Charles

Greville, Clerk to the Council, an older man who had been a regular guest for a good many years, have left us lively accounts of what happened at some of these famous entertainments.

Dinner at Holland House was at seven o'clock, and all the guests were expected to be punctual. They drove up the fine avenue of elms and came into the noble entrance hall, then followed the liveried footmen up the grand staircase to the library, which, Macaulay told his sisters, was a long room containing all the books that one ever wished to read. Here they talked together until all were assembled. Mr Allen, Lord Holland's librarian, with his big head, broad face, thick legs—" the thickest legs I ever remember," said Sydney Smith—and bright, intelligent eyes looking through enormous round silver spectacles, was always there, and Samuel Rogers, white-faced and cadaverous, and a little past the height of his fame, was such a frequent and honoured guest that he seemed almost part of the house.

The rest of the company varied from day to day. Most of the prominent Whig statesmen came frequently, and there were a few Tories. Lord Grey, the Prime Minister, was always welcome, because he had great influence with Lady Holland, and stood between her and the victims of her arrogant temper. Brougham, the Lord Chancellor, " looking like an old-clothes man and dirty as the ground " ; Palmerston, the Foreign Secretary, smiling and debonair ; good-natured, lazy Lord Melbourne of the Home Office ; and the Paymaster of the Forces, " that dangerous little Radical, Lord John Russell "—these came as often as they could. Byron during the brief years of his London popularity was a frequent guest, and dedicated his *Bride of Abydos* to Lord Holland " with every sentiment of regard and respect " ; Crabbe and Wordsworth and Walter Scott paid at least one visit to Holland House whenever they came to London. Thomas Moore was welcome for his eloquent Irish tongue, and handsome Thomas Campbell for his battle songs. Then there were the rival wits, Sydney Smith, portly and smiling, and the brilliant, popular Henry Luttrell. Of foreign visitors the most remarkable was Talleyrand, the French

THE HOLLAND HOUSE LIBRARY
C. R. Leslie

250

Ambassador, then nearly eighty years old. "He is certainly the greatest curiosity that I ever fell in with," said Macaulay.

> His head is sunk down between two high shoulders. One of his feet is hideously distorted. His face is as pale as that of a corpse, and wrinkled to a frightful degree. His eyes have an odd glassy stare quite peculiar to them. His hair, thickly powdered and pomatumed, hangs down his shoulders on each side as straight as a pound of tallow candles. His conversation, however, soon makes you forget his ugliness and infirmities.

Not many ladies came to the dinners at Holland House, but Macaulay tells of the beautiful Marchioness of Clanricarde, Canning's daughter, and the Duchess of Richmond and Mrs Vernon Smith, who came with their husbands, and Charles Greville mentions Mrs Tierney and Lord Holland's daughter, Lady Lilford. Macaulay speaks of one occasion when the guests were "all lords but me," but as a rule the company was a varied one, and lords were not preferred before commoners, other things being equal.

When nearly all the guests were assembled Lady Holland came in. Macaulay noticed, as an interesting fact to tell his sisters, that she was not rouged, according to the fashion of the day, and that her dress was sober and handsome, befitting her years. Lord Holland seldom appeared in the library before dinner. During the last thirty years of his life he was hardly ever free from gout and dropsy, and often he was unable to join his guests at table, but came in, in a wheeled chair, after the meal was over.

As the clock struck seven they all proceeded to the dining-room. It was a big, oblong apartment, the wainscot richly ornamented with old gilding, and through a large and beautiful window at one end could be seen the waving branches of tall trees, and beyond them a glimpse of the Surrey hills, all golden in the light of a summer evening. The dinner was excellent, and served by well-trained servants; the wines were up to the great reputation of the house. Lady Holland was waited upon by her own favourite page, Edgar, whom she always spoke of as "a dear little creature," though he was, as one of the guests has recorded, "a great hulking fellow of about twenty."

THE ENGLISHMAN AND HIS BOOKS

One evening in February 1832 Mr Charles Greville happened to come in late, and, doing his best to ignore his hostess's heavy frown, slipped quietly into an empty seat between Macaulay, whom he did not know, and Sir George Robinson. When he had recovered from the slight confusion he had felt because of his late entry he glanced at his neighbour. "A common-looking fellow, badly dressed, and all in black," he said to himself, "some obscure man of letters, probably, or perhaps a doctor of medicine." For a little while the common-looking fellow went on eating his dinner in silence. The conversation turned on early and late education, and Lord Holland said he thought that self-educated men were usually conceited because, never having been to a public school, they knew little about the acquirements possessed by other people. Mr Greville's neighbour observed that he thought the most remarkable example of self-education was Alfieri, who reached the age of thirty without having acquired any accomplishment except that of driving.

Lord Holland instanced Julius Cæsar Scaliger, who married and commenced learning Greek the same day, and Mr Greville found to his surprise that the dull-looking fellow beside him knew all about Scaliger. "I suppose," he said, "that his learning Greek was not an instantaneous act like his marriage"; and from that he started on a brilliant discourse concerning Scaliger and his wound, illustrating from all sorts of sources and finishing with a reference to Loyola, who was wounded at Pampeluna. "Who could this be?" thought the amazed Mr Greville— this man who looked so insignificant, yet showed such a marvellous range of information and talked with such assurance?

"Mr Macaulay, will you take a glass of wine with me?" said Lord Auckland (brother of Emily Eden), who was sitting opposite; and Mr Greville's neighbour rose and bowed.

This, then, was the much-talked-of Mr Macaulay, this vulgar, ungainly looking fellow, with not a ray of intellect beaming from his countenance! Thus Mr Greville, in his diary, described the famous essayist; and he would doubt-

252

less have agreed cordially with *Blackwood's*, which a few months before had called him " a little, splay-footed, ugly dumpling of a fellow, with a mouth from ear to ear."

Mr Greville, like most other persons who became intimate with Macaulay, soon learned to disregard the young Whig lawyer's lack of beauty, but his amazement at the young man's conversational powers mounted higher and higher. He records that on one occasion the talk turned on India, and Macaulay discoursed brilliantly on the different Governors-General and the details of their administrations, until Lady Holland got bored and demanded a change of subject. A little later some reference to the Fathers of the Church gave him another chance, and he held the company entranced by a vivid account of Athanasius and Chrysostom, and, going from one subject to another, came at length to dolls, and rapidly, but very entertainingly, outlined their origin and history, with illustrations drawn from all the ancient peoples and most of the modern ones.

Macaulay became rather a favourite with Lady Holland, and she would argue with him without any of the overbearing temper that she showed to poor Mr Allen and Mr Greville. One evening they talked of the meaning and use of certain words, a subject on which Lady Holland considered herself an authority. " We talked about the word ' talents ' and its history," said Macaulay.

> I said that it had first appeared in theological writing, that it was a metaphor taken from the parable in the New Testament, and that it had gradually passed from the vocabulary of divinity into common use. I challenged her to find it in any classical writer on general subjects before the Restoration, or even before the year 1700. I believe I might safely have gone down later. She seemed surprised by this theory, never having, so far as I could judge, heard of the parable of the talents. I did not tell her, though I might have done so, that a person who professes to be a critic in the delicacies of the English language ought to have the Bible at his fingers' ends.

" As a slight but imperfect sketch of the talk of Holland House," wrote Greville, in September 1834,

> I will put down this. They held Wordsworth cheap, except Spring Rice, who was enthusiastic about him. Holland thought

Crabbe the greatest genius of modern poets.   Melbourne said he degraded every subject.   None of them had known Coleridge ; his lectures were very tiresome, but he is a poet of great merit. . . . After dinner they discussed women's works : few *chefs-d'œuvre* : Madame de Sévigné the best ; the only three of a high class are Madame de Sévigné, Madame de Staël, and (Bobus Smith said) Sappho, but of her not forty lines are extant ; these, however, are unrivalled ; Mrs Somerville is very great in the exact sciences.   Lady Holland would not hear of Madame de Staël.   They agreed as to Miss Austen that her novels are excellent.   There was a great deal of very good talk, anecdotes, literary criticism, and what not, some of which would be worth remembering, though hardly sufficiently striking to be put down, unless as forming a portion of a whole course of conversations of this description.   A vast depression came over my spirits, though I was amused, and I don't suppose I uttered a dozen words.   It is certainly true that the atmosphere of Holland House is often oppressive, but that was not it.   It was the painful consciousness of my own deficiencies and of my incapacity to take a fair share in conversation of this description.   I felt as if a language was spoken before me which I understood, but not enough to talk in it myself.   There was nothing discussed of which I was altogether ignorant, and when the merits of Wordsworth, Coleridge and Crabbe were brought into comparison, and Lord Holland cut jokes upon Allen for his enthusiastic admiration of *De Moribus Germanorum*, it was not that I had not read the poets or the historian, but that I felt I had not read them with profit.

Poor Mr Greville was not a bookish man.   Too much of his time was taken up with gambling and horse-racing to leave him leisure for solid reading.   He was always lamenting this, and always resolving to turn over a new leaf, but he never did so.   His part at Holland House was mainly that of a listener, and very often he only imperfectly understood what he heard.   Occasionally the talk got too deep for all except the most scholarly among the company ; but when this happened Sydney Smith or Henry Luttrell would bring it back to the surface with a jest.   Sydney Smith himself was not in the strict sense of the word a scholar.   He was widely read, and his quick brain made it easy for him to follow an argument even when it was on a subject concerning which he was not very fully informed, but the conversation in which he most delighted was brilliant and superficial rather than profound. " I read," he told a correspondent,

> four books at a time ; some classical book, perhaps, on Monday, Wednesday, and Friday mornings. The History of France, we will say, on the evenings of the same days. On Tuesday, Thursday and Saturday Mosham or Lardner, and in the evenings of these days Reynolds' *Lectures* or Burns' *Travels*. Then I have always a standing book of poetry, and a novel to read when I am in the humour to read nothing else. Thus I avoid that gloom which proceeds from hanging a long while over a single book.

It was not, however, through the books that he read that he shone at Holland House. " I sit in my study, looking upon a thousand flowers, in order to keep up arguments with Allen and Lord Holland," he wrote ; but when his chance came he carried the conversation out of the region of argument, and made it a succession of jests and puns and exquisite foolery, until all round the guests were helpless with laughter. Macaulay (that " book in breeches," as Smith described him) was actually shouting, and strange explosions were coming from the grave Sir James Mackintosh, while some of the servants were seen to leave the room hurriedly that they might not disgrace themselves by joining loudly in the merriment. Only Samuel Rogers sat irritated and unenjoying. His own fine caustic wit could make no way against the Canon's robuster humour, and it was only when those overwhelming talkers Smith and Luttrell and Macaulay were all absent that his weak voice could gain attention for the polished, cultured, bitter sayings, drawn from wide reading and long experience, for which he was famous.

Lord Holland died in 1840, and in the fine and eloquent tribute that Macaulay paid to his memory is contained such an account of the Holland House meetings as will prevent them from ever being forgotten. He laments the passing of " that circle in which every talent and accomplishment, every art and science, had its place." He recalls how

> the last debate was discussed in one corner and the last comedy of Scribe in another ; while Wilkie gazed with modest admiration on Reynold's Baretti ; while Mackintosh turned over Thomas

Aquinas to verify a quotation; while Talleyrand related his conversations with Barras at the Luxembourg or his ride with Lannes over the field of Austerlitz.

And he concludes by speaking of the joy that the guests at that house may justly feel " if, in looking back on many troubled years, they cannot accuse themselves of having done anything unworthy of men who were distinguished by the friendship of Lord Holland."

CHAPTER XVI

MELODRAMA AT THE SURREY AND TRAGEDY AT COVENT GARDEN

WHEN the year 1829 opened it found the managers of the London theatres inclined to take a gloomy view of the prospect it offered to them. The public was in no mood to be greatly attracted by anything that they could put before it. A play that commanded the thrilled attention of an audience made up of the entire nation was being played on a stage wider than that of any theatre ; and men called it " Catholic Emancipation." The first scenes had already been acted, and the actors —George IV and O'Connell, Sir Robert Peel and the Duke, supported by a large and powerful company—had given the public a taste of their quality. The most exciting scenes were to come, and an absorbed though clamorous audience watched the opening of Parliament, listened to the King's Speech, and shouted because it foreshadowed the ending that most of them desired. They saw Peel unseated at Oxford University and re-elected for West-bury, they watched the confusion in the Ministry, held their breath when Wellington was dismissed, but released it with a sigh of profound satisfaction when he was almost at once recalled ; and when the great final act was staged, and at last the Bill became law, there was much applause and only a few hisses. By this time it was the middle of April, and there was still the epilogue to come, in which O'Connell took the part of a patriotic Irishman ; and when that was over the people turned with zest to preparations for the other great drama—Parliamentary Reform—which had been on the bills almost as long as many of them could remember. So that still there seemed little chance for the smaller plays of the theatre.

Looking back over the past five or six years, the managers

R   257 of the two great licensed theatres of London—Drury Lane and Covent Garden—saw little that could hearten them. This preoccupation with politics was not a new thing; it had been going on since the beginning of the century, but it was only during the last few years that it had so spread among the middle classes—who were now the chief patrons of the theatre—as to affect seriously the London audiences. There had been other reasons, too, for the falling off of the theatre's popularity. The plays produced had somehow failed to suit the public taste. Few new ones of any merit had been written, and the old ones had proved unattractive. At Drury Lane all sorts of experiments had been tried. There had been old plays and new plays, tragedies and comedies. Some had been brilliant successes, but others had failed to attract an audience for more than two or three performances. Miss Mitford's tragedy of *Rienzi* had been played for thirty-four nights, and the engagement of Grimaldi, the popular clown, had filled the theatre. But successes and failures together had produced but a moderate average.

At Covent Garden the situation was more unfortunate. A lawsuit was proceeding between the partners in the ownership of the theatre—Charles Kemble, brother of the more famous John Philip, and a certain Mr Harris—and in 1823 the property had been thrown into Chancery. The theatre had remained open, and several successful plays had been produced, including *King John*. But the difficulties were very great, and at the beginning of 1829 poor Charles Kemble saw ruin coming upon him surely and swiftly.

There were, besides the two recognized houses, several unlicensed theatres in London, which managed to evade the law by introducing music, or performing dogs, or acrobats very freely into their dramas, and so pretending that they were not dramas at all, but musical or acrobatic performances. None of these produced anything very characteristic or noteworthy except the two theatres " over the water "—the Coburg and the Surrey. Each stood near the southern end of one of the great bridges—the Coburg near Waterloo, the Surrey near Blackfriars—and they had some hope of drawing part of their audiences from the north side of the river, for, as the poet of *Carols of Cockayne* sang :

> frequent buses start
> From Charing Cross and Gracechurch Street,
> (An inexpensive ride),
> So if you want an evening's treat,
> O, seek the Surrey side.

But people from the other parts of London did not " seek the Surrey side " in any numbers, so the proprietors of the two theatres were forced to seek their patrons among the ladies and gentlemen living round about the New Cut and the Blackfriars Road. These patrons demanded a fine, stirring drama, crammed full of murders and abductions and hair-breadth escapes. They liked realistic effects, and enjoyed seeing the scene bespattered with blood—an off-stage murder they would have resented as an attempt to cheat them of their lawful rights. They loved to have an occasion given them for copious tears and bitter sobbing. They were strong on morals, and would have no weak dabbling in half-tones ; the wicked, who were always rich, must be inky black, the good, who were always poor, must be of a dazzling whiteness. If any manager had ventured to allow the wealthy villain even a small triumph at the end of a play the stage would immediately have been filled with orange-peel, nutshells, the corks of ginger-beer bottles, or even the bottles themselves, thrown by a righteously indignant audience.

> Can I forget those wicked lords,
>   Their voices and their calves ?
> The things they did upon those boards,
>   And never did by halves.
> The peasant brave, though lowly born,
>   Who constantly defied
> Those wicked lords with utter scorn,
>   Upon the Surrey side.

The Surrey and the Coburg became noted for a particular variety of drama, or melodrama, which ran along certain conventional lines to a recognized end, with many divergences and shocks and alarms, but no slackening of its headlong speed.

> They nearly always end the same,
>   Upon the Surrey side.

The proprietors were therefore relieved of the strain, which tried their West End brethren severely, of deciding what type of play would ' take.' Their difficulty lay rather in providing variety with sameness, for a transpontine audience demanded a frequent change of bill, and had good memories for detail. Moreover, there were the musical, acrobatic, or other foreign elements to be worked in, in order to satisfy the authorities that the law was not being broken.

At the beginning of 1829 Davidge was the proprietor of the Coburg, and Elliston—Charles Lamb's Elliston, the great Robert William—was the proprietor of the Surrey. The district could not maintain two theatres, and neither of them was prospering. Douglas Jerrold, the playwright, was engaged at the Coburg, and he offered Davidge a new play which he believed would be a success. Davidge would not offer a sum that Jerrold thought sufficient, so he went to the opposition theatre, and was engaged by Elliston as hack writer to the theatre at five pounds a week. Then he produced his new play, *Black-eyed Susan*, founded on Gay's ballad. Elliston saw its possibilities at once. Here was a part that was made for the popular actor T. P. Cooke ; and here was a play which, if he was not mistaken, would charm the whole town, north, south, east, and west.

On Whit Monday, June 8, while at Westminster Parliament still held high debate concerning O'Connell's election, and while George IV in his palace lay nearer to death than any of his loving subjects imagined, the audience assembled for the first performance. The pit, which held over nine hundred people, was crowded, and quite a large proportion of its occupants had clean faces and wore decent clothes. There were small tradesmen or workmen in regular employment, with their wives and one or more of their children. Each mother held a large bag of oranges in her lap, and each father carefully arranged several bottles of ginger-beer under the seat, out of the way of his own and his neighbours' heavy boots. There were slatternly factory-girls and maids of all work having their evening out, bluejackets on leave, and youths who worked at the wharves by the river or at the Lambeth potteries. These made some attempt at

SURREY THEATRE.

UNDER THE DIRECTION OF MR. ELLISTON.

First Night of Mr. T. P. COOKE,
IN AN ENTIRELY NEW NAUTICAL PIECE.

WHIT-MONDAY, June 8th, 1829, and DURING the WEEK.

Will be presented (NEVER ACTED) an entirely new NAUTICAL AND DOMESTIC MELO-DRAMA, (by the Author of Bampfylde Moore Carew, Ambrose Gwinett, Luke and Laura, and John Overy,) founded on the popular Naval Ballad, and entitled

BLACK-EYED SUSAN:
Or, "ALL IN THE DOWNS!"

It will perhaps be necessary to state, that this Piece has been for some Weeks in preparation, and that its announcement was taken advantage of by another establishment, which, in pirating the title of "Black-Eyed Susan," has committed a contemptible and unprincipled infringement on Private Property.

The OVERTURE and the whole of the MUSIC selected from DIBDIN's SONGS,
Adapted and arranged by Mr. BLEWITT.

The Scenery designed and executed by Mr. MARSHALL.—The Machinery by Mr. E. HAGLEY.—The Properties, Naval Trophies, and Decorations, by E. BRIDWELL, assisted by Mrs. FREELOVE.—The Dresses, (the Costume of which are correctly copied from authority,) by Mr. and Miss SHAKSPEARE, and the Messrs FREELOVE and the Scene-Dressers.

CHARACTERS.

Captain Crosstree, Mr. FORESTER, Hatch, Mr. WARWICK, Halrblot, Mr. YARDLEY, Doggrass, Mr. DIBDIN PITT, Admiral, Mr. GOUGH, Jacob Twig, Mr. ROGERS, Gnatbrain, Mr. GLADSTONE, (his First Appearance at this Theatre)

William, (with an introduced Song) Mr. T. P. COOKE,
(His First Appearance at this Theatre these Ten Years, who is engaged for a limited period.)

Blue Peter, (with the original Ballad of "Black Eyed Susan,") Mr. WILLIAMSON, Seaweed, Mr. Quid, Mr. Lee, Lieutenant Pike, Mr. Hicks, Yarn, (a Smuggler) Mr. Upcroft, Ploughshare, (a Rustic) Mr. Webb, Seamen—Messrs Boulogne, Goomer, Broadfoot, Smith, Gunner, Wild, Harris, Phillips, &c.

MIDSHIPMEN, Master Ellis, Mr. WEBSTER, Miss PINCEY, and Miss RAYNER.
Black-Eyed Susan, Miss SCOTT, Dolly Mayflower, Mrs. VALE, Girls—Misses James, Ramsey, Yates, Horton, Oldfield, Houldon, &c.

NEW SCENERY.

VIEW NEAR DEAL. THE TOWN OF DEAL. BLACK-EYED SUSAN'S COTTAGE.
COUNTRY NEAR DEAL. SMUGGLERS CAVE—Attack by the Revenue Officers and Crew of the Hedbreast.
VIEW OF THE DOWNS—all as the Downs the First was seen &c.
Landing of William, and Restoration of Susan—Capture of Seaweed and Rescued by Pike, &c.

VIEW NEAR DEAL—DOUBLE HORNPIPE, by Mr. T. P. COOKE and Miss BARNETT.
Unexpected return of Captain Crosstree—Revenge of William.

THE STATE CABIN—NAVAL COURT MARTIAL, and TRIAL OF WILLIAM,
Evidence in behalf of William—Condemnation and Fate of the Prisoner.

OFFICERS ATTENDING THE COURT MARTIAL—Captain Wandesford, Mr. Abson, Captain Offl, Mr. Henry, Captain Raylor, Mr. Martin, Capt. Howe, Mr. James, Capt. Mackay, Mr. Johnston, Capt. Lawrence, Mr. Brockton, Capt. Baylrue, Mr. Clarke, Capt. Wilson, Mr. Charles, Capt. Gainly, Mr. Thompson, Capt. Sherriffe, Mr. Clifford, Capt. Alford, Mr. Peters, Capt. Stroughton, Mr. Upcroft, Master al Arms, Mr. Price.

THE GUN-ROOM—William's Requests to his shipmates—Villainy and Fate of Doggrass.
THE COCKPIT—Parting of William and Susan—Preparations for the Execution. VIEW OF THE FORECASTLE, with the
SCAFFOLD, RIGGED OUT BETWEEN THE CAT-HEAD AND THE FORE RIGGING.
FUNERAL PROCESSION ALONG THE GANGWAY.
Appearance and production of Captain Crosstree, and Denouement.

After which, NEVER ACTED HERE, a new Young, the laughable Interlude, (by the Author of John Overy &c.) entitled

THE SMOK'D MISER.

Screw, (the Miser) Mr. WILLIAMS, (his First Appearance in that Character), Ned, Mr. MUNN, Daring, Mr. ROGERS,
Giles Sawdford, Mr. YARDLEY, English against Frenchmen, Mrs. VALE, who will introduce The Good Old Days of Adam & Eve.
Polly Curry, Mrs. VALE, Anne, Miss VINCENT.

The whole to conclude with the Nautical Melo-Drama, (invented by E. Fitzball, Esq. Author of The Farragge Boll, Devil's Elixir, &c.) which has also been in preparation for some time, and is not announced in the Nautical piece, at the Amphitheatre, namely, &c., entitled

THE PILOT.

Produced under immediate Superintendance of Mr. T. P. COOKE.

Colonel Howard, Mr. GOUGH, Captain Borroughcliffe, (a regular Tasker) Mr. VALE, Marry, Mr. HICKS,
The Captain of the American Frigate, (Munson) Mr. WARWICK, Captain Manual, Mr. ALMAR, Sergeant Drill, Mr. ASBURY,
Corporal Tomm, Mr. VALE, Tar Point, Mr. DIBDIN PITT, Lieutenant Barnstable, Mr. FORESTER, Lieutenant Griffith, Mr. BENSON.

Long Tom Coffin, the Coxswain, - - - - - Mr. T. P. COOKE,

Sailor Boy, Miss ELLIS, Captains Hartman &c. &c. Messrs. Boulogne, Price, Williamson, Smith, Boulogne, Goomer, Webb, &c.
Kate Plowden, Mrs. FITZWILLIAM, Cecilia, Miss SOMERVILLE, Lady Baynes, Miss HORTON.

ORDER OF THE PRINCIPAL SCENERY AND INCIDENTS.

SEA VIEW, with a Distant View of the American Frigate, (the Alacrity)
THE FORE AND AFT VIEW OF THE SCHOONER, ARIEL,
The original (and no inapplicable to close a breachless scene)

TREMENDOUS STORM!

THE CABIN OF A BRITISH MAN-OF-WAR, WITH LONG TOM'S HORNPIPE.
Court-Yard of Colonel Howard's House, adjoining the Sea, with the Rescue of his British Officers, through the courage and ingenuity of Tom
In America—a Colonel Howard's House, with the defeat of Captain Borroughcliffe by Long Tom.
MOONLIGHT VIEW OF THE SEA OFF THE COAST OF AMERICA,

Desperate Combat between Long Tom & the American Sergeant!
Long Tom Storm, &c. in prison.

THE QUARTER DECK OF THE AMERICAN FRIGATE, ALACRITY,
With its preparations for the Death of a released American, who is taken Tom to slay, and the British schooner, and rescue by the spirit aboard
the Quarter-deck of the American schooner, to her Rescue, and the Party overcome, &c.

A GENERAL COMBAT AND FINAL TRIUMPH OF THE BRITISH FLAG.

Tickets, Places, and Private Boxes for the Season, to be had of Mr. CURRIER, at the Box Office of the Theatre, from Eleven o'Clock, until Four.
Private Boxes and Stalls, &c. to be had at Royal Library, 81, James's Street.

---

smartness as well as cleanliness, for they considered them-selves, and were considered, as the aristocracy of Blackfriars Road. Some were smoking, some were audibly sucking highly scented sweets. All were generously supplied with refreshments to sustain them during the long evening, for the patrons of the Surrey demanded from the management at least four hours of continuous entertainment.

Upstairs in the gallery, where over a thousand people were gathered, the air was even thicker with smoke and odours than it was in the pit. Here were navvies—magnificent fellows, with great brawny limbs and the shoulders of Hercules; bargemen, the rough monarchs of the Thames-side; loud-voiced costermongers, who all the week pushed their barrows through mean streets and on Sunday mornings presided over a stall in the New Cut; pickpockets combining business with pleasure; pot-boys and loafers; and thieves from the dark recesses of riverside alleys. Few of them had thought it necessary to wash their faces and hands, and quite a number had neglected to put on their coats or turn down their shirt-sleeves. The recognized theatre-going toilette of the ladies included, it appeared, a large apron, white in its origins, and a shawl worn over the head; and in a corner of the shawl or the apron was carried the indispensable store of oranges and apples. In the pocket of nearly every one in the gallery, men and women alike, were the coins which would pay for one or for several drinks that the man at the bar would bring round, in response to their shouted orders, during the performance.

On this first night of the new play the boxes as well as the pit and gallery were filled, for T. P. Cooke had his admirers in all parts of London, and some of them had thought it well worth while to cross the river and pay four shillings to see him in his new part. These, if they were strangers to the Surrey side, must have felt some surprise, perhaps a little consternation, as they looked round the theatre. At Covent Garden and Drury Lane they had seen noisy and disorderly audiences, but only during the famous O.P. riots had there been anything like this. It seemed as if every person in the place was bawling or singing or cat-calling, or laughing the loud laugh that makes unseasoned hearers shiver. How could T. P. Cooke or anybody else reduce this riotous crowd to silence and attention ?

The actors of the Surrey knew better than to attempt any such impossible task. They were quite prepared for interruptions and comments and outspoken remarks on their personal appearance and their acting. They realized that it was occasionally necessary to attempt to shout down the shouters. But a moderate degree of quietness, such as would allow everybody to follow the play, they knew would be enforced by an audience determined to get its money's worth, and with that they were satisfied.

Punctually—to keep a Surrey audience waiting most managers understood to be unwise—the curtain rose, and showed, according to the playbills, " a view of country in the vicinity of Deal." Doggrass and Gnatbrain, a friend of Susan's, are discovered in conversation, and the audience, on the look-out for the villain, are not long in deciding that here they have him. Doggrass, the uncle of Black-eyed Susan, is clearly the wicked uncle whom they have met more than once before. He has, for his own wicked purposes, forced William to go to sea, and now he is persecuting Susan ; and nothing that Gnatbrain can say serves to soften his heart.

Doggrass has a trading partner, Tom Hatchet, the smuggler of Deal, and Hatchet is in love with Susan ; and in the next scene he appears and tries to persuade Raker—an old sailor who cannot speak two sentences without introducing strange nautical terms that delight the audience—to join in a wicked plot. " Listen to my story," says Hatchet.

> It shall be short—short as a marlin-spike. I must marry Susan ; she knows not you—you must swear that you were her husband's shipmate—that you saw him drowned. Susan now lives with old Dame Hatley—she has no other home, and if she refuse, Doggrass will seize, for long arrears of rent, on the old woman's goods and turn Susan adrift ; then the girl has no chance left but to marry.

It is clear that there are to be two villains in this piece —which generosity on the part of the author the audience greatly appreciates.

In the next scene Susan is seen in Dame Hatley's cottage. She sings a verse of the ballad *Black-eyed Susan*, then stops to lament over her absent William, of whom she has had no news for "twelve long tedious months." She wears a brown open gown, white petticoat, and muslin apron, and a white gipsy hat trimmed with pink, and she looks the very picture of the favourite Surrey heroine :

> That maiden in distress,
> So unimpeachably correct
> In morals as in dress.

Then comes Gnatbrain to say that his attempt to move Doggrass from his purpose has been unsuccessful, and then Doggrass himself, insisting on payment of the money due to him. Susan defends Dame Hatley vigorously.

"Uncle, the old woman is sick, I fear dangerously. Her spirit, weakened by late misfortunes, flickers like a dying light—your sudden appearance might make all dark. Uncle ! Landlord ! Would you have murder on your soul ?"

This is the sort of thing the audience appreciates, and some of them are already in tears. Their attention is secured, and they follow the play eagerly. Doggrass leaves a bailiff in possession ; and then Hatchet, appearing just at the right moment, pays the money and earns Susan's tearful gratitude.

In the next scene the fleet is seen at anchor off the Downs, and soon William appears with a party of his shipmates. The women crowd to meet them, and before long every one has found his wife or his sweetheart—except William. William at once shows his quality as a magnificent speechmaker—his eloquence is astonishing. It is only after he has held forth at great length on his love and his disappointment that he manages to put a plain question concerning Susan and learns that she is well and faithful, but in dire distress through poverty—or, as he puts it, "short of ammunition to keep off the land sharks." Meantime Captain Crosstree, William's commander, has seen Susan, fallen in love with her beauty, and resolved to win her for himself.

Next is seen William bursting into Dame Hatley's cottage, just as Hatchet is calling upon Raker to tell the false story of the death of Susan's husband, and there is an exciting struggle between the two men.   Sailors rush in, and Hatchet is recognized as a smuggler and taken off for forced service with his Majesty's fleet.   Then Doggrass comes in with a pretence of friendship for William, but is ignominiously sent about his business.   William tells Susan he has applied for his discharge, and has great hopes of getting it, since he saved Captain Crosstree's life during the late voyage, and the officer has promised to do all he can for him, as a mark of gratitude.

There follows a scene in a public-house where the sailors are making merry, and William gains great applause by his singing of *Black-eyed Susan*.   Captain Crosstree enters, and tells them they must all be aboard again that night, and after dancing with their sweethearts and passing a joyful evening they prepare to go.   There enters again Captain Crosstree, now a little the worse for wine.   He begins to make love to Susan and attempts to embrace her; she shrieks, and William rushes in with a drawn cutlass and strikes the captain down. All cry in dismay, " The Captain ! " and the curtain goes down to slow music.

When it rises again the audience gathers from a conversation between Gnatbrain and Doggrass—who is rejoicing over William's misfortunes—that although Captain Crosstree will probably recover from his wound a court-martial is ordered and William must die for the offence of striking his officer. Gnatbrain goes out overcome with grief, and Doggrass draws out a packet, looks at it, and says : " The postman brought this packet to my house for Captain Crosstree.   What can it contain ?   No matter ; it is a virtue on the right side to be over-cautious ; so go you into my pocket until William is settled for."

By this time almost every one in the theatre is weeping bitterly, and there are cries of pity from all parts of the house. Many have relieved their feelings by pelting Doggrass with orange-peel and nutshells, and they are prepared to take more extreme measures should occasion arise.

The court-martial opens.   In the state cabin sits the Admiral, a Union Jack flying over his chair.   William is led in, and the trial begins.

Mr T. P. Cooke as William in
"Black-eyed Susan"
From a contemporary drawing
Gabrielle Enthoven Collection, Victoria and Albert Museum

264

MELODRAMA AT THE SURREY

Nothing could be more touching than are William's speeches and nothing more emphatic than the witness of his comrades to his good character. Nevertheless he is found guilty, and though he explains his conduct in another eloquent speech he is sentenced " to be hanged at the fore-yard arm of this his Majesty's ship at the hour of ten o'clock." " Heaven pardon your sins and have mercy on your soul," says the Admiral, and he shakes hands with William, who falls on his knees, then rises, and walks firmly away with his guards ; and the curtain goes down to the sound of noisy sobbing.

The audience spends the interval in imprecating Crosstree and Doggrass and Raker with great energy of language, and proclaiming loudly what they would have done in the way of rescue had they been William's comrades.

When the curtain rises it shows the gun-room of the ship and William taking leave of his comrades. He distributes small articles among them to be kept in memory of his friendship, and makes more edifying speeches ; then he attempts to sing a verse of *Black-eyed Susan* as his wife is being brought in to say good-bye. Susan shrieks and rushes into his arms.

The navvies and bargees in the audience are by this time reduced to a pitiable state, and several of the girls are very near hysterics. If the farewell speeches of the heartbroken husband and wife are sometimes interrupted by the popping of ginger-beer corks it is not because the owners of the ginger-beer are indifferent to their sufferings, but because emotion always makes them thirsty.

Then comes the last scene of all, in which William is led out to his death. It is only a short scene, so it can be given in full :

> *Master-at-Arms.* Prisoner, are you prepared ?
> *William.* Bless you ! bless you all [*mounts the platform*].
> 　　　　　　[*Captain Crosstree rushes on from gangway.*
> *Crosstree.* Hold ! Hold !
> *Admiral.* Captain Crosstree—retire, sir, retire.
> *Crosstree.* Never ! If the prisoner be executed, he is a mur-dered man. I alone am the culprit—'twas I who would have dishonoured him.

Admiral. This cannot plead here—he struck a superior officer.

Crosstree. No !

Admiral. No ?

Crosstree. He saved my life ; I had written for his discharge— villainy has kept back the document, 'tis here dated back ; when William struck me he was not the King's sailor—I was not his officer.

Admiral (taking the paper—music). He is free !

[*The seamen give three cheers. William leaps from the platform. Susan is brought on by Captain Crosstree.*

CURTAIN

The excitement is intense, and several ladies shriek shrilly. First they call out to Captain Crosstree in terms of rich vituperation, then they applaud his eleventh-hour repentance. But they reserve their choicest epithets for Doggrass, and it is with great satisfaction that they hear that the boat from which he has been watching for the signal that tells that all is over with William has gone down and he is drowned. There are shouts of delight, and the hubbub goes on until the curtain rises once more and the funny man of the theatre in a few minutes changes sobs and curses into roars of laughter.

Black-eyed Susan was played for forty evenings in succession, and all London crowded to see it. The sobs and the hysterics continued ; there was no heart so cold that it did not feel for the woes of the lovely heroine and her gallant sailor. Fine old Robert Stephenson, father of the inventor of the steam-engine, came on his birthday with a party of friends, and wept through half the performance. Charles Lamb almost certainly came to rejoice with his friend Elliston over the great success. We can think of him in one of the boxes trying, at the most touching moments, to stifle a loud burst of laughter that would have outraged the audience, for he had, he confesses, " an unseasonable disposition to levity on the most awful occasions." Hazlitt most likely came in his office of theatrical critic, but the notice he would write for his paper next morning would not help the play very much, for Hazlitt hated " the Surrey side," and said that the audiences there were made

up of " Jew-boys, pickpockets, prostitutes, and mounte-
banks," and that the actors showed a "heartless indifference
and hearty contempt" for their parts, and the people a
heartless indifference and hearty contempt for the players
and the play.

For Cooke and Elliston and their colleagues *Black-eyed
Susan* was an unmixed triumph, and it set the fashion for
a new type of nautical play which was identified with the
Surrey Theatre, and brought popularity and gold in its train.

> Can I forget those hearts of oak,
> Those model British tars,
> Who crack'd a skull or crack'd a joke,
> Like true transpontine stars ?
> Who hornpip'd *à la T. P. Cooke,*
> And sang—at least they tried—
> Until the pit and gallery shook
> Upon the Surrey side.

The Surrey side during this summer of 1829 was clearly
having the best of it ; across the water there had been
nothing to rival *Black-eyed Susan.* Drury Lane at the
opening of the autumn season reduced the price of its boxes
to six shillings, and hoped great things from its new actress,
Miss Faucit, who appeared as Ophelia in *Hamlet.*

At Covent Garden the blow, so long threatened, fell
toward the end of August. A paragraph in the newspapers
stated : "The affairs of Covent Garden continue in a bad
state—yesterday the magistrate at Bow Street signed distress warrants for £896 for parish rates and taxes, and the
King's tax-gatherer is in possession for assessed taxes due
to the amount of £600."

Fanny Kemble, now home from her Paris boarding-school,
tells how one day in September her mother came in from
a walk, threw herself into a chair, and burst into tears.

" Oh, it has come at last !" she cried. " Our property is
to be sold. I have seen that fine building covered with
placards and bills of sale. The theatre must be closed, and
I know not how many poor people turned adrift without
employment."

Poor frightened Fanny wept with her mother. She had
known for a long time that things were going badly at the

267

theatre, but there had always been the hope of some splendid success that would save it from ruin. Now ruin had come, and they must face it. She implored her mother to let her find a situation as a governess that she might at least earn her own living. But Mrs Kemble in her desperation suggested another plan—a wild one it seemed to Fanny and to every one else when first they heard it. How if they made one last desperate venture and produced a play with Fanny as the heroine ? Fanny had never acted since she had taken part in the plays at school. She disliked everything connected with the theatre and had rejected decidedly all idea of becoming an actress. Yet within a few days after her mother first made the suggestion it was decided that she had talent and that she should make an attempt to bring back prosperity to Covent Garden.

The kindness of generous friends made this further venture possible. Large sums were contributed by " three or four persons of high rank and consideration." The King's Theatre gave a performance in aid of the fund, and several of the chief actors and actresses of Covent Garden offered their services free for the first weeks of the new production.

The play chosen was *Romeo and Juliet*. Fanny was to play the heroine, her father Mercutio, and her mother Lady Capulet for the first night. Romeo was to be taken by a Mr Abbot, a good but not a brilliant actor, and now growing elderly. Less than three weeks was allowed for rehearsal, and on October 5 the play was produced.

Every seat in the theatre was filled. The threatened ruin of the old and well-known house had made a great stir in London, and the public was anxious to show its sympathy with this gallant attempt to retrieve a cause that was almost lost. " I love and respect Miss Kemble for giving her active support to her father in his need, and preventing Covent Garden from coming down about their ears," said Sir Walter Scott, and a great many other warm-hearted people felt the same. Friends of the Kembles had been busy spreading tales of the twenty-year-old Miss Fanny. It was felt that this was not an ordinary first night, but something far more adventurous and thrilling.

268

Romeo and Juliet suited well with this mood of generous and ardent excitement and with the thoughts uppermost in the minds of those who gathered to see it. Here were desperate measures to attain a great end ; here were courage and faithfulness, and youth waging its battle against tremendous odds. The end was tragedy, but it was tragedy that elevated instead of depressing the feelings, and it left all the fires of enthusiasm unquenched.

For Fanny Kemble herself the inspiration of the play was at once more necessary and more potent than it was for her audience. She had no natural love for acting, and she had had no time to learn the technique of the stage. Her greatest gift was her wonderful power of losing herself in the character she represented, and it followed that she would be most successful in a play that appealed to her strongly. All that the audience felt with regard to *Romeo and Juliet* she felt in a far higher degree, and it gave her just what she needed. Shakespeare's tragedy of youth was surely the ideal play for an occasion such as this.

Miss Kemble was not beautiful. Charles Greville described her as " short, ill-made, with large hands, and feet, an expressive countenance though not handsome, fine eyes, teeth, and hair, not devoid of grace, and with great energy and spirit." Fanny herself acknowledged her lack of beauty. When, after the London season was over, she went to play in Edinburgh, she remarked that the newspapers said more about her diminutive stature and her irregular features than they did about her acting. " Jeffrey, I hear," she said, " like other of his fellow-townsmen, complains piteously than I am not prettier. I am very sorry for it and I heartily wish I were."

As Juliet she wore a plain white satin gown, with short sleeves, low neck, and long train, and a girdle and comb of brilliants. Mrs Jameson, the author of *Christian and Legendary Art*, shivered, as she watched from one of the boxes, at the inartistic and inappropriate costume. But Mrs Kemble had insisted that Fanny should be dressed according to stage tradition. An attempt to robe her in the Venetian dress of the period of the play would, she said, distract the actress's attention and do more harm than good. The audience, except for a few of its more highly artistic members, like Mrs Jameson, seemed to see nothing wrong with Fanny's dress. As for the train, that was not allowed to cumber her movements, for at her first entrance she snatched it up and flung it over her arm, and she kept it there all the while she was on the stage, though when next morning she was laughed at for her undignified action she was perfectly unconscious of what she had done.

When she first appeared she was, she said, stunned by the tremendous shout that greeted her, and for the first two scenes, while her self-consciousness lasted, she scarcely managed to make herself heard. After that the play took hold of her ; she was no longer Fanny Kemble, but Juliet ; she loved and dared and suffered not only in show, but in fact.

The applause that came at the end of the play was almost frantic in its enthusiasm. There was no doubt that a great triumph had been won. It was, in all its aspects, a triumph of youth. The heroine of a boy and girl tragedy had been played by an actress scarcely out of her teens, and it was the boys and girls among the audience who had understood it best and received it with the highest rapture. Here and there a carping or a critical voice was heard, but it came from sober middle age or elderly insensibility. From Miss Kemble's own generation there was nothing but praise.

Young James Stuart Wortley, just down from Christ Church, Oxford, wrote to his mother a few weeks after the first performance of *Romeo and Juliet* :

> There is as yet no announcement of Miss Kemble in anything but *Romeo and Juliet*. I believe Belvidera is quite ready, but the crowds that flock to see Juliet are so undiminished that they think it in their interest to reserve the additional excitement of a new part till the public curiosity begins to flag. I hear there are some heretics about her merits. The only one for whose opinion I would give twopence, however, is Charles Greville, who, I believe, professes to have been disappointed. The fact is that now her renown is so great that people go expecting to see an angel perfect.

Scene from "Romeo and Juliet," Covent Garden, 1829
Miss Fanny Kemble as Juliet, Mrs Davenport as the Nurse.
Gabrielle Enthoven Collection, Victoria and Albert Museum

TRAGEDY AT COVENT GARDEN

Charles Greville was at this time thirty-five years old, so that it was generous of the youthful James to value his opinions even as high as twopence; the other "heretics" were probably old. Greville recorded his disappointment in his journal. "Miss Kemble," he said, "wants the pathos and tenderness of Miss O'Neill, and she excites no emotion; but she is very young, clever, and may become a very good, perhaps a fine actress." And, he added, "She fills the house every night."

We do not know if James Stuart Wortley belonged to the band of young men who went night after night to Covent Garden and waited long hours in the queue so that they might get seats in the front of the pit. These ardent admirers of Miss Kemble applauded her with such fervour that their neighbours first laughed at them and then grew annoyed, and complained that these demonstrations hindered the general enjoyment of the performance. But the enraptured young men could think of no one but Fanny. Walking home one night through the quiet streets near Cavendish Square, they loudly expressed their disgust that no better Romeo could have been found for this divine Juliet than Mr Abbot. They ridiculed his ungainly deportment and imitated his "damned faces" and uncouth gestures, then laughed until the whole street rang. A solitary figure that had for some time been walking in front of them turned round. "Gentlemen," said Mr Abbot, "no one can be more aware than myself of my unworthiness to play Romeo to Miss Kemble's Juliet. But the part was given to me, and I will continue to take it to the best of my ability." The young men were stricken dumb, and before they could recover the use of their tongues Mr Abbot had walked away. Next evening it was remarked that the applause that came from the front of the pit was a little subdued and that some of it was for Romeo.

One of these young men was a personal friend of the Kembles, and was at the time preparing for ordination as a priest of the Church of England. His conscience was a little troubled as to whether his extreme enjoyment of the play was not, under the circumstances, wrong. He consulted

Mrs Kemble, who put the question to Canon Hughes, that delightful and genial friend of Sir Walter Scott, who with his kind-hearted, autocratic wife came more than once from his house in Amen Corner to see Fanny in *Romeo and Juliet*. " That," said this young-hearted old gentleman, looking down into the pit where the enraptured youth was sitting, " depends upon his own convictions and nothing else. Meantime, pray give him my compliments and say that *I* thoroughly enjoyed the performance."

Clarissa Trant saw the play on November 11. " Went to Covent Garden with the Campbells," she wrote in her journal, " to see Miss Fanny Kemble in Juliet." The Campbells were Sir Archibald Campbell, her brother's old general, and his wife. " I never could have believed," went on Clarissa, " that so young and inexperienced a creature could have formed so accomplished an actress. I was delighted. But my companions all so devoid of enthusiasm—it was quite chilling not to have a single idea in common between us."

Night after night a fashionable and splendid audience gathered to applaud Miss Kemble. The boxes could not take all the people of rank and position who crowded to see the play, and they overflowed into the pit, and well-to-do City people thought themselves fortunate if they managed to get a good seat in the gallery. The Duke of Devonshire had a box and filled it with parties of friends. He was not one of Miss Kemble's admirers, but he belonged to the elder generation, and James Stuart Wortley declared he did not " value his judgment a *straw*." The Earl and Countess of Bristol and their family occupied another box, and Lord and Lady Dacre, staunch friends of the Kembles, another. The fat, good-natured, vulgar Duchess of St Albans, who had once been Miss Harriot Mellon, came in the most wonderful toilets to the most expensive box in the theatre, and brought her fashionable step-daughters ; and afterward she made her way behind the scenes to congratulate Miss Kemble as one artist to another. Stately Mrs FitzGerald was there, magnificent in her velvet and diamonds, and her son Edward managed to come from Cambridge to see the play of which everybody was talking.

TRAGEDY AT COVENT GARDEN

Mrs Siddons, majestic still in spite of her years and her sorrows, was taken with all privacy to a small box on the stage, to see her niece triumphing as she herself once had triumphed. It had been said by some that Miss Kemble was merely a copy of her greater kinswoman, and that she owed everything to Mrs Siddons' teaching. But the great tragic actress herself declared that this was not so. Not only had she never given the slightest instruction or assistance, but after she had seen her niece act she admired her so much and thought her conceptions so powerful that she would not presume to interfere. Fanny had never seen her aunt act except once when she was four years old, so that, as James Stuart Wortley maintained, "if there are parts where she resembles Mrs Siddons it must be from congenital inspiration, and not from any want of originality." Old playgoers declared that there was such a resemblance, and, as was natural, they gave the palm to the aunt. "Fanny Kemble wants her beautiful countenance, her fine form, and her matchless manner," declared Sir Walter Scott. "On the other hand, Miss Fanny Kemble has very expressive, though not regular features, and, what is worth it all, great energy mingled with and chastised by correct taste."

As soon as it became certain that Miss Kemble was to be a success, the management of Covent Garden began to consider with what play they could best follow up *Romeo and Juliet*. There was no modern tragedy that seemed to them worth a trial, and they decided to produce Otway's *Venice Preserved*, which had been first acted in 1682. It had been a popular play in its own time, and had been revived at intervals during the hundred and fifty years that had passed since then. Mrs Siddons had played Belvidera, its heroine, and so had Miss O'Neill, and now Miss Kemble was to follow.

She did not like the play, and dreaded the part of Belvidera. It was a painful and a terrible one, and there was little beauty in it to soften its horrors. Fanny prepared for it with feelings very different from those which she had experienced when she was rushed into her great part of Juliet.

s

THE ENGLISHMAN AND HIS BOOKS

" I am of course going to see Belvidera," wrote James
Stuart Wortley to his mother on November 26,

> and am just going to dine in order to be in good time. There
> will be a tremendous crowd ; the Orchestra is all let in *guinea*
> tickets ! a thing not known since the night when John Kemble
> took his leave.   I have got a ticket, and as I have not now seen
> her for some time, I look forward with the most eager pleasure
> to the rising of the curtain.   When will the *frondeurs* give in ?
> She has acted Juliet 30 times, I think, with constantly increasing
> applause and bursting houses ! If she succeeds to-night they
> must be entirely silenced.   I have such an opinion of her that
> I don't feel the smallest fear for the result.   You shall hear.
> Everybody that I know is going, and I never knew so much
> excitement about a thing of the kind, nor do I believe that it
> has been known since the time of Mrs Siddons.

That night a packed and breathless house watched a
Fanny Kemble they had not known before show them a
woman tried and tortured by the weakness and treachery
of man.   It was not a tragedy of beauty but of horror.
The heroine, sombrely grand in black velvet with crimson
linings and gold and pearl embroidery, a long veil hanging
from her beautiful hair, became, as scene followed scene,
more moving in her suffering and her terror ; and when at
last her brain gives way and she fancies herself digging for
her husband's body, hidden in the earth, the woes of
Belvidera proved too great for the endurance of Fanny
Kemble.   She should have shrieked aloud, then fallen sense-
less, but horror took hold of her, shriek followed shriek,
and she rushed from the stage, past her amazed and stupefied
fellow-actors, and down the stairs, and would have run
screaming into the street if some of them had not pursued
her and brought her back.

" I am just returned from the theatre," wrote James
Stuart Wortley that same night,

> and sit down to give you my impressions whilst they are fresh.
> Never was anything more brilliant or triumphant than Miss
> Kemble's success in Belvidera.   She surpassed all that I had
> been able to imagine or anticipate.   It is decidedly a more
> powerful and commanding performance than her Juliet, but
> only because the part affords better opportunity for display, for
> both are perfect.   If I was to instance the passages in which she

274

shone I should have to mention every fine piece in the play. Several times she was interrupted by thunders and regular rounds of cheers, which prevented her proceeding with her part for above a minute, and at the end the applause was perfectly terrific; one general shout and cheer which continued till Charles Kemble appeared to announce the play for repetition when the whole pit became one moving mass of raising hats. I never raised my hat in a theatre before, but as I was in the Orchestra, and on the critic's bench, I felt free, and both cheered and waved my hat most lustily. There is an end to all the cavillers and false critics. She is now established, and you must see *her* to know the pleasure of once more seeing a first-rate, great, magnificent actress.

" Don't fancy that I am in love," he went on, anticipating parental comment,

and that this is a rhapsody flowing from the extravagance of my admiration. I admire her only as an actress, for I have had no opportunity of admiring her otherwise, and you will find that I am justified in all that I have said.

Next day he was writing again.

There is a good critique in the *Times*, and I enclose you another from the *Chronicle*, both of which will show you that I have not understated the effect upon the audience. . . . The house at the end of the play presented the most extraordinary appearance I ever saw. Amidst the stunning thunders of applause it seemed as if it reeled from the number of hats and handkerchiefs which were floating backward and forward in every part. I saw a man to-day who spoke to poor Charles Kemble afterward, who said it was the happiest day of his life. You really must come up and see her.

Think of *Alexander Baring* confessing that he cried his eyes out at Belvidera. I saw him *in a state*.

We do not know if Lady Wharncliffe did come up in response to this rapturous letter, but Lord Wharncliffe saw Fanny, and does not seem to have been as deeply impressed as his enthusiastic son. But London as a whole heartily agreed with the younger critic, and tragedy on the stage of Covent Garden Theatre averted the real tragedy which had threatened its proprietors.

CHAPTER XVII

DRAWING-ROOM BOOKS

THE drawing-room was one of the most cherished of nineteenth-century institutions. It had its conventions, its code of manners, its regulation dress, its particular style of conversation. It stood both as a symbol and a safeguard of the refinements and elegances of social life. Women ruled over it ; men entered only as subjects, offering homage. Mrs Grundy made its laws, and my Lady Fashion ordered its ceremonial. Its constitution was handed down by each class to the next below it, and adopted with only such modifications as narrowing incomes or inferior breeding made inevitable. Lady Catherine de Burgh might be proud of her grand drawing-room at Rosings, with its chimney-piece that had cost eight hundred pounds, but Mrs Pullet looked with equal complaisance upon the handsome carpet and brilliantly polished furniture of her apartment at Garum Firs.

Books were to be found in every drawing-room, and these, like the other articles of furniture, were chosen with due regard to certain well-established conventions. As it was generally recognized that the drawing-room was designed, not, primarily, for the use and enjoyment of the family, but for the entertainment of visitors, so the drawing-room books were not necessarily such as the owner loved, but such as she thought would make a good impression on her guests. They must be ornamental—shabby bindings were as much out of place in a drawing-room as shabby frocks. They must be in the fashion. They must be such as visitors could turn over with polite interest when conversation languished. They must suggest, subtly or openly, the favourite ideas of the particular set of which the hostess was, or would like to be, a leading member.

In the closing years of the eighteenth century the five

volumes of *Camilla* had the place of honour; but a new generation grew up and found this masterpiece "monstrous tedious," so it passed to the top shelf of the library or the family bookcase. In 1805 came *The Lay of the Last Minstrel*, and in 1808 *Marmion*, taking the drawing-rooms as well as the world outside by storm. "Have you read *Marmion*?" and "Do you like it better than *The Lay*?" were the questions asked in every drawing-room during the season of 1808, and the books must be displayed to witness to the hostess's first-hand knowledge of their contents. Small boys reluctantly accompanying their mammas on morning calls pounced upon them and found the usually tedious half-hour too short for their delights. Thomas Babington Macaulay at the age of eight learned the greater part of the *Lay* on one such occasion. In 1810 *The Lady of the Lake* came to join the others; but all three were swept aside when, two years later, *Childe Harold* captivated the reading public and London society was given up to rapturous admiration of the book and of its noble author. "It is not, say all the gentle damsels of my acquaintance, that we like Scott less, only we like Byron better"—thus Miss Mitford explained the poetic situation. Another two years passed and *Waverley* appeared to win back the allegiance that the poems had lost; and for the next ten years Scott and Byron jostled each other on the drawing-room tables, competing for the best place. A *Rokeby*, then a *Giaour*; a *Corsair*, followed by a *Guy Mannering*; a *Siege of Corinth*, outdone by a *Heart of Midlothian* and a *Rob Roy*—so it went on.

In 1826 the fashionable drawing-room novel was Disraeli's *Vivian Grey*, in 1828 it was Bulwer's *Pelham*. Wordsworth attained only very slowly to the rank of a drawing-room poet; pre-Victorian society knew him chiefly as the author of poems that had occasioned some entertaining articles in the *Edinburgh*. There were ladies who appreciated at their true value *Pride and Prejudice, Mansfield Park*, and the rest of Miss Austen's works, but in most drawing-rooms they had their place on the side table with the latest Minerva novels.

Some ladies had special attachments and enthusiasms, which resulted in a particular class of book finding its way to their drawing-room tables. The Princesse de Montcontour —born Miss Higg—in Thackeray's *The Newcomes* spread the table of her magnificent apartment in a Jermyn Street hotel with " pretty little books in Middle Age bindings, in antique type many of them, adorned with pictures of the German School, representing demure ecclesiastics, with their heads on one side, children in long starched nightgowns, virgins bearing lilies, and so forth." Devotion to a favourite clergyman sometimes influenced the choice of books, as in the case of Mrs Sherrick. On the drawing-room table of her handsome villa in St John's Wood were to be found

> the Lives of St Botibel of Islington, and St Willibald of Bareacres ; with pictures of those confessors. Then there was the *Legend of Margery Dawe, Virgin and Martyr*, with a sweet double frontispiece, representing (1) the sainted woman selling her feather-bed for the benefit of the poor ; and (2) reclining upon straw, the leanest of invalids. There were *Old Daddy Longlegs, and how he was brought to say his Prayers ; a Tale for Children, by a Lady*, with a preface dated St Chad's Eve, and signed "C. H." *The Rev. Charles Honeyman's Sermons, delivered at Lady Whittlesea's Chapel. Poems of Early Days, by Charles Honeyman, A.M. The Life of Good Dame Whittlesea*, by do. do.

Miss Maria Hanton, in Miss Edgeworth's *Patronage*, shocked many of her friends and acquaintances by covering her table with French and German novels, while at Glastonbury Castle, in *Vivian*, by the same author, nothing was to be seen except Toplady's *Sermons*, Wesley's *Diary*, and *The Pilgrim's Progress*.

The perfect drawing-room book, specially designed and constructed for the distinguished position it was to occupy, arrived at the beginning of the nineteenth century, and remained in favour until long after Victoria had begun her reign. It belonged to the genus annual, and there were a number of species, which differed only slightly, such as *The Keepsake, The Book of Beauty, Friendship's Offering, Forget-me-not, The English Annual*. Charles Greville, in his *Memoirs*, describes these books as

> those gorgeous inanities called Books of Beauty, and other trashy things of the same description, to get up which all the

TITLE-PAGE OF "THE KEEPSAKE," 1829

fashion and beauty, the taste and talent of London are laid under contribution. The most distinguished artists and the best engravers supply the portraits of the prettiest women in London, and these are illustrated with poetical effusions of the smallest possible merit, but exciting interest and curiosity from the notoriety of their authors.

The most successful editors of such books were beautiful ladies of rank and fashion, who used their position and their charms to cajole the most famous writers of the day into giving them " just a few lines " for the next issue of their exotic publication, and, having done this, they proceeded to flatter rich or titled nonentities who imagined they could write with a similar request. There resulted an extraordinary collection of feeble, sentimental effusions, with here and there a shining poem or a piece of finely wrought prose standing out strangely from its shoddy background.

The Countess of Blessington and the Honourable Mrs Norton, one of Sheridan's three lovely granddaughters, were among the most famous of these lady editors. Sir Walter Scott was asked in 1828 to become the editor of *The Keepsake*, but he declined, though he consented to contribute two or three short tales. He refused, however, all subsequent entreaties, and was sorry, Lockhart tells us, that he had ever " meddled in any way with this toyshop of literature." There were few writers of any note who were not at some time or other persuaded or entrapped into giving a contribution. Thomas Hood's *I remember, I remember*, appeared in *Friendship's Offering*, and his *Ruth* in *Forget-me-not*, both in 1823. Readers turning the pages of *Friendship's Offering* for 1833, and enjoying—as we suppose—such gentle inanities as *Lines to a Window that has been Frozen—*

> Pellucid pane, this morn on thee,
> My fancy shaped both tower and tree—

came suddenly upon the ringing numbers of Macaulay's *Armada*. Edward FitzGerald had two poems in the *Keepsake* of 1834, not up to the standard of the translator of Omar Khayyám, but, as Thackeray said, no worse than the " sweet things " contributed by " Lord Diddle " and his aristocratic brethren. They were certainly much better than the poem contributed by Miss Landon to the next year's issue of Fisher's *Drawing-room Scrap-book*, which began :

> He wandered on a weary way,
> A weary way he wandered on.

There were two poems written by John Ruskin at the age of sixteen in *Friendship's Offering* for 1838, and contributions from Landor and Dickens in the *Keepsake* of 1843. Thackeray would do nothing but make fun of these productions. A picture of the sickly sentimental sort, he said, was first procured ; then

> Miss Landon, Miss Mitford or my Lady Blessington writes a song upon the opposite page about water-lily, chilly, stilly, shivering beside a streamlet, plighted, blighted, love-benighted, falsehood sharper than a gimlet ; recollection, cut connexion, true-love token, spoken, broken, sighing, dying, girl of Florence, and so on. The poetry is quite worthy of the picture, and a little sham sentiment is employed to illustrate a little sham art.

Charles Lamb stood out stubbornly against the wiles of those who would have made him a supporter of those " combinations of show and emptiness yclept Annuals." Only once was a contribution beguiled from him. " Yes, I am hooked into the *Gem*," he wrote in 1828,

> but only for some lines written on a dead infant of the editor's, which being as it were his property, I could not prevent them appearing. But I hate the paper, the type, the gloss, the dandy plates, the names of contributors poked up into your eyes on the first page and whistled through all the covers of the magazines, the barefaced sort of emulation, the immodest candidate-ship brought into so little space. . . . In short I hate to appear in an Annual.

But, in spite of some railing and ridicule, " by all this puffing and stuffing and untiring industry, and practising on the vanity of some and the good-nature of others," says Greville, " the end is attained." The books were produced, and bought—at a preposterous price—by all who had any pretensions to fashion, including the scoffers. There were copies on the beautiful enamel tables of the Countess of Blessington's luxurious drawing-room at Gore House, with its yellow satin sofas and ottomans. They were to be seen in Mrs Norton's pretty, untidy room on the first floor of her little house at Storey's Gate, mixed up with her drawing-paper and coloured chalks. They had an honoured place in stately Mrs FitzGerald's magnificent apartment at the White House, Bradfield. The lively, brilliant group that assembled in Mrs Dickens' drawing-room in Devonshire Terrace had great fun over them, and Lady Scott listened with amusement to the caustic comments of her son-in-law, John Lockhart, on the masterpieces of *The Keepsake*, which lay upon the table of her handsome, spacious apartment, with its antique ebony furniture and crimson silk hangings, at Abbotsford.

Becky Sharp had a lavish supply of annuals in her charming little drawing-room in Mayfair—offerings, doubtless, from some of her many devoted admirers. When the crash came and the bailiffs were in the house Fifine, the French maid, went off with as much spoil as she could gather, including six gilt albums, *Keepsakes*, and *Books of Beauty*. They had a place even in the chaste *salon* where Mrs Brian Newcome gave her famous intellectual parties and where charming little Rosey Mackenzie, gushing though shy, pronounced the prints in them " very sweet and pretty " and the poetry " very pretty and sweet," and really couldn't say which she liked best, Mr Niminy's *Lines to a Bunch of Violets* or Miss Piminy's *Stanzas to a Wreath of Roses*, and must ask Mamma. Mr Ned Plymdale, who was " one of the good matches in Middlemarch, though not one of its leading minds," brought the latest *Keepsake* to Mrs Vincy's drawing-room, to entertain her lovely daughter Rosamond. He was brimming over with complacency at having found such a suitable offering, and congratulated himself that there was the very thing to please a nice girl. Miss Rosamond listened amiably while he pointed out various ladies and gentlemen with " shining copper-plate cheeks and copper-plate smiles," and declared the comic verses to be capital and the sentimental stories interesting. But his satisfaction was shattered when the rival suitor, Lydgate—poor, but well born, and a doctor—came up and laughed scornfully at the book, while Miss Rosamond, with smiling discretion, avoided expressing her own sentiments and talked lightly of the Countess of Blessington and L. E. L.

Clarissa Trant read *The Keepsake*, with some misgivings as to whether its contents were quite suitable for a modest young lady. Her friend, Mary Spring Rice, had a story in the issue of 1837. " I certainly read it with almost a beating heart," says Clarissa,

> and with more regret than pleasure, for though the story is very interesting and the language such as I should have expected from her, still the subject is a tale of passion, and the description of highly wrought feelings somewhat too glowing for public exhibition.

Friendship's Offering for 1829 travelled as far as the homely sitting-room of Haworth Parsonage, and Charlotte Brontë, then a girl of thirteen, wrote a paper, which is still in existence, recording minute details of its engravings, with criticisms upon them. The 1835 issue we hear of even farther afield, in the United States of America, where a good many years later a little girl named Caroline Hewins read with great delight a poem by Mary Howitt, two poems signed J. R. (which stood for John Ruskin), and " a highly sentimental and improbable tale " by Mrs Norton, called *The Brazilian Bride*.

The annuals had other uses in a drawing-room besides helping enamoured young gentlemen to pay their addresses to charming girls. Mrs Gore, in her *Diary of a Désennuyée*, tells of a dinner-party where all the guests, save two laggards, were assembled in the drawing-room. They chatted politely and turned over the pages of *The Keepsake*. The hour of dinner struck, and still the two tardy guests had not arrived. The host grew more furious each minute, the hostess more embarrassed. Something must be done. ' The album was accordingly reopened and read by those nearest the table ; the *Keepsake*, the *Book of Beauty* were commented on according to individual taste." What polite fictions did the Désennuyée murmur ? Her real opinion she recorded in her diary: " So weary am I of the embroidered-cambric-handkerchief school that the sight of a table covered with tabbyfied Annuals is to me more nauseating than an Apothecary's Shop."

DRAWING-ROOM BOOKS

The mention of the album introduces another class of book very popular in drawing-rooms. What is an album? Charles Lamb, an unwilling authority on the subject, shall answer.

> Those books kept by modern young ladies for show,
> Of which their plain Grandmothers nothing do know,
> A medley of scraps, half verse and half prose,
> And some things not very like either—God knows.
> The first soft effusions of beaus and of belles,
> Of future Lord Byrons and sweet L. E. L.'s ;
> Where wise folk and simple both equally join,
> And *you* write *your* nonsense that I may write mine.

Albums seem to have come in with the century, and to have had their flourishing period in the reign of his Majesty King George IV. The object of each album-owner's ambition was to make a collection larger and containing more celebrated names than the collection of her friends. The owners were usually young ladies, though we hear of gentlemen who took great pride in their albums. Beau Brummell's album was famous. They importuned all their acquaintances, especially such as had a reputation for being 'literary,' and the victims, usually after much labour, produced a few verses or a few lines of prose, sentimental or humorous according to their individual tastes. They importuned famous writers with whom they had no acquaintance at all, and the writers, if they were good-natured, scribbled the first thing that came into their heads, and received enthusiastic thanks in payment. The book was laid on the drawing-room table, and visitors made a point of turning its pages, looking for fresh contributions, laughing or sighing over them as their nature demanded, praising the author, and envying the owner of the album. The young ladies of Reading when they came to pay a morning call on the Misses Beetham Edwards, in the autumn of 1805, must have been immensely fluttered by the poem which Captain Beetham Edwards had written in the album of one of his sisters, which began :

> I'm six foot two above my toes,
>   My age is over thirty,
> Blue are my eyes, straight is my nose,
>   Sunburnt my face, not dirty.

My carriage good, I'm just the size,
    My fame abroad is spreading,
Some ladies can't be very wise,
    For I am leaving Reading.

They say I'm straight, and strong and tall,
    A model of a figure,
If smaller, I should be too small,
    Too big, if I were bigger.
And yet they know I'm taking flight,
    Packed is my chest and bedding;
'Tis Leap Year too, why don't they write,
    Before I go from Reading.

" So witty ! " the young ladies would say, as they giggled and blushed over this effusion. It was the sort of thing that made a young officer popular; and Thackeray's Major Dobbin ought to have felt acutely—though apparently he did not—his lack of such drawing-room accomplishments when the blooming Miss Glorvina O'Dowd asked for lines for her album and he could only copy into it lines made by somebody else, instead of by himself. Dobbin had not been brought up in drawing-rooms, and their ways were strange to him. Aristocratic young gentlemen born into fashionable society acquired such graceful accomplishments almost without effort. Henry Temple, afterward Lord Palmerston, could turn a verse to the admiration of the fine ladies who thronged Lady Cowper's exclusive drawing-room and were privileged to read her album :

Cease, mortals, to consume your Prime,
In vain attempts at killing Time,
For Time, alas ! whate'er you do,
Is sure to end in killing you.

Instead of signing his name to this verse he drew a sketch of a cupid, for he was called Cupid by his intimate friends because he was fair-haired, blue-eyed, and boyish looking.

Another darling of society—nearly twenty years later—was Edward Bulwer, who, besides being handsome, well born, and of fascinating manners, had lately sent London wild over his novel *Pelham, or The Adventures of a Gentleman*. He received the homage offered to him a trifle superciliously, and affected extreme annoyance at the attentions of the learned ladies, the Blue-stockings of his day. " ' Write something in my album,' said a celebrated Blue to me the other day," he told a friend. " Teased into compliance I wrote :

> Fools write here to show their wit,
> And men of sense to laugh at it.

I need not tell you that the Blue looked exceedingly black."

Young gentlemen who had not the pleasant knack of writing verses found themselves sometimes considerably embarrassed by the unwelcome though flattering requests of fair ladies. Lady Harriet Duncan, the " light Blue " of Lister's novel *Granby*, drove poor Lord Chesterton almost to despair by refusing to accept any of the excuses he was trying to make, until at last he " retired to a bow window, paper in hand, and began casting up his eyes, knitting his brows and drumming upon his chin with a golden pencil in all the agonies of inspiration "—but with no result.

Thackeray, as a literary lion, was constantly implored to write " just a few lines " in the albums of his young lady admirers, and he found it very difficult to refuse, though he evaded the requests whenever he could. On one occasion he had been beguiled into promising a verse, and, turning over the pages to see what had already been written, he came upon a contribution signed " Albert Smith ":

> Mont Blanc is the Monarch of Mountains
> They crowned him long ago,
> But who they got to put it on,
> Nobody seems to know.

Thackeray could not resist the temptation, offered in such delightful fashion, for a retort. He wrote underneath :

> A HUMBLE SUGGESTION
> I know that Albert wrote in a hurry,
> To criticize I scarce presume,
> And yet methinks that Lindley Murray
> Instead of " who " had written " whom."

285

THE ENGLISHMAN AND HIS BOOKS

" John Lockhart and Anne and I," wrote Sir Walter Scott in 1825,

> are to raise a Society for the Suppression of Albums. It is a most troublesome shape of mendicity. Sir, your autograph— a line of poetry—or a prose sentence ! Among all the sprawling sonnets and blotted trumpery that dishonours these miscellanies a man must have a good stomach than can swallow this botheration as a compliment.

But the society does not seem to have been very effective. The young ladies had no pity for the poor authors, and went on industriously collecting spoils to lay on their drawing-room tables. " We have got something from every modern poet worth having—all the galaxy of *The Keepsake*," cried the young ladies triumphantly in Mrs Gore's *Female Domination*, and Theodore Hook in *The Parson's Daughter* shows the three all-accomplished Miss Gorgons—who all had albums—relentlessly gathering in contributions from willing and unwilling victims.

Not only in fashionable drawing-rooms, but in those humbler apartments, the " parlours ten feet by ten," which Charles Lamb declares to be his natural home, were albums a coveted adornment. " We are in the last ages of the world," wrote Lamb to Bryan Procter in 1829, a few days after he had moved into lodgings at Enfield,

> when St Paul prophesied that women should be headstrong, lovers of their own will, having albums. I fled hither to escape the albumean persecution and had not been in my new house twenty-four hours when the daughter of the next house came in with a friend's album to beg a contribution ; and the following day intimated that she had one of her own. Two more have sprung up since. If I take the wings of the morning and fly into the uttermost parts of the earth, there will albums be.

A sterner man would have scattered the importunate damsels with a decisive refusal, but " gentle-hearted " Charles Lamb was born to be imposed upon, and he submitted, with good-humoured groanings. He had a pretty knack of turning out verses which pleased his lady suppliants and gave him little trouble. In the album of Lucy Barton, daughter of Bernard Barton, the Woodbridge

286

Quaker poet and banker, he wrote a poem of nine verses, of which the first two are :

> Little book, surnamed of white,
> Clean as yet and fair to sight,
> Keep thy attribution right.
>
> Never disproportioned scrawl,
> Ugly blot, that's worst of all,
> On thy maiden clearness fall.

When Emma Isola, Lamb's beloved adopted daughter, set up an album he became in his turn an importuner of others. " Dear Dib," he wrote to J. B. Dibdin, the playwright, " bring some verses with you for it on Saturday evening. Any fun will do. . . . Has your Pa any scrap ? " And to Bryan Procter: " I have another favour to beg which is the beggarliest of beggings—a few lines of verse for a young friend's album—make 'em light. They need not be very good, as I chiefly want 'em as a foil to mine."

The Keepsake and the other varieties of the annual began to decline in favour about the middle of the century. The album, in a modified form, is still with us, though its place is now the schoolgirl's desk rather than the drawing-room, and authors are no longer pestered by strangers for contributions. Elderly people to-day can still remember the Victorian drawing-room of the type of Mrs Thornton's in Mrs Gaskell's *North and South,* where " in the middle of the room, right under the bagged up chandelier, was a large circular table with smartly bound books arranged at regular intervals round the circumference of its polished surface, like gaily coloured spokes of a wheel." But the large centre table has now disappeared from the drawing-room, and the books have gone with it ; except in a few country parlours, where the children's prizes are proudly displayed, this arrangement is seen no more. The drawing-room book, as a class by itself, is dead.

INDEX

T

INDEX

INDEX

293

INDEX

295

INDEX

INDEX

INDEX